What Are Schools For?

HOLISTIC EDUCATION IN AMERICAN CULTURE

What Are Schools For?

HOLISTIC EDUCATION IN AMERICAN CULTURE

Ron Miller

Holistic Education Press
Brandon, Vermont

Holistic Education Press
Brandon, Vermont 05733-1007

ISBN 0-9627232-0-7

Contents

Introduction

As the twentieth century enters its final decade, Americans are examining their schools with an intensity — even a sense of desperation — rarely experienced before. It is increasingly clear to a growing number of educators, political leaders, businesspeople, journalists, and parents that our system of education has fallen into a severe and possibly fatal crisis. In recent years, we have seen a torrent of highly publicized and influential critiques pour forth from nationally recognized foundations, commissions, and scholars. The foreboding message of most of these reports is that the United States is "a nation at risk" (the title of the landmark report of 1983) because the schools are turning out citizens who lack the skills to compete with the well-trained scientists and workers of other nations. Scholars like E.D. Hirsch, Allan Bloom, and others have reached the bestseller lists by charging that our cultural heritage is being eroded by the failure of education; they claim, in other words, that our students simply do not know enough.

The criticisms have spawned a number of reforms in the education world. Under the banner of "excellence," educators and politicians have pressed for more strenuous, more effective, more professionally controlled means of teaching the young generation. They have called for more stringent graduation requirements, more homework, longer school years and longer days, more discipline and moral training, and stricter training and evaluation of teachers, combined with higher pay and professional autonomy. Under the rubric of "accountability," standardized testing — for teachers as well as students — has been given a central and exalted place in the educational endeavor. Other reforms, such as opening school districts to parental choice, are receiving increasing attention and are seen by some as magic keys to a better educational future.

Yet in all this political and academic turmoil, there is virtually no serious questioning of the fundamental assumptions and purposes that underlie contemporary educational practice. It is simply assumed that "education" means imparting certain facts and skills to those students smart enough (and disciplined enough) to learn them. It is simply assumed that the primary purpose of education is to enhance the economic and technological capacity of the nation so that we can compete with other nations and ultimately defeat them. And it is further assumed that there is a direct connection between these first two assumptions: once we impart enough facts and skills to our youth, our nation will not only prosper, but prevail over all others.

It is the aim of this book to raise two fundamental questions about these unquestioned assumptions:

(1) Since the United States is a diverse community of individuals, ethnic heritages, economic interests, and religious and ideological positions — many of which are often in conflict — how is it actually decided which facts and skills, which beliefs and values, are the essential ones to be perpetuated through schooling? Who makes these decisions, and why? Whose interests are served, and whose are not?

(2) Regardless of *how* these decisions are made, should education in fact be defined as the endeavor to impart an established body of facts and skills? Shouldn't "education," in keeping with the Latin root of the word, aim to *draw forth* the latent intellectual, moral, social, and spiritual qualities that lie within the human personality? Is *any* predetermined curriculum capable of nurturing the fullest human possibilities of a new generation?

The first question — how educational goals actually are determined —has been addressed by social historians of education, particularly in recent years. The implications of their research are profoundly significant, yet the political dialogue on education in this country has utterly failed to take these implications into account! In the beginning chapters of this book, I will review this field and draw conclusions that educational reformers should find sobering.

The second question — whether education should be a *drawing forth* of human potentials rather than a *handing down* of preselected facts and skills — is even less commonly asked. Indeed, this question leads to conclusions that are beyond sobering; they would completely transform educational practice in the modern world. In the past two centuries, this question has not been seriously addressed by mainstream educators, but only by a small, fragmented group of dissident educators whose ideas have always remained on the fringes of educational practice. It is the major purpose of this book to give this group of educators the serious attention their ideas deserve. I will argue that this group of educators, whom I call "holistic," offers a profound philosophy that may be a genuine solution to the educational and cultural crisis we are now suffering.

I will further argue that an examination of both these questions is vital for understanding — and solving — our modern educational crisis. To ask the first question without the second leads to a merely ideological critique of education; conservative educational goals may be replaced by radical educational goals, but the end result is still indoctrination. On the other hand, to ask the second question without the first leads to an overly optimistic approach that is easily caricatured as "romantic," "child-centered," or "New Age" thinking. My major thesis is that a truly holistic approach questions the social context as well as the ultimate purposes of education.

Social History and the Concept of Culture

Generally speaking, there are three major approaches in the field of educational social history. The first is laudatory; it celebrates public education as the brilliant expression of a uniquely free and democratic society. It sees the founders of the "common schools" (Horace Mann and his colleagues) as great benefactors of progress, prosperity, and democracy, and critics of public education as unenlightened or reactionary cranks. This historical interpretation was popular earlier in the twentieth century (its champion was the highly influential E.P. Cubberley), but it has been largely discredited by recent scholarship that takes a more critical look at the social, political, and ideological origins of public education. Still, many conservative scholars and many professional educators retain a certain affinity for this view. There may be some truth in it, but as I intend to demonstrate, it is highly oversimplified.

The most severe critics of this view are the "revisionist" historians and a group of educational thinkers who espouse a "critical pedagogy." These are radical scholars — some explicitly Marxist, others not — who claim that American society is not the paradise of freedom and social harmony that conservatives claim it is. They point out that the ideals of liberty and equality have never been fully achieved in American society, that there has in fact been much discord and conflict — real and fundamental disagreement between economic interests, social classes, and ideologies. There has been, they argue against the conservatives, no Golden Age when public schooling smoothly turned out enlightened, productive, happily free citizens.

The revisionists claim that public schooling was a deliberate effort by those with social and economic power to protect their interests and impose their values on the mass of the population. This is a serious charge, and it has been criticized by other scholars (especially conservatives) for exaggerating and distorting historical evidence. But many of the revisionists' claims deserve serious attention. In this book, I will draw selectively from writings I consider to be more balanced (most of these authors are not Marxist); I have found the work of Joel Spring, David Nasaw, Clarence Karier, Michael Katz, and Marvin Lazerson especially useful. The critical pedagogy approach, represented by Paulo Freire, Henry Giroux, Stanley Aronowitz, Michael Apple, and Ira Shor (among others), is unquestionably an important and much needed movement in educational scholarship today. I have, however, chosen not to incorporate it into this study, for I find it to be heavily colored by leftist ideological assumptions and arcane academic terminology (e.g., "hegemony," "deconstructionist," "praxis") and therefore more narrow and technical than the holistic approach I am developing here.

The third historical interpretation, which dominates the field today, is a middle ground between the laudatory and revisionist approaches. These historians recognize that public education represents a complex mix of democratic ideals and a variety of social, political, economic, technological, and religious forces. Their work is an attempt to sort out and describe these various influences. For this study, the work of Carl Kaestle, Robert L. Church and Michael Sedlak, Merle Curti, R. Freeman Butts, David Tyack, and Rush Welter were especially helpful. I have enlarged upon their work on education with broader studies of social historical issues, such as immigration, labor, race relations, and religion. This book is based upon the interdisciplinary perspective of American Studies, and was originally written as a doctoral dissertation in that field.

Out of this interdisciplinary emphasis, my focus moved from *social* history — the study of institutions and movements — to *cultural* history —an exploration of the worldview that underlies and gives meaning to institutions and movements. "Culture" is the set of basic assumptions about reality, nature, and human nature through which a group of people make sense of the world. Anthropologist Clifford Geertz (1973, chaps. 1 and 2) defines culture as the "webs of significance" that implicitly give meaning to experience. For Geertz, culture is not a collection of material artifacts, it is the implicit belief system, the ultimate values, the *ways of perceiving* that determine our social reality. Psychologist Charles Tart (1986, chaps. 1 and 10) adds another perspective to this concept of culture in his discussion of "consensus trance" or "consensus consciousness." He points out that the way we understand and interpret our experience is largely predetermined by implicit preconceptions that we derive from the social group. These preconceptions are generally unstated and unconscious, yet they are nonetheless compelling.

The social historical literature does not directly address the issue of culture. We learn from these studies which individuals and groups had the power and influence to make decisions about schooling, but we do not get a clear picture of the fundamental beliefs and values that moved these individuals and groups. For example, to find out that Horace Mann was an upper middle class lawyer and Whig politician is important, but it does not explain why a man in his position would hold the particular beliefs and values that he did. In this book, I will attempt such an explanation. Obviously, American culture is tremendously complex and there are many possible ways to describe it, but I will focus here on five general cultural themes that I believe have demonstrated their profound influence on educational thinking and practice: Protestant Christianity, scientific reductionism, restrained democratic ideology, capitalism, and nationalism.

The Emerging Paradigm Shift

Because mainstream scholarship has not adequately dealt with the underlying culture, and the radicals (who have) are largely occupied with leftist themes, little serious attention has been paid to the *paradigm shift* that appears to be emerging in American — indeed, global — civilization today. Technically, a paradigm is an implicit, fundamental interpretation that governs understanding within a particular field of thought, especially in science (Kuhn, 1970). In physics, for example, it involves assumptions about basic foundational concepts like gravity, matter, and energy. If we stretch the concept a bit, we can see *culture* as the basic underlying paradigm of paradigms: the unifying worldview from which particular interpretations arise.

Both Geertz and Tart observe that any worldview is only one possible interpretation of experience; there are always other possible interpretations. And yet a paradigm — or a culture — seems complete and permanent. It is tightly held, jealously guarded, and generally unquestioned, because it is the ultimate foundation for all our beliefs and social practices. A paradigm changes only when the events of experience contradict our understanding so severely that we are forced to question basic assumptions. The discoveries of Copernicus, for example, did not simply add new facts to our knowledge, they revolutionized our way of thinking about the universe. This transformation of perception itself — this shattering of "consensus consciousness" — is a paradigm shift.

We may have reached such a cultural crisis today. The massive social problems of drugs, crime, corruption, and poverty; the growing awareness of impending ecological disaster; the struggles of third world peoples; the dramatic political realignments in the developed world; the continuing refinement of communications technology; and (perhaps more than symbolically) the first actual view of planet Earth suspended, alone, in the black void of space have all dramatically shaken the implicit assumptions of the scientific/nationalistic worldview that has dominated the modern era. There is mounting evidence that a new paradigm — an entirely new worldview — which is more ecological, global, spiritual and, in a word, *holistic*, is rising to meet the challenges of the late twentieth century.

Mainstream scholarship has largely ignored this emerging paradigm. Conservatives, especially religious fundamentalists, have scorned it as a dangerously romantic "New Age" heresy. Even the radicals have missed the profound significance of the evolving culture. Instead, we must turn to a body of scholarship and criticism that has emerged only in the past twenty years. A growing number of thinkers from a variety of disciplines — from physics to psychology, from economics to theology — have been exploring the meaning of the holistic paradigm. They tell us that the industrial age — the age of fossil and nuclear fuels, powerful nation-states, and mass public education — simply cannot continue very much longer if humankind is to survive on this planet. These thinkers are, for the most part, outside the academic and political mainstream; few of them even work at universities. Yet it is a serious mistake to dismiss this emerging movement as "New Age" romanticism. I believe these writers are the advance scouts of a new, post-industrial civilization. We have a great deal to learn from them, and we ignore them at our peril.

This book aims to apply the holistic cultural analysis to problems of contemporary education. If this analysis is correct, then surely the education reform movements of the past few years are woefully shortsighted and inadequate. Our nation is not "at risk" because the schools are failing; schools are failing because our nation, and our culture, have entered a period of serious decline. If the holistic analysis is correct, then educating our youth for the sake of national economic superiority is a profoundly self-destructive mistake! To put it bluntly, educating our youth with the assumptions and methods of the industrial age is, at this crucial point in history, dangerously obsolete. Such is my argument in this book.

My focus in these pages will be on the philosophical foundations of education. I do not address concrete problems of curriculum, organization, or classroom management. My purpose here is to elaborate a holistic vision of education. It is out of this vision that creative educational solutions to the present crisis may arise.

Themes of
American Culture

CHAPTER 1

Before we can fully appreciate the cultural significance of holistic education movements, we need to understand the cultural roots of mainstream American society. Without this understanding, holistic education appears simply as a gentle "child-centered" approach which seems too "romantic" to address the educational demands of our society. But a critical understanding of the dominant American worldview, which I will present in these first three chapters, reveals that holistic education is a profoundly radical movement which we need to take far more seriously than we have so far.

How shall we describe this vast, complex worldview that is American culture? One of the distinctive features about American history is that a worldview which was new in the eighteenth century — Enlightenment rationalism and republicanism — here encountered a huge, sparsely populated continent rather than an entrenched social order of monarchy, aristocracy, and established churches, and so had an opportunity to thrive. The American myth proclaims that this frontier-nurtured culture is uniquely democratic, egalitarian, and free. Early historians of education assumed this was so and sought to demonstrate that public schools embodied the uniquely American democratic faith.

There is much truth behind this myth. The United States has been a dynamic, open, mobile society which, to a great extent, has offered individual rights and opportunities denied in many other parts of the world. Millions of immigrants have come to this country seeking relief from oppression and poverty, have wept at the sight of the Statue of Liberty, and have become grateful, loyal citizens. However, the full truth is far more complex, and historians in the twentieth century, especially since the culturally unsettling 1960s, have taken a closer look at the many crosscurrents and undercurrents of American life. It turns out that the worldview which moved the founding fathers and which has evolved over two centuries is not entirely democratic, tolerant, and liberal, but contains other elements as well.

For the purposes of this study, I will pay particular attention to how this worldview has restricted the possible meanings of human experience — how it has served as a cultural limit to the growth and expression of our

innate possibilities. Certainly the cultural themes I will discuss have contributed in positive ways to people's lives, but we can acknowledge their
value without celebrating them blindly. We need to recognize that in
important ways they have also been barriers to further human development,
and that it is a major task of the emerging cultural transformation to
overcome these barriers.

Protestant Christianity

The colonies had been settled by an overwhelmingly Protestant population. Indeed, many colonists had emigrated from Europe in order to
establish a more purely Christian society (according to their definition) than
they could find at home. Protestantism has continued to pervade American
culture. The "Great Awakening" of the mid-eighteenth century and the
"Second Great Awakening" at the turn of the nineteenth were major cultural events which left a lasting impression on the evolution of American
society. Historian Warren Susman claims that

> No analysis of American culture makes any sense if it fails to realize that this
> was from the start and largely remains a Protestant nation in which the role of
> religious ideology in the shaping of other ideological positions is key. (Susman
> 1984, 56)

Other, more secular cultural themes, such as Enlightenment philosophy,
commercial expansion, and political agitation also characterized late colonial and early national society. But as Susman argues, each of these themes
had close ties to the Protestant worldview.

In some ways this religious heritage has contributed to the democratic
ideals of American culture. The Judeo-Christian tradition emphasizes the
moral and spiritual dignity of the person; if the human being is made in
God's image, then every person has value. Protestantism, with its emphasis
on the moral responsibility of the individual, has had a significant impact on
the evolution of democracy as we know it. Nevertheless, American Protestantism — indeed, Christianity in general — is an exceedingly complex
social phenomenon which incorporates many diverse ideas and groups of
people. Christian ideals have been interpreted and applied in many, often
contradictory ways. It is my belief that American culture has been deeply
influenced by a theme of Christian theology which has sought to control
and even suppress inherent human possibilities; this is the "Fall/Redemp-
tion" theology of St. Augustine, which has been fervently adopted by the
Calvinist, Puritan movement in Protestantism (Fox 1983; Karier 1986, 3-4). In
American culture especially, this "orthodox" Protestantism is characterized
by a particularly narrow and pessimistic view of nature and human nature.
In several ways, this view has had an important influence on mainstream
American education.

Most basically, the orthodox tradition has emphasized an *utter separation between the material and spiritual realms* — between natural and supernatural, profane and sacred, human and divine, person and God. The material
world is "fallen," meaning non-sacred; it is the realm of depravity and sin.

Consequently, human nature is seen as a never-ending battle between the "fallen" state of our physical being and the elusive ideal of divine grace. In relation to the absolute perfection of the divine, the human being is, in the words of many an orthodox minister, a "poor worm." To the Puritans, the person was by nature a seedbed of depravity and corruption, and in order to deny the personal, physical self, they practiced intense, guilt-inducing introspection (Bercovitch 1975, 15-23; Karier 1986; Roszak 1973, chap. 4; and Roszak 1978, 89-90).

According to Charles Leslie Glenn, in a recent study of American education from an evangelical perspective, orthodox Protestantism teaches that sin is an *inborn* "corruption of human nature cutting man off from God and from his own happiness." The individual cannot redeem oneself because we are all tainted by original sin; rather, we must accept Jesus Christ as our Savior and wait for God to bestow grace as He chooses (Glenn 1988, 48, 132).

This extreme Calvinist pessimism was challenged in the eighteenth century by the rising influence of secular rationalism and in the nineteenth century by romantic influences. Indeed, Glenn's main argument is that these secular and romantic trends were embraced as the religion of American public education (This is the basis for the fundamentalists' complaint that the religion of "secular humanism" permeates the schools.) I will discuss the role of religion in public education later; the important point here is that *despite* these liberalizing trends, orthodox views of nature and human nature have remained embedded in American culture. First of all, secularization and public education did not extinguish the vitality of orthodox sects. Even Glenn recognizes, in numerous references, that the orthodox were "greatly in the majority among the population" during the formative years of American culture; that "in fact evangelicalism was evolving and expanding rapidly"; that "powerful revival impulses ... were shaping American Protestantism"; and that orthodox leaders were confident "that they spoke for the nation." Orthodox Protestantism continued then and continues now to be an active force in American culture (Glenn 1988, 150, 162, 182, 195).

Furthermore, this hostile attitude toward nature and human nature has permeated the American worldview well beyond the boundaries of the orthodox sects themselves. The mistrust of the natural human being, of the physical body, of esthetic pleasure and sexuality, has remained a constant theme in American culture (not unchallenged, certainly, but nevertheless pervasive). Because the "Fall/Redemption" theology has had such an impact on Christian thinking, even the liberalization of American religion had its limits, and the growing influence of Roman Catholicism did not challenge this basic separation of the human from the divine. It has been left to small dissident sects in American Christianity — such as the Unitarian movement led by William Ellery Channing, the Creation Spirituality movement of the present-day Dominican teacher Matthew Fox, and the

Quaker tradition — to reject the natural/supernatural dualism and reclaim a spirituality of the whole person. As we will see, such movements are closely related to holistic educational approaches.

Believing that human beings are cut off from the divine and are, instead, moved by innate evil impulses, American culture has become highly *moralistic*; it is commonly believed that a rigorous moral code, and vigilant enforcement of social mores, standards of behavior, and civil laws are all that stand in the way of social upheaval and anarchy. As some historians have observed, American politics and reform movements have traditionally defined social problems as problems of personal morality and discipline, and therefore have often failed to address the ideological or economic sources of social conflict. This moralistic approach has chronically prescribed religious authority and education rather than consider fundamental institutional change to remedy serious social problems.

This moralism is further reflected in the traditional Puritan attitude toward work and success. Work is seen as a necessary discipline of the naturally slothful human being. Therefore, those who undertake this discipline most diligently exhibit a superior moral status, and are consequently favored by material prosperity. Private property is, in this sense, sacred. Poverty — the absence of property — is not attributed to social factors (especially given the presumably open opportunities available to all) but is seen as the inevitable result of personal moral failure.

Another general tendency in American religion is its emphasis on intellectual debate and interpretation (often literal interpretation) of scripture, creeds, and catechisms. It is true that various sects have sanctioned emotional conversion experiences and genuine moral sentiment. But overall, American religion has relied more heavily on conceptual, verbal, and doctrinal paths to truth than upon those which are more subjective, esthetic, contemplative, or mystical. This emphasis on authoritative texts and creeds has had a profound effect on the educational practices of our culture. When religious beliefs encourage a more personal or mystical communion with the divine, ideas of education are vastly different.

Finally, American Protestantism has always been charged with a sense of mission, a deeply held belief that America was the New Jerusalem, the "city upon a hill" which would bring forth God's kingdom on earth. Robert Handy observes that "from the beginning American Protestants entertained a lively hope that someday the civilization of the country would be fully Christian" (Handy 1984, ix-x). Converting others in the national community was an urgent task; there was a sense that if they failed to build a holy commonwealth, God would judge them severely. When the western frontier was opened to massive migration in the nineteenth century, Protestant sects hastened to send ministers, Bibles, inspirational tracts, and circuit riders to the wilderness to ensure the perpetuation of Christian morality.

For this reason, we should be skeptical of the historical thesis that the frontier inspired a self-reliant democracy in the American character. The pioneers did not experience the frontier with innocent awe but through the filter of their Protestant worldview. In this view, the pioneers had to be even more vigilant than the settled kinsmen they left behind. Nature was a howling, Godless wilderness; the Indians were uncivilized pagans; the land existed to be tamed; and the community must be bound by a strict moral code or degenerate into lawlessness. Thus, while the frontier may have dissolved some of the pioneers' previous class distinctions in an economic or social sense, it did not erase the moralistic Puritanism of their ancestors. *American culture — on or off the frontier — has not encouraged true self-reliance in a moral or spiritual sense, because it disdains nature and so mistrusts an unconverted, uncontrolled, undisciplined human nature.*

Scientific Reductionism

In the so-called Enlightenment of the eighteenth century, the "natural philosophy" of Bacon, Descartes, Galileo, and Newton became firmly established in Western thought. According to this view, nature is a system of lawful regularities, best understood through *reason* — the careful use of induction and deduction (ideally expressed through mathematics) rather than subjective experience. Truth is not tested by personal revelation but by actual effectiveness in practical use. Knowledge of natural laws would give humankind power to *control* physical events — the highest aim of science. Applied to human affairs by Hobbes, Locke, Montesquieu, Adam Smith, and others, the scientific worldview was a major underpinning of the republican vision which moved the American revolutionaries and founding fathers. In an important book, *Individualism and Nationalism in American Ideology,* Yehoshua Arieli says the Enlightenment taught that

> man was capable of reshaping himself and his social life according to the dictates of reason and could reflect in his society the harmony of the laws which maintained the universe. (Arieli 1964, 110-111)

In this sense, the scientific worldview offered a more progressive social philosophy and a more optimistic image of human nature than did orthodox Protestantism. The Baconian-Cartesian movement was in part a response to the religious warfare that had torn Europe, a hope that a universally valid method of gaining truth would supplant endless doctrinal strife. Those who were most enthusiastic about the scientific worldview, such as Jefferson, Franklin, and Paine, argued that "unalienable" natural rights applied to all men, and thus called for a broadly democratic society with limited concentrations of political, social, or religious authority. The view that a rational scientific approach is the most authentic means for achieving a humane, democratic society was echoed over a century later in the thought of John Dewey and taken up by the Humanist movement.

But in a very important sense, the scientific revolution was not so much a repudiation of Protestantism as a secularized extension of it. *Scientism retained the religious dichotomy between matter and spirit.* The material world is ruled by impersonal, amoral laws, not by any transcendent, self-creative purpose; the spiritual realm is wholly supernatural, and thus not the concern of science. The scientific emphasis of reason over subjective, mystical experience was an exaggeration, but not a rejection, of mainstream Protestant epistemology. The early scientists could — and did — pursue their rational approach towards nature while remaining devoutly religious in their personal and social beliefs. And except for the most implacable Biblical literalists, a religious American culture could accommodate and even complement the rise of scientism.

During the early, formative years of American culture, in social and political thought the secular view remained subordinate to the Protestant. Few of the founding fathers took the natural rights philosophy to its democratic extremes. In general, the ruling Federalists retained what Arieli calls a "Protestant nationalism" which was jealously protective of public morality and order. The more radical followers of Enlightenment ideas such as Paine, who attacked Christianity directly, were unpopular, and the violence of the atheistic French Revolution gave conservatives a rallying cry for purging whatever influence the radicals did have. Some historians suggest that conservatives' horrified response to the French Revolution led directly to the wave of revivals which comprised the "Second Great Awakening." So even as the Enlightenment radical Jefferson was elected to the Presidency in 1800, American culture was reembracing Protestantism, delaying a more secular worldview for well over half a century.

But after the middle of the nineteenth century, the scientific worldview became more aggressive and pervasive. Religion began to share its central cultural role with a consuming scientific positivism; it was believed, with ever greater fervor, that the scientific method could solve all the riddles of the universe and all the problems of society. This echoed the hope of the Jeffersonian republicans — except that nineteenth century science, freeing itself from all religious concern, veered toward *materialism*, the belief that all reality is essentially physical matter (which is measurable and manipulable) without *any* spiritual, transcending force. It became more *mechanistic*, presuming that natural events are produced by lawful cause-and-effect relationships rather than any overarching purpose. And it became more *reductionistic*, seeking to explain phenomena by breaking everything into component parts and measuring the pieces. By the early twentieth century, even the human sciences had become positivist, and still today behavioral and quantitative approaches remain the preferred methods for studying human and social problems. As scientism has moved alongside religion as a dominant influence on American culture, the result for society, as we will see in Chapter Three, has been the "culture of professionalism," which is actually a serious erosion of the Jeffersonian democratic faith.

Restrained Democratic Ideology

Still, even before the rise of elitist professionalism, American culture had always harbored a tension between radical Jeffersonian ideals and far more conservative principles. Historians have debated which ideology was the most basic in the formation of American culture. Louis Hartz (1955) and "consensus" historians claimed that an individualistic liberalism, based on John Locke's ideas, pervades American culture; other historians, such as Gordon Wood (1969), have argued that the more conservative ideals of classical republican virtue were very influential. Charles Beard and Progressive historians earlier in this century argued that the founding fathers were opportunistic businessmen. Clearly, there has been an ongoing conflict between conservative elements — represented by the Federalist, Whig, and Republican parties, which are oriented to commercial expansion, traditional morality, and obedient citizenship — and liberal elements — inspired by Jefferson, Jackson, and various populist movements, which tend to emphasize personal freedom and opportunity.

Although both tendencies are represented among mainstream, patriotic Americans, the differences between the conservative and liberal elements should not be taken lightly. These are different ideals of social order, based on different images of human nature. In conservative/republican thought, human excellence is limited to a select few, who naturally tend to rise to economic and social prominence and who should be entrusted with guiding the affairs of state and society. The masses, especially immigrant masses not schooled in national traditions, are often feared as subversive elements. Excessive liberty granted to individuals is seen as a dangerous threat to the social order. Therefore, freedom must go hand-in-hand with discipline. The welfare of the community — the common good — supersedes the personal freedom of the individual.

Liberal democratic ideology, on the other hand, argues that most (if not all) people have the potential to conduct their own lives and do not need to be controlled from above. If people were free from economic, social, and religious injustice, they would, willingly, be hard-working and moral citizens. While this ideology is arguably the majority, mainstream view of American culture (it is certainly the core of the American myth), there is no question but that it is held in check, and in certain periods seriously compromised, by the more conservative tradition. Throughout American history, large numbers of people, notably women, African-Americans, non-Anglo-Saxon immigrants, native Americans, and children, have been denied the "natural rights" promised to them by the liberal ideology. Conservative attitudes toward poverty and other social problems, strongly influenced by Puritan Protestantism, tend to be moralistic rather than sympathetic toward those who fail to attain prosperity or power. As we will see, the ongoing tension between conservative and liberal interpretations of democracy is reflected, and has played a major part, in the development of American education.

Capitalism

American culture, however, has never accepted extreme doctrines of either the right or the left, because the core values of capitalism are shared by the vast majority. In fact, perhaps more than any other theme, it is capitalism that defines the identity of American culture. It is the almost unanimous acceptance of capitalist ideology — by the worker as well as the entrepreneur, by the followers of Jefferson and Jackson no less than those of Alexander Hamilton — which distinguishes the United States from most other nations. The vast majority of Americans eagerly defend capitalism both for its effectiveness (it has, after all, produced unprecedented material prosperity for the nation) as well as for its moral virtues (to a large extent capitalism does reward ingenuity, initiative, and effort, and the economic freedom it engenders is historically related to the political freedom offered by democratic government).

But in significant ways, capitalism also places limitations on human experience. First, let me state that what follows is not a Marxist or socialist critique. My concern here is not ownership of the means of production, but with capitalism as an all-encompassing worldview, a body of beliefs that involves far more than economic considerations. As a worldview, capitalism involves the belief that nature exists to serve human needs and wants; consequently inventiveness and audacity in taming nature are highly valued, and quality of life is measured in terms of how quickly raw nature is converted to human use — the gross national product. Furthermore, capitalism involves the belief that there are no inherent limits to human progress and comfort; therefore, the most ambitious and wealth-producing entrepreneurs are widely honored, and technological innovations are almost always welcomed. Another core belief is that in an open society there are no unfair barriers to opportunity; it is only one's own talent and initiative that determine one's status (the life of Franklin and the stories of Horatio Alger are thus important myths in American capitalism).

Capitalism as a worldview is based on *meritocracy*, that is, an almost unchecked competition between individuals for social and economic status. And the standards for measuring success are overwhelmingly *materialistic*; whole realms of human experience, notably the esthetic, emotional, and spiritual, do not count as qualifications for the job market or as emblems of achievement. Capitalism promotes individualism and self-assertion in social and economic terms, but places far less value on self-understanding, critical intelligence, or spiritual discovery. Practicality and productivity are more important than contemplation or inner questing; meditative practices are disdained as "contemplating one's navel." Intellectuals have long complained that American culture is "anti-intellectual" and hostile to the life of the mind; ruled by an unrelenting competitiveness, American culture is suspicious of contemplation that does not demonstrate its immediate practicality. Just as the religious tone of the culture encourages practical moral discipline rather than mysticism, capitalism demands tangible results, not inward seeking or self-realization.

Capitalism is closely intertwined with the other themes of the American worldview as well, including the restrained democratic ideology of

American culture. On one hand, capitalism does promise, and often provides, opportunities for social and economic advancement. Class distinctions are not imposed by law or custom; the meritocracy invites aspirations and achievement by anyone who is capable. Certainly there is truth in the Franklin/Alger myth. Yet it cannot be denied that the competition for wealth and status results in some highly undemocratic consequences. If clever entrepreneurs represent the heroic ideal of American culture, it is not surprising that we have robber barons and corporate raiders, men (generally white Protestants) with enormous concentrations of wealth and power. Today the richest 1% of the population control something like 30% of the national wealth. It is considered normal for a corporate executive to be paid twenty or fifty or even a hundred times what most of his employees make. This is far beyond the personal success to which Franklin or Alger's heroes aspired.

Under corporate capitalism, only a small number of people can reach this pinnacle of success, no matter how many people are talented or motivated to succeed. Capitalism preaches democracy for all, but clearly some people enjoy more actual democracy, in the form of more access to quality education, more influence on economic and political decisions, more freedom to pursue happiness and personal meaning, and more opportunities to acquire still further wealth.

This is not a call for a revolution or legislation to forcibly guarantee equality. That misses the point, but we ought to reconsider seriously the cultural beliefs which allow us to place such incredibly disproportionate values on the worth of entrepreneurial cleverness versus even the most diligent physical work, and which allow us to accept placidly such concentrations of wealth and leisure when over 20% of our nation's children are growing up in poverty. The point is that capitalism as a worldview does not sufficiently address the extreme effects of its cherished meritocracy. The conservative version of capitalism accepts these effects as perfectly natural; it assumes that only a select few can actually attain the pinnacle of success because human nature is lazy and untrustworthy; those few who discipline themselves to achieve should be amply rewarded, and the mass of people should simply be content to share in the general prosperity by respecting private property and the rule of law. During the surge of corporate industrial expansion in the late nineteenth century, the doctrine of Social Darwinism was used to justify the extreme polarization of society; to some, natural law dictated the survival of the fittest, and it was considered healthy for society's failures to be weeded out altogether! (Hofstadter 1955b).

The liberal version of capitalism has been more generous, asserting that there is room for everyone to succeed — if not a particular individual, then surely one's children. Society's major obligation, then, is to provide education in order to equalize economic and social opportunities. Significantly, the liberal capitalist view shares with the conservative the belief that social problems and cultural discontent are best solved by stimulating personal ambition and increasing individual opportunity, rather than by radically questioning the cultural values that may be their root cause. Consequently, the use of education as a panacea for social and cultural problems is a consistent pattern in American history.

One of the root cultural causes of modern social problems is that capitalism, in its materialist urge to control nature, is aligned with scientific reductionism and technocracy. This materialism is a major source of personal spiritual alienation and the disintegration of family and community life. All industrial age cultures — even socialist countries — share this faith in scientism and hence share its social problems, but in American culture, Protestant teachings give materialism (ironically enough) a distinctly religious fervor; the moral and vocational responsibility of the individual, the discipline of work and saving, and the sanctity of private property clearly distinguish capitalism from socialism, and they are especially pronounced in American culture. Historian Bernard Wishy has observed that "the will for righteousness and will for success ... [a] complex play of moralism and materialism" have been strongly ingrained into the American character (Wishy 1968, 20). I believe that a genuine concern for human potentials and their attainment must include a penetrating analysis of such a religiously sanctioned materialism.

Nationalism

Finally, an unusual urgency is given to all these cultural themes because they are so completely tied to national identity. Unlike European countries, in which national loyalty is inherited through deep-seated historical, mythical, religious and artistic traditions, to be "American" is to overcome such given distinctions in order to identify oneself deliberately with a certain body of ideals: the American worldview, or as it has frequently been called, the "American Way of Life." In the writings and speeches of early American leaders, a deeply felt conviction was expressed again and again:

> This society was unique, absolutely different from all the historic societies. Only here had the universal rights of man been translated into a living reality. (Arieli 1964, 78-79)

This self-righteous nationalism has had positive as well as negative connotations. Since European societies were considered to be corrupted by tyranny of church and state, by poverty, ignorance, and superstition, emerging American nationalism was a secular restatement of the Protestant urge to create a holy commonwealth, a model society to inspire the rest of the world. Early Americans, religious and rationalist both, were exhilarated by the sense of being on the verge of a monumental human experiment. Paine captured this feeling in *Common Sense*:

> We have every opportunity and every encouragement before us, to form the noblest, purest constitution on the face of the earth. We have it in our power to begin the world over again. (in Arieli 1964, 72)

American nationalism has, ever since, had an aggressive, missionary tone. According to the American worldview, no other nation offers humanity a better example to follow.

The negative meaning of nationalism, however, is a nagging insecurity. Other nations have ancient traditions and to be a citizen is to have a lifelong motherland and a secure national identity. Americans, however, are people who have surrendered their ancestral ties to come to the new world. They need to *prove* their loyalty to a set of abstract ideals. Seen in this light, assertive nationalism is a defensive gesture to reassure Americans that they do, indeed, belong to the national community. Furthermore, especially in the early years, the ideals themselves needed to be proven: not since antiquity had citizens forged a successful republic. The American experiment was not an assured success. As a result of this insecurity, American culture has generally mistrusted foreign cultures and periodically resorted to xenophobic crusades against immigrants and dissidents. This has taken the form of federal laws, political parties, outright violence, and the notorious Congressional "unAmerican activities" investigations. And, of course, education has been a major weapon in these crusades.

I would argue that these five themes — Protestant Christianity, scientific reductionism, restrained democratic ideology, capitalism, and nationalism — are defining characteristics of the common, middle class American worldview, the "consensus consciousness" through which most Americans interpret their experience of the world. If there is a common thread which ties these themes together, it is the need for social discipline. Despite the emphasis on "liberty," "freedom," "independence," and "individualism" in the American myth, the dominant worldview actually does not trust the spontaneity and self-expressive creativity of the individual. The proper beliefs and proper ways of acting which lead to social and economic success are predominantly moral, rational, entrepreneurial, and "professional"; in short, they impose rational discipline on the deeper, more impulsive, intuitive, mystical, and emotional aspects of human nature.

Certainly all cultures impose discipline and a degree of conformity; in many ways American culture *is* individualistic — even atomistic — in comparison to more traditional cultures. But this individualism is almost exclusively economic, competitive, and superficial. The issue here is American culture's pervasive mistrust of the deeper subjective facets of human experience. Specifically, American culture does not value the truly *spiritual* element of human life. By "spiritual" I mean a receptivity to the more subtle, interior aspects of existence: a search for deeper meaning to existence than is offered by the intellect or by social convention alone. The American worldview imposes a moralistic, materialistic, rational discipline on this inward receptivity; in this culture, the truly spiritual is dismissed as "mystical" and "romantic." The holistic paradigm is an effort to regain this essential element of our being.

Obviously, American culture is far more complex than this brief sketch has indicated. These five themes are by no means a complete description of our worldview. But for the purpose of understanding the foundations of

American education, I believe these particular themes are especially relevant. Their influence is particularly evident in the early history of American schooling.

Education in Early America

CHAPTER 2

The educational ideas and practices of early America were direct expressions of the emerging culture. To begin with, schooling was thoroughly Protestant. Continuing the colonial tradition, religious instruction was an essential component of education at all levels. Well into the nineteenth century, most college presidents were ministers. In fact, in the rural, preindustrial world of colonial and early national America, religious indoctrination was a main purpose of elementary schooling. Children learned to read in order to read the Bible; practically anything else that most people needed to know was learned in daily life in the community. Only a small minority went on to "grammar" school and college to prepare for the professions of the ministry, law, and medicine. The mass of people, some historians say, were not only indifferent to schooling but suspicious of the overly educated (an indication of the "anti-intellectualism" of the culture.) Schools played a small role in early American life — except to ensure the continuity of Protestant moral values.

Pedagogical practices were determined by Protestant ideas. Since Calvinism taught that the individual is tainted at birth by original sin, that an innate tendency toward wickedness could only be curbed by stern discipline, it followed that the child's spontaneity must be highly discouraged, if not altogether crushed. "A playful, energetic, pleasure-loving child would surely be on the road to perdition," according to Bernard Wishy (1968, 11). Thus absolute obedience, reinforced by corporal punishment, characterized the classrooms of early America. The prevalent method of instruction was rote memorization of long Bible or textbook passages, to be recited before the teacher. People believed, says Carl Kaestle, that this method "helped children develop habits of discipline and industry" (Kaestle 1983, 46).

Some historians argue that this discipline, rather than learning, was the primary concern of early schooling. Kaestle, in fact, quotes one teacher's observation that keeping a schoolroom quiet was "the very summit of pedagogic excellence" (Kaestle 1983, 18). There are many stories of rebellious children and incompetent teachers, but the ideal was a silent, still, well-controlled classroom. The legendary one-room schoolhouses were actually drab, uncomfortable places where childrens' developmental needs and interest in learning were subordinated to discipline and order.

However, as Enlightenment ideas were slowly seeping into the intellectual life of the period, they were gradually beginning to affect Americans' attitudes toward education. The leading advocate of Enlightenment rationalism, secularism, and scientism in education was Benjamin Franklin. His conception of education as practical training for a life of enterprise and self-improvement was a reflection of a rising urban middle class consciousness. Private tutors and academies were beginning to spring up in the commercial centers of the colonies, and Franklin has come to represent this middle class tendency to use the school for personal advancement. Merle Curti points out that this was a "revolutionary" cultural development. Still, it did not soon replace traditional attitudes toward education because until the mid-1800s America remained a predominantly religious, agrarian culture.

Early educational ideas reflected the ambiguity of the founding fathers' attitudes toward democracy. Most of them agreed that a republican society simply could not survive unless the public was sufficiently educated; but the liberals held that education is vital for citizens to appreciate their liberties under natural law, while the more conservative republicans, concerned with restraining the people's more impulsive tendencies, thought schooling should teach them to choose, and then obey, the most qualified leaders. In the early years of the nation, the conservative view prevailed. An essay published in 1786 by Benjamin Rush presented one of the clearest statements of republican educational thought (in Rudolph 1965, 9-23):"Man is naturally an ungovernable animal," he declared. Therefore, in order to maintain social stability, reduce crime, promote agriculture and commerce, and foster religion and good government [Note that these are a conservative's priorities], it was necessary to teach the individual "that he does not belong to himself, but that he is public property."

Rush's ultimate goal was to "render the mass of the people more homogeneous and thereby fit them more easily for uniform and peaceable government." It is to the state that each person must owe his primary allegiance. This can be taught in the schools by having "the authority of our masters be as *absolute* as possible." He adds:

> I consider it as possible to convert men into republican machines. This must be done if we expect them to perform their parts properly in the great machine of the government of the state.

Historian Glenn observes that such republican ideas on education (expressed in similar essays by other early American leaders) were analogous to the radical Jacobin ideology of the French Revolution, which also saw children as the property of the state. National unification was the goal of both groups, and in America both Federalists and Republicans subscribed to this patently undemocratic view of education.

Although early American political thinkers talked of "equality" and did begin to break down traditional structures which had upheld an inherited aristocracy, the founding fathers were not interested in a complete levelling of society; they retained property qualifications for voting, for example.

Schools continued to perpetuate a divisive class structure, in which the wealthy obtained the best available schooling and the working class was funneled into apprenticeships. It is quite evident that early Americans did not consider it necessary to educate women, African-Americans, or native Americans for participation in public life. Furthermore, as Curti observes, educational practice itself,

> emphasizing as it did dogmatism, authoritarianism, and memorization, and aiming to impose "good order" by fear and physical brutality, was more suitable to a class society than to a republican one that claimed to be democratic. (Curti 1968, 29)

When we look at urban schools as they developed after 1800, we find additional evidence to support Curti's assertion. The commercial elite and rising middle class, as I have said, were turning to private tutors and academies to prepare their sons for economic success. Although old-fashioned pedagogical methods were still in use even in these schools, there was an evident contrast between their instructional goals and those of the charity schools provided for the urban poor. Instead of personal advancement, the charity schools promised social stability. Nasaw writes that in contemporary reports on these schools

> what was emphasized time and time again was not what the children learned but their clean and orderly appearance, the precision with which they marched into and out of school and classroom, the readiness with which they obeyed their teachers ... the rapid improvement in their morals, "docility and gentleness." (Nasaw 1979, 24)

Kaestle says that philanthropists offered "little pretense to providing equality of opportunity or intellectual enlightenment" and notes that charity schools, rather than serving parental expectations for their children (as upper class schools did), sought instead to counteract the influence of poor children's family environment (Kaestle 1983, 36, 55).

One manifestation of the growing rift between the educational opportunities of the elite and the poor was the enthusiastic adoption of Joseph Lancaster's "monitorial" system in the charity schools. This method brought four to five hundred students under the direction of a single teacher who controlled the school through teams of student monitors. They enforced a rigid, programmed routine; not only lessons but children's movements were directed on command. The method was popular because of its efficiency and economy and because it seemed ideally suited for preparing workers for the newly emerging factory system. The Boston School Committee reported in 1828 that the method's

> effects on the habits, character, and intelligence of youth are highly beneficial; disposing their minds to industry, to readiness of attention, and to subordination, thereby creating in early life a love of order, preparation for business.... (in Spring 1972, 46)

Historians disparage the monitorial system as "lockstep and mechanical," "a mode of riot control" that was "more appropriate to a feudal kingdom than a New World republic" (Kaestle 1983, 41-44; Greene 1965, 92; Nasaw 1979, 20). Yet it was widely adopted in the cities of republican

America. To me, this is an important indication that among the early leaders of American education, democratic idealism was mixed with a strong dose of conservative capitalism. The rising urban middle class used education to expand opportunities for its children, but to limit opportunities for children of the poor. We will discover this theme again later in the history of American education.

As for nationalism, R.F. Butts points out that the fulfillment of the Revolution required the "development of self-sacrifice, loyalty, patriotism, and moral regeneration on the part of the people...." Educating the people to place the public good above their personal interests (turning them into "republican machines," as Rush put it), was a nationalistic goal (Butts 1978, 11ff). Early American leaders, as noted above, saw public education as a force for national unification. In practice, school systems were slow to develop because the young nation was working out the delicate balance between federal and state powers, and education was left to the states, who left it to local districts. It took half a century, until the 1830s, for the states to get actively involved in schooling. But once they did, national unity remained an important goal.

The Rise of Public Education: 1830s-1870s

Many historians have observed that the "Age of Jackson" (1829-1837) represented an important watershed in American society. Social structures and values with their roots in the eighteenth century faced the arrival of the industrial age. What we consider "modern" institutions and beliefs became established in these years. Mass public education is one of these institutions, and it is important to understand the context of social and cultural change in which it emerged.

Industrialization

The Industrial Revolution, in the United States as elsewhere, was far more than the appearance of factories on the landscape. It was a transformation of society. First of all, it was a shift from the self-sufficiency of the family farm to the interdependence of mass producers and markets. Innovations in transportation — canals, railroads, steamships — made long-distance trade more feasible. The personal interaction of the village marketplace, which bound a small community together, began to give way to impersonal, non-local trading connections. Kaestle refers to this as the "world of cash" and says that its emphasis on calculation and written communication was one important stimulus of the demand for schooling (Kaestle 1983, 24, 65).

Workers began to specialize and, instead of being wholly responsible for their own needs, began to offer specific skills on the labor market. This shift to a market economy had substantial consequences for human relations. An important point is made by historians Church and Sedlak: In an impersonal social network there are different means for establishing one's status; instead of ancestry, personal character, and craftsmanship defining one's place in the community, it is *material success* which serves as a visible badge of identity in a fast-paced, mobile, non-local society. These authors suggest that a major impetus behind the public school movement was status anxiety on the part of men from agrarian backgrounds who faced the competition of urban life (Church & Sedlak 1976, 170-171). The rise of industrial capitalism placed a premium on education as an aid to economic and social success; and educational attainment itself became a more important status symbol.

Industrialism changed the very nature of work. Nasaw writes that in an agrarian/artisan economy

> the rhythm of work was set by the season, the day of the week, the amount of orders accepted, and the desires of the craftsmen/artisans. "Blue Mondays," long meal breaks, time off for electioneering, family festivities, and public and church holidays were not a sign of bad work habits as much as of a distinct style of work.

However, the organized routine of the factory demanded a change.

> The employer and his paid agents alone set the work hours, the work tempo, and work rules according to the logic of productive efficiency. The decision-making process was two steps removed from the worker. The machine dictated to the employer who arranged work patterns and conditions accordingly. (Nasaw 1979, 36)

Nasaw's assessment is supported by other critical studies in social history. Herbert Gutman (*Work, Culture, and Society in Industrializing America* [1976]) and Paul Faler (*Mechanics and Manufacturers in the Early Industrial Revolution* [1981]) both discuss the transformation of work habits in this period. It is clear that the habits demanded by the machine and the clock —punctuality, obedience, discipline, and so forth — needed to be deliberately instilled in workers from an agrarian/artisan culture. As will be shown, this was one of the primary aims of the public school movement.

Closely related to the new work pattern was a widening division between employer and worker. Faler describes how the "mechanic" ethos encouraged solidarity among workingmen, even between the owners of shops and their employees. But as the factory/mass market system grew, and workers became subordinate to entrepreneurs and managers who did not share their work or even personally know them, class lines became more sharply defined. For example, until this period, cities were not as clearly separated into wealthy and poor residential areas as they have since become. The widening gap posed a severe challenge to Jacksonian America's egalitarian self-image. Republicanism was founded upon a society of property owners with their "stake" in the social order, not upon property-less masses. Alexis de Tocqueville clearly saw the emerging repercussions:

> In proportion as the principle of the division of labor is more extensively applied, the workman becomes more weak, more narrow-minded, and more dependent.... On the other hand ... wealthy and educated men come forward to embark in manufactures.... Thus at the very time at which the science of manufactures lowers the class of workmen, it raises the class of masters.... The friends of democracy should keep their eyes anxiously fixed in this direction; for if ever a permanent inequality of conditions and aristocracy again penetrates into the world, it may be predicted that this is the gate by which they will enter. (Tocqueville [1840] 1954, 2:169, 171)

From this period on, American educators have struggled to preserve the ideal (or the illusion) of a classless society, even as industrialism, just as Tocqueville prophesied, has sorted Americans along distinct lines of social, economic, and political power.

Industrialization also meant urbanization. Employment opportunities were concentrated in cities, so beginning in the 1830s the population of the United States began a dramatic shift from rural to urban environments. This was alarming to an agrarian culture; De Witt Clinton expressed a key Jeffersonian belief that

> cities are, at all times, the nurseries and hot-beds of crimes.... And the dreadful examples of vice which are presented to youth ... cannot fail of augmenting the mass of moral depravity. (in Spring 1972, 64)

Church and Sedlak comment that in small agrarian communities, social cohesion was more effectively exercised through person-to-person contacts, while in cities people are more anonymous to each other. In addition, the arrival of masses of unskilled workers — and in coming years, of immigrants — did actually contribute to urban social problems.

> Social leaders in the cities saw pressing and potentially dangerous problems arising among resourceless or alien groups.... Newly established almshouses filled.... Incipient slums and deteriorating sanitary conditions alarmed city leaders. (Kaestle 1983, 32)

Reinforced by their Protestant worldview, social leaders believed that poverty was a sure sign of "moral depravity." In addition to a crusade of moral reform (described below), they sought to protect social order through new civic institutions; among these were police departments and public schools.

I suggest that American society's response to industrialization was a cultural choice. Perhaps the development of industrial technology was inevitable, and perhaps the promise of cheaper, more diverse goods and regular wages was irresistible. But the social organization of industrialism could have taken other forms. Robert Owen had built a model industrial community in Scotland — New Lanark — and in 1824 and 1825 he toured America, presenting his "new view of society" to many leading intellectual and political figures, including Congress and Presidents Monroe and Adams. But instead of taking this community-centered approach, industrialism was largely grafted onto the existing Protestant-capitalist culture.

Industrialization and urbanization created a Pandora's box of social problems and personal stresses, but Americans were willing to pay this price. Again, calling upon Protestant values, mainstream America treated the new social problems with moralistic rhetoric. For example, even as Tocqueville was foreseeing the social consequences of industrialism, a leading Massachusetts Jacksonian, Robert Rantoul, was proclaiming that "We are travelling onward towards perfection, and nothing can retard our progress but our own wickedness or our own folly" (in Meyers 1957, 167). With their faith in the fairness of a competitive, meritocratic social order, middle class Americans spurned criticism of the new industrial age. There were problems, to be sure, but since they were caused by "wickedness" and "folly," they could be solved with moral and rational discipline. Education would substitute for any meaningful social change and it would become the social cure-all of industrial capitalism.

Institutionalization of Family Roles

As the self-sufficient family farm yielded to industrialism, many of its economic functions were absorbed by larger enterprises. As Kaestle indicates, this increased the importance of schooling because a whole set of skills, not generally acquired in daily family life, were required to participate in the "world of cash." In addition, the family also surrendered many of its nurturing functions. David Rothman's *The Discovery of the Asylum* (1971) explores how the decline of preindustrial communal life brought about an institutional approach to the care of social deviants such as criminals and the insane. The family was no longer considered adequate for the task, so public institutions were created to isolate the deviant from the community. This growing acceptance of the state's responsibility for care-giving functions extended to schooling as well. As urban industrial society was beginning to loosen personal and family relationships, reformers saw a burgeoning need for public institutions to maintain social stability. It is significant that Horace Mann, before becoming a crusader for public education, had been instrumental in establishing the first state mental hospital in Massachusetts.

As if in compensation for the loss of family nurturance, Jacksonian society created a "cult of domesticity" which defined the role of women in early industrial society. This was the belief that women were inherently more nurturing and more spiritually refined than men and were therefore best suited for the home — and for teaching young children. Nancy Cott (*The Bonds of Womanhood* [1977]) notes that the woman's role in the home and school was considered to be an antidote to the selfishness and ruthless competition of the man's world of business.

This attitude toward women calls our attention to four different points:

1. It helps show how preindustrial family functions were changing. The woman's maternal role assumed greater importance just at the time fathers were beginning to spend many hours each day away from home.

2. It is further evidence that Jacksonian Americans substituted moralistic rhetoric for active confrontation with social problems.

3. It was a great advantage to the leaders of the public school movement. The feminization of the traditionally male role of schoolteaching, which made public schooling more economically feasible (women could be paid less) was rationalized as a moral reform.

4. It was a middle class idea. Many working class women — and children — spent most of their waking hours in factories. For the middle class reformer, this was all the more reason to introduce the moral influence of the school into working class family life.

Immigration

Until the mid-1800s the United States was not a truly pluralistic society. Enclaves of non-English cultures existed, but they were small, and most were of northern European Protestant origin. Franklin and other early leaders had been concerned with the German-speaking population of Pennsylvania, but not until the 1840s was Anglo-Protestant homogeneity seriously challenged by the beginning of mass immigration. In that decade the Irish began arriving in large numbers. The social history of immigration, and the nativist, often xenophobic response to it has been well described by scholars (Archdeacon 1983; Jones 1960; Higham 1970; Glenn 1988, 64-73), and from this literature I have drawn the conclusion that three particular characteristics of the new immigrants had profound effects on American culture and education:

1. They were Catholic, and if they were to be integrated into American society either their faith or Protestant nationalism would have to yield.

2. They were from an alien culture that did not appear to share American attitudes toward work, morality, or republican government.

3. Most were uprooted, uneducated, and quite desperate people — refugees, really — who, out of necessity, were more willing than most natives to take on the dirty work of industrialism.

These characteristics were shared by many other immigrant groups who followed the Irish during the next eighty years. There were two important consequences of mass immigration for American society: Americans were (a) further distracted from considering the problems of class stratification — because working class difficulties could be attributed to immigrants' supposed moral inferiority — and (b) further propelled into self-righteous nationalism, because many immigrants themselves, despite nativism and other problems, found in American society the freedom and opportunities they had sought and joined the chorus of patriotism.

Popular Politics

The 1820s and 1830s saw the "rise of the common man." Property qualifications were relaxed, so that almost all white adult males could now vote in most states. The Jacksonians proclaimed that public offices could be filled by any (white male) citizen, because the voice of "the people" must not be muted by elite control. The first true party convention was held in 1831. Workingmen's parties emerged in the major cities and called for broad economic and social reforms, including free public schooling. This movement redefined eighteenth century republicanism, placing less emphasis on self-sacrifice for the common good and more on the individual's aspirations and opportunities. In attacking "aristocratic" or "monopolistic" institutions, including many functions of government, Jacksonians sought to open the social and economic arena to all would-be entrepreneurs. The sense of boundless opportunity was expressed in the concept of Manifest Destiny; a whole continent was available for the exercise of democratic ambition.

Although it was accompanied by Protestant proselytizing, Manifest Destiny reflected a romantic nationalism which exalted the wisdom of the American people.

However, many traditional, conservative Protestant views were upheld by the anti-Jackson party, the Whigs. To some extent they accepted the advent of mass politics and the more democratic rhetoric; they had to, in order to win elections. Rush Welter (1962) argues that the Whigs joined a "liberal consensus," but I believe the revisionists make a more convincing case: the Whigs represented the emerging industrial elite and simply did not trust the uncontrolled will of the masses. They supported centralized rather than local power because, contrary to Jacksonian claims, they expected the more established elements of society to gravitate to positions of prominence. Like their predecessors the Federalists, they believed the government ought to be actively involved in economic development and protection of social order. Thus, the Democrats, who conceived of free public schooling for egalitarian ends, were not successful in organizing school systems because they mistrusted state authority, but the Whigs, who like Daniel Webster tended to see public schooling as a "system of police," went on to create the state school systems in the form we know them. Most of the reformers and politicians who led the public school movement in various states — Horace Mann, Henry Barnard, Calvin Wiley, William Seward, Thaddeus Stevens, Samuel Lewis, and Horace Eaton — were *not* Jacksonian Democrats; they were Whigs.

In most of the South during the antebellum period, political and social developments followed a somewhat different course. In the slave states public school movements lagged behind their northern counterparts because southern society resisted many of the economic and political developments which were transforming the north into an urban, industrial society. The Civil War, as Edwards and Richey (1963) contend, was in part a conflict over the direction American culture would take. The South was not ready to become an urban, industrialized society comprised of middle class entrepreneurs and working class wage earners, but ultimately the North — and industrial capitalism — prevailed.

Crusades for Social Reform

The public school movement cannot be understood outside the context of the larger social reform movement that swept the northern states during these years. A widespread temperance (anti-drinking) movement, abolitionism, communal experiments and perfectionistic sects, the reform of asylums and prisons, Sunday schools, a nascent women's rights movement, socialism, anarchism, pacifism, vegetarianism, and phrenology (a quasi-scientific psychology based on the shape of a person's skull) — all claimed enthusiastic followers during the second quarter of the nineteenth century. There were three major sources of the crusading impulse: evangelical Protestantism, elites seeking social control, and genuine criticism of the effects of industrialization.

The Second Great Awakening rekindled the Protestant dream of a Christian America spearheading God's kingdom on Earth. In 1801, the Congregational and Presbyterian sects formed a "Plan of Union" for a joint missionary effort. Historians have called this the "evangelical united front," and it led to a proliferation of missionary efforts such as distributing Bibles and religious tracts, supporting ministers' training, and proselytizing the new settlements in the Midwest. Meanwhile, frontier-oriented sects like the Methodists and Baptists were gaining thousands of followers through their camp meetings and circuit riders. A more liberal theology emphasized universal salvation through personal piety. In fact, many of these evangelical Protestants were inspired by a messianic belief in the imminent Second Coming of Christ and turned to perfectionistic sects and social movements to prepare the way for God's ultimate triumph. Some of the more radical movements, such as abolitionism, religious communes, and extremist sects, reflected a belief that American society must be cleansed of its growing materialism.

Yet most Americans were not radical. For most, Protestant piety was already in alliance with the other pillars of the American worldview. It is more likely that the overall effect of the evangelical revival was to heighten respect for property and industriousness, for capitalism and entrepreneurship, for Manifest Destiny and self-righteous nationalism. Jacksonian middle class ambition was fueled, not dampened, by the resurgent Protestantism. And conservatives — as represented by the Whig party — used this to their advantage. Clifford Griffin argues that the nation's self-appointed moral stewards used religious enthusiasm as "an instrument for molding the country to conform to God's — and the stewards' — ideas," while Walter Hugins says flatly that religious benevolence was adopted "by a conservative elite to use morality as a means of social control over the population in a changing America" (Griffin 1960, xii; Hugins 1972, 7).

This is most evident in the temperance crusade. Says Faler, "Temperance reform must be viewed as an integral part in the larger process of social disciplining" that was necessary to turn agrarian people into reliable industrial workers (Faler 1981, 130). Rather than question the industrial social order, community leaders blamed poverty, vice, and urban squalor on drinking habits. One active advocate of temperance reform was Horace Mann. His major biographer, Jonathan Messerli, says that Mann, like other temperance crusaders, lost his faith in voluntary temperance and called for legal enforcement as it became clear that moralizing alone was not having the desired effect. When even legal measures failed, Mann and the others turned to another promising approach: public education (Messerli 1972, 117ff).

The other source of reform enthusiasm was a more critical and more secular awareness of the social changes wrought by industrialism. There were a few individuals and groups who questioned the very Protestant-capitalist basis of the social order. These included Orestes Brownson, Henry

David Thoreau, Frances Wright, Brook Farm and other experimental communities, and the Workingmen's parties, among others, who explored new
ideas such as anarchism, socialism, and feminism. But they were largely
unheeded. Industrial capitalism was becoming firmly established in American culture. Both the secular critics and the radical religious opponents of
materialism were destined to fail. Hugins summarizes the outcome of
antebellum reform by noting that it was

> a minority movement, and hence in contradiction to the majoritarian temper
> of the time. The mass of Americans during the Jacksonian era had a more
> optimistic and less critical vision of America's future.... Seekers after economic
> opportunity, they generally had little sympathy for intellectuals who seemed
> unduly critical of the materialistic mainstream of American life. (Hugins 1972,
> 19)

Mass public education arose during a fertile period of social reform move-
ments, but it endured while the others faltered. What made the difference?
It is, I suggest, that the schools were more in harmony with the dominant
American culture.

Goals of the "Common" School Movement

My reading of the historical literature suggests that the antebellum
educational reformers had five major goals: moral training, responsible
citizenship, cultural uniformity, the advancement of industrialism, and
enhanced economic opportunity.

Moral Training

There can be little doubt that the foremost aim in the minds of the
leading educators in the mid-nineteenth century was the moral rejuvena-
tion of American society. They were devout Protestants, they were Whigs,
and they saw the problems of urban industrialism as problems of personal
morality. For them, as for their culture, morality was inseparable from
Protestant Christianity; only the teachings of Protestantism could ensure
social order. (As late as 1838 Massachusetts convicted a man of the crime of
blasphemy for preaching atheism.) Curti writes that

> No great educational leader before the Civil War would have denied that
> intellectual education was subordinate to religious values. None would toler-
> ate any non-Christian beliefs in the schools. (Curti 1968, 20)

Even Welter, despite his "liberal consensus" thesis, admits that

> most pedagogical innovations arose amid Whiggish rather than Democratic
> surroundings, and they drew on theological rather than secular perspectives
> on man and education. (Welter 1962, 90)

Indeed, Horace Mann himself, commenting on teacher training, said

> Moral qualifications, and ability to inculcate and enforce the Christian virtues,
> I consider to be even of greater moment than literary attainments. (in
> McCluskey 1958, 38; see also Glenn 1988, chap. 6)

The morality which the reformers sought to instill was intended to
ameliorate the excesses of competition and materialism without questioning the social order itself. "The morality of the social system as a system was

beyond question; the moral quality of the society was therefore to be improved by improving the moral quality of individuals" (Kaestle 1983, 81). If schooling could instill personal piety and respect for law and order, if it could prevent intemperance, laziness, and vice, then Americans could pursue their entrepreneurial ambitions with a clear conscience.

The pervasiveness of Protestantism in American culture is revealed by the educators' struggle to remove denominational — but not religious — influence from the public schools. Mann, a Unitarian who subscribed to a more liberal theology, fought bitterly with orthodox ministers who accused him of introducing infidelity and atheism into the schools. Yet Mann steadfastly insisted on keeping the Bible and moral training in the classroom. For him "common" schooling was not a secular but a nonsectarian Protestant crusade. Glenn's recent study, *The Myth of the Common School*, written from an evangelical perspective, helps us define more clearly the issues involved here. Glenn argues that Mann's liberal Unitarian approach was indeed sectarian, that it deliberately excluded orthodox beliefs about sin and redemption. He associates Mann's beliefs with several liberal and romantic figures, including the philosopher Rousseau, the educator Pestalozzi, and the Unitarian minister William Ellery Channing, in order to demonstrate that the common school movement sought to impose a liberalized religion on the public, especially the poorer and more rural populations who tended to favor conservative religious beliefs.

Glenn is right that Mann and his colleagues offered a diluted, idealized version of Protestant morality, and that its inclusion in public education was discomfiting to those with strictly orthodox beliefs. Clearly it would be a mistake to say that the common school movement endorsed *orthodox* Protestantism. However, it is only from the orthodox point of view that common school moralism can be described as secular or romantic; from the holistic point of view, Mann's ideas remained quite religiously conservative — that is, quite traditionally moralistic — compared to the essential teachings of Rousseau, Pestalozzi, and Channing. It is true that each of these particular thinkers, in some ways, influenced Mann's approach; but like many original thinkers, these men were not always consistent in their views, and it was their more conservative statements, certainly not their holistic ideas, that Mann adopted.

As Glenn himself argues, the orthodox public, even some of its leaders, accepted the common school program because Mann's inclusion of religious moralism — even if diluted — was to them clearly preferable to a secular state-run education (such as Jacobin/republican programs of the 1790s) and preferable to allowing Catholics and atheists to teach their own children in separate private schools. As I pointed out previously, Glenn himself emphasizes the dominance of Protestant principles in American culture. Mann and his colleagues

> presented the mission of the common school in essentially religious, salvific terms to a Protestant majority that was quite prepared to identify the institutions of American society with the Kingdom of God. (Glenn 1988, 205; see also 91, 97, 100, 215, 288)

So the common school movement did advocate a Protestant moralism. The Bible was part of the curriculum for many years, and textbooks were permeated with moralistic advice; the McGuffey readers are a prime example. When Catholics protested the use of the King James Bible — and textbooks which maligned immigrants and Catholicism — Protestants were indignant; the ensuing conflict continued for years, and even after overt religious teaching was removed from public education, tensions between the Protestant culture and Catholics and other minorities, were expressed in bitter disputes over public funding and control of schooling.

Responsible Citizenship

Many social historians conclude that the leading educators — devout Protestant Whigs that they were — held a conservative rather than liberal democratic vision of American society. Schools were expected to cultivate an unquestioning loyalty to the American state.

> Political education consisted of stressing common beliefs and glorifying the exercise of intelligence in a republic, while urging respect for laws and downplaying the very issues upon which citizens might exercise their intelligence. (Kaestle 1983, 80)

The reformers discouraged teachers from raising controversial issues, so, observes Nasaw, the textbooks

> provided the only point of view, which was no more or less than the Whiggism preached and practiced by the reformers themselves: it was a republicanism that emphasized the need for public obedience rather than public participation.... The American Revolution was a conservative revolution led not by "rebels" but by men of law and order.... The republic that had survived into mid-century was sacrosanct in form and function. (Nasaw 1979, 41, 42)

Another way of teaching obedient citizenship, as Curti points out, was "the maintenance of rigid discipline and authority in the classroom ... [as] the best means of inculcating respect for law and order." He says that "the vast majority of teachers" agreed with this approach (Curti 1968, 60).

An important aspect of good citizenship was respect for property. As we have seen, conservative republicanism as well as Protestantism placed great emphasis on property ownership. The Rev. Timothy Dwight, president of Yale, expressed the union of religious and social conservatism when he declared that

> the love of property seems indispensable to the existence of sound morals.... The secure possession of property demands, every moment, the hedge of law, and reconciles a man, originally lawless, to the restraints of government. (in Kaestle 1983, 90)

Respect for property was a high priority in the educational rhetoric of the public school movement. Just to give one illustration, in 1847 the secretary of the Maine board of education wrote:

> What surer guaranty can the capitalist find for the security of his investments, than is to be found in the sense of a community morally and intellectually enlightened? (in Curti 1968, 80)

Whigs — and Whig educators — were concerned that the emerging working class would resort to "levelling" to improve their status, unless they were taught respect for the social order.

Yet was this not the "Age of Jackson" and the rise of popular democracy? We should expect the Whigs' educational program to be challenged by the voice of the people. But except for small pockets of protest among radical Democrats and intellectuals, American culture fostered a fierce loyalty to the "sacrosanct" nation which the founding fathers had created, and to the inviolability of private property. Welter finds that

> most Americans were interested not in analyzing the nature and tendencies of their institutions but in reinforcing habitual institutional behavior through proper training in schools. (Welter 1962, 121)

As long as the middle class experienced economic and social mobility, they shared the Whigs' determination to preserve the republic. The American has been called, with good reason, the "venturous conservative."

Cultural Uniformity

The growing ethnic diversity of the cities worried the Anglo-Protestant elite, and they sought to overcome it through the public schools. In the face of an urban population increasingly made up of unfamiliar peoples, Mann and his colleagues attempted "to maintain a set of common values and reestablish the older community of consensus on a newer urban and industrial foundation" (Messerli 1972, 249).

As another historian put it, for Mann

> the function of the school is to build into the coming generation a common set of beliefs and attitudes. This function logically follows from his conception of the good society wherein all men adhere to the same basic moral, economic, political and social values. Mann's good society, in this respect, was distinctively a secularized Puritan society. (Karier 1986, 64)

Thus the goal of acculturation was intimately tied up with the goals of moral training and responsible citizenship —especially so because it was the working class immigrant who most threatened social order. The Boston School committee spelled out this belief in 1858, stating its goal of

> taking children at random from a great city, undisciplined, uninstructed, often with inveterate forwardness and obstinacy, and with the inherited stupidity of centuries of ignorant ancestors; forming them from animals into intellectual beings, and ... from intellectual beings into spiritual beings; giving to many their first appreciation of what is wise, what is true, what is lovely and what is pure. (in Katz 1968, 120; see also Glenn 1988, 64-73)

The thinly veiled implication is that immigrant people are morally and intellectually inferior to the Anglo-Protestant-American culture and must be brought up to par by the schools. This sentiment was widely shared and frequently expressed.

Advancement of Industrialism

Not only did educational leaders hold Whig ideals themselves, but they also recognized that the successful adoption of their programs required the political and financial support of the emerging capitalist elite in each of their states. Hence, they made direct appeals to manufacturers — as in Mann's Fifth Annual Report (1842) — claiming that public schooling would benefit industry. In part, their appeal rested on the contention that education would contribute to the resourcefulness and productivity of the whole community, an argument that has been used with increasing fervor in the 1980s. But the main thrust of their argument was that schooling would produce "tractable," dependable, sober employees. Through the schools' emphasis on moral training, educated workers would be more punctual, respectful of authority, willing to accept the factory routine, as well as be cleaner and more orderly. As we have seen, this concern was the result of rapid industrialization which required the replacement of agrarian work habits with wholly new attitudes toward work. Faler's intensive study of one industrializing city reveals that the school committee deliberately sought to instill industrial work habits — and encountered resistance among people who were not used to such discipline (Faler 1981, 117-120).

Enhancement of Economic Opportunity

During the previous century, the middle class had begun to turn to schooling as a preparation for more lucrative commercial careers. As industrialization and urbanization transformed the nature of work, the schools became ever more indispensable to personal success. It seems that the public school crusaders were more concerned with training and acculturating the poor, the immigrant, and the working class: these were the immediate threats to the social order. But what culture did the reformers want to instill in these people, if not the competitive capitalist values of the middle class? An important part of the "common" school ideology was that public schools would ensure social cohesion by educating children of all classes together. The reformers apparently believed that schooling the immigrant working class in Anglo/Protestant/middle class values would simply eliminate class divisions in American life; the immigrant children would learn from their classmates the benefits of hard work and thrifty habits. Then they, too, could participate in the race for wealth and status. Horace Mann expressed this faith in his Twelfth Report (1849), his final statement as Secretary of the Board of Education:

> According to the European theory, men are divided into classes, — some to toil and earn, others to seize and enjoy. According to the Massachusetts theory, all are to have an equal chance for earning, and equal security in the enjoyment of what they earn. (in Hugins 1972, 140-142)

Mann saw the public school as "the great equalizer of the conditions of men." This was a role that reformers would assign to the schools for the next century and a half. As Kaestle observes, "educational reformers struck a strong chord in American culture when they articulated the opportunity theme" (Kaestle 1983, 91). It is here that Welter's thesis of a "liberal consensus" applies: although the public school crusaders were conservative Whigs, they shared with Jacksonians a commitment to the individualistic economic and social striving characteristic of capitalism. With the burgeoning use of education as "the great equalizer," Americans could feel confident that no drastic political or social measures would be necessary to address class divisions or poverty — much less the materialistic striving that was being denounced by a few dissidents.

Assessment of the Public School Movement

By the 1870s, tax-supported public school systems were well established in most states. Preindustrial attitudes toward schooling had been overcome; the school year was lengthened and more attention — and money — were being given to school buildings, equipment, textbooks, and teacher training. Administration was organized and centralized, schools were divided into grades. Educators developed a professional identity, with their own journals, organizations, and conferences. While school attendance did not rise dramatically, it shifted considerably from private to public institutions, and compulsory attendance laws were beginning to appear. Pedagogical methods had been somewhat liberalized; in place of rote memorization and sectarian indoctrination enforced by frequent corporal punishment, the reformers had called for milder approaches.

However, although the reformers succeeded in putting an educational system into place, we must take a critical look at what kind of system it was. In my view, several major issues need to be recognized.

Probably the most serious issue was the failure of educational leaders to address class divisions in American society. Whether it was a deliberate strategy to protect elite interests, or a genuine but naive faith that social mobility depended on personal moral virtue, the educators seem to have been oblivious to Tocqueville's warning that industrialism was hardening the class structure. When they did express concern over the extremes of poverty and wealth, as in Mann's Twelfth Report, they offered education as the primary solution. Equal educational opportunity, they believed, would ensure that no permanent underclass would develop. They did not see that an unequal distribution of wealth virtually assures an unequal distribution of education, and they failed to address the problem of child labor. Working class children left school early in life — or never attended at all — because they were a vital source of income for their families. It was futile even to offer "common" schooling to all children when the poor, who needed it most, simply could not avail themselves of it. As Nasaw observes, the educators dared not propose child labor legislation because this would have risked losing the manufacturers' support.

Essentially, public schooling was offered as a panacea that would substitute for more fundamental social reform. The statement of Horace Eaton, Vermont's superintendent of schools, that education "will do more to secure a general equality of condition, than any guarantee of 'equal rights and privileges' which constitution or laws can give" (in Welter 1962, 118) was echoed time and time again not only by the public school crusaders, but even by labor leaders, and it was a theme that has dominated American social thought ever since. There is a broad consensus among historians that Americans have habitually resisted addressing social problems as *social* problems. Some see this as a reflection of Protestantism, which holds individuals rather than institutions morally accountable (Susman 1984; Elkins 1968). The revisionist interpretation is that

> most Americans have been too absorbed in the enjoyment or pursuit of
> possessions to take much notice of the exactions of the system.... Any radical
> attack on social problems would compromise the national optimism.
> (Duberman 1965, 395)

Church and Sedlak, Katz, and other writers observe that during periods
when social problems have appeared impervious to educational solutions
(such as the 1870s, 1920s, and 1970s), reformers have turned in despair to a
pessimistic determinism: If education cannot rescue depressed ethnic or
racial groups from poverty, the problems are blamed on their genetic
inheritance rather than the social structure, and therefore nothing further
can be done.

Another flaw of the public school movement was that it maintained the
religious, racial, and sexual prejudices of nineteenth century American
society. Anti-Catholic agitation reached a feverish pitch in the antebellum
years, even resulting in a major political party, the Know-Nothings. Rather
than promote mutual understanding, the "common" schools, with their
blatantly nativist goals and textbooks, only inflamed the situation. In fact,
according to a leading historian of immigration,

> No portion of the program to Christianize America caused more bitterness
> between the native stock and the immigrant than the public school move-
> ment. (Archdeacon 1983, 77)

"Common" schooling excluded blacks as well; social historians have demonstrated that the North, even more than the South, insisted on an almost
complete segregation of society out of a gripping fear of racial "amalgama-
tion." Even educators who tried to set up integrated *private* schools in the
1830s were boycotted, imprisoned, and violently attacked — even in the
heart of New England. Finally, the schools reinforced the "cult of domesticity" by making it clear, especially through textbooks, that women had a
narrowly defined place in American life.

In certain respects the public school movement was implicitly anti-
democratic. Although most Jacksonians were satisfied with the patriotic
content of public education, some put up a fierce struggle against its political
structure. They resented paying taxes to educate other families' children,
especially, as Katz has shown, when it became clear that early public high
schools only benefited a small proportion of the community. More importantly, educational authority was removed from the local districts and
vested in the states. Decisions over teaching personnel, curriculum, and
ethnic and religious issues had, in the district system, reflected the wishes of
the community; public participation was active, according to Church and
Sedlak, and there were even proposals in the Jacksonian period to choose
teachers by popular election. (While the educational merit of this idea is
questionable, it reflects a willingness to involve the community in public
schools in a highly democratic way.) But under the new systems more
and more decisions would be made by distant administrators. Rural
communities feared that urban values would be imposed on them, and
ethnic enclaves — for example, the Germans of Pennsylvania and later the

Irish — were soon to feel the pressure of cultural homogenization.

An even more fundamental issue was raised by Orestes Brownson: in America, he suggested,

> the people do not look to the government for light, for instruction, but the government looks to the people.... To entrust, then, the government with the power of determining the education which our children shall receive is entrusting our servant with the power to be our master. (in Nasaw 1979, 64)

Opponents of Horace Mann's crusade, which included a state legislative committee as well as orthodox Protestant leaders, argued that having the state educate is equivalent to having it dictate religious beliefs: "a strange doctrine in a free country" (in Glenn 1988, 183; see also 122, 133).

Such opposition to public education was dismissed by the reformers — and early historians — as unpatriotic and selfish, or worse, as merely backward or unenlightened resistance to progress. But the opponents saw what was coming: As the educational bureaucracy became established in American society, it became a vehicle for political interests which were often insensitive to the wishes of individuals or communities. The public schools would be severely affected by the "culture of professionalism" that arose later in the nineteenth century; by the 1850s educators were frequently asserting that parents (especially working class and immigrant parents) were unfit to raise their own children. As a Massachusetts educator put it, "the children must be gathered up and forced into school" (in Nasaw 1979, 78). From this attitude it was only a small step to the confirmation of Brownson's fears: in 1865 the Wisconsin Teachers' Association could proclaim that "children are the property of the state" (in Kaestle 1983, 158). For a society that prides itself on its individualism and claims to be democratic, such an assertion is indeed chilling.

It should also be recognized that the reformers' efforts to modernize the old-fashioned pedagogy had limited effect. Throughout the nineteenth century

> it was common belief that there was a relatively fixed body of knowledge and certain basic 'skills' to be mastered eventually by all students.... Intellectual mastery came through conquering the material in textbooks under the teacher's guidance and drill. (Wishy 1968, 73)

Butts says that the role of the teacher was that of

> authoritative conveyer of the knowledge, manners, and morals most highly approved by the dominant society.... Teachers almost everywhere pressured students to learn the value of conformity to law and regulations, and stressed obedience and submission to authority. (Butts 1978, 106)

Church and Sedlak suggest that most (middle class) nineteenth century parents supported this approach, believing that "obedience to authority must be forcibly inculcated in children" (Church & Sedlak 1976, 103). Corporal punishment was less frequent, but it was still accepted.

Each of these limitations in the public school movement illustrates the extent to which the reformers' ideals were ultimately realized in terms acceptable to American culture. The most democratic and humanistic element in their program, the reform of classroom practice, was largely ignored; but such goals as moral training, acculturation, advancement of industry, and centralization of administration, which were to a large degree undemocratic, were institutionalized on a massive scale. Church and Sedlak maintain that the public schools were "captured" by the Protestant, nativist middle class, who used education to advance their social and economic interests at the expense of the immigrant working class (Church & Sedlak 1976, 156). Glenn puts it another way:

> At its heart, then, the common school agenda was — and to some extent continues to be — concerned above all with the muting of strongly held passions, the sentimentalizing of deeply felt convictions. Its "truth" had to do more with the process of social accommodation than with the drama of a living religion. (Glenn 1988, 61-62)

Although Glenn's idea of a living religion is quite different from a holistic view of spirituality, his statement is entirely in accord with my major thesis that American culture, through its schooling, has sought to impose a social discipline on the nonrational passions of human nature. This was the overriding mission of the common school movement.

So it is a mistake to simplistically characterize Mann and his colleagues as democratic humanitarians, which is how most educators (and until recently most historians) have seen them. For they were middle class Protestant Whigs who sought to maintain a moral, stable, capitalist social order in the face of the severe human problems brought on by industrialization, and to promote cultural uniformity in the face of immigration and religious diversity. Still, I cannot totally agree with the revisionists that the common school leaders were simply agents of class oppression. They appear, sometimes, to have been genuinely disturbed by human suffering; perhaps their understanding of social problems was inadequate (after all, industrialization and mass immigration were wholly new phenomena), or perhaps they tempered their concern for political reasons, so as not to jeopardize the social elite's support for public education.

Horace Mann was elected to Congress after his service on the Board of Education, and it is interesting that while there, he was an eloquent abolitionist and critic of capitalist materialism. That Mann waited until he left education to express his deeper convictions may tell us something about the cultural and political pressures on American schools at the time.

Education
in the Modern Age

CHAPTER 3

Professionalism and Progressivism: 1870s–1910s

By the 1870s, the agrarian image of America as a community of independent farmers and craftsmen was obsolete. Industrial capitalism was firmly established, and with it came an increasing acceptance of a social class structure based on increasingly specialized labor. By 1900, says Welter, it was clear that education was not going to remake American society. Instead, the educational developments of this period actually promoted the widening rift between the aspiring middle class and the perpetually immigrant working class.

The middle class ensconced itself in what Burton Bledstein has called the "culture of professionalism." A professional is a specialist with a high degree of intellectual expertise: the ability to apply a special technique or scientific approach to control the physical or social environment. Professional expertise assumed the new prestige — we might even say mystique — that was beginning to surround science during the latter half of the nineteenth century. The new professions sought, and received, legitimacy by applying "scientific" (i.e., quantitative, analytical, reductionistic) techniques to their work. The social sciences, which promised to explain human nature and control social problems, emerged as important professional applications of scientific technique.

The aspiring middle class made a "culture" of professionalism by defining social success more and more in terms of professional status. In a society becoming increasingly technological and impersonal, professional credentials became a visible badge of personal attainment, a rational and standardized way of defining elite status in contrast to the common herd. By the 1870s, Bledstein explains, the medical, legal, engineering, and education professions had evolved their own associations, terminology, codes of ethics, and more standardized training, which set them apart from, and above, the nonprofessional.

> The citizen became a client whose obligation was to trust the professional. Legitimate authority now resided in special spaces, like the courtroom, the classroom, and the hospital; and it resided in special words shared only by experts. (Bledstein 1976, 78-79)

Middle class professionalism was an important element in the emergence of the urban, secular society we have come to identify as "modern." Yet Protestantism remained a major theme in American culture. Alongside the rise of scientism and professionalism, the Social Gospel and Prohibition movements of the late nineteenth and early twentieth centuries demonstrated the persistent influence of traditional religious moralism. The culture of professionalism itself reflected this influence: the acquisition of specialized expertise has been considered desirable not only because it assures scientific precision, but also as a sign of moral character and self-discipline. Professionals, like property owners in preindustrial society, are often considered to be morally as well as intellectually superior to other people.

Professionalism had profound implications for education. Since admittance into one of the specialized fields required extensive schooling, education assumed greater and greater importance as the primary avenue to professional and social success. The middle class use of education for economic advancement was greatly expanded by the need to attend high school, college, and graduate school in order to secure professional status. Nonprofessionals were increasingly disdained as unqualified to conduct the affairs of society, including education. Consequently, the role of educator itself became highly professionalized, with all the trappings of specialized training, "scientific" techniques, and an aura of superior expertise.

The culture of professionalism contributed to what is known as the Progressive movement. In the 1870s, a group of patrician intellectuals including E. L. Godkin, Charles Francis Adams, and Carl Schurz became disgusted with the corruption of Gilded Age politics and launched a crusade for civil service reform —essentially a call for professionalism in government. By the 1890s a group of university presidents, including Charles W. Eliot of Harvard, Nicholas Murray Butler of Columbia, Daniel Coit Gilman of Johns Hopkins, James Angell of Michigan, and others, were advocating the view that social affairs should be entrusted to a university-trained elite. These men were instrumental in developing professional education at the university level, and also sought to align the public schools to the universities' requirements. In addition, they were active leaders of the emerging Progressive movement.

Progressivism was a multi-faceted political and social movement which has lent itself to various, even contradictory, interpretations by historians (Ostrander 1970; Link & McCormick 1983, Hofstadter 1955a). Still, a few generalizations can be reasonably supported: I believe we can understand Progressivism as *a reaffirmation of American culture* in the face of new challenges such as ethnic pluralism, urban social problems, corporate industrialism, and threatening new ideologies spreading from Europe. The persistent themes of American culture were all present in Progressive approaches. For instance, although religion was yielding to science, Progressives sought to uphold traditional Protestant moral values; even their

social science and their political theory retained concepts of personal morality and sin, good, and evil. It is no coincidence that Prohibition — the
twentieth century name for the temperance movement — emerged from
the Progressive years.

Yet Progressives also had an optimistic, positivist faith in science as the
answer to social problems; what some historians have called the "revolt
against formalism" was the adoption of the scientific method in place of
moralistic dogmatism in intellectual life. In many cases, this faith in science
only fed an anti-democratic professionalism. Many leading Progressive
intellectuals argued that the egalitarian ideals of Jefferson and Jackson were
obsolete in a complex industrial, technological world. Herbert Croly's *The
Promise of American Life* (1909) and Walter Lippmann's *A Preface to Politics*
(1913) argued that modern society needs scientific, efficient social planning
by well-trained professionals. Social scientists like Edward A. Ross, Charles
H. Cooley, E.L. Thorndike, and Lewis Terman also supported "a rationally
organized, corporate state" which meant "the establishment of a meritocracy and the assignment of each individual to the functional slot for which
he was best suited" (Karier, Violas, & Spring 1973, 41, 42; see also Karier 1986,
174-175). New "scientific" techniques like intelligence tests would help the
experts manage society efficiently. While some historians see this faith in
science as a forward-looking aspect of Progressivism, it seems to me more a
reassertion of an established cultural pattern of social discipline, using a
potent blend of Protestant moralism and scientific positivism to keep the
nonrational impulses of human nature under control.

The Progressives espoused the traditional republican belief that "the
people" have a common good which requires self-discipline and qualified
leadership to protect it from private self-interest. There is in this formulation
little recognition of class interests or conflict, and even in an age of unprecedented labor strife and violence, even as anarchism, socialism, Bolshevism,
and other radical answers to urban industrial problems were being brought
to the United States, the Progressives continued to express faith in the
"common good" and "the people" (Goldman 1966, 83). Furthermore, they
upheld the nationalistic equation of America with liberty; Wilson, after all,
entered the First World War to "make the world safe for democracy," and
the other leading Progressives cheered him on.

The First World War, in fact, stirred up an unprecedented binge of
"100% Americanism." This was the climax of a steadily rising tide of racial
and nativist prejudice. Jim Crow laws were tightened in the South. Immigration restrictions aimed deliberately at southern and eastern Europeans
who seemed to threaten the Anglo-Saxon identity of American culture were
passed by Congress. "Scientific" evidence (like intelligence testing) was
gathered to demonstrate the superiority of the Anglo-Saxon race, and a
eugenics movement gained a great deal of attention. In many cases, the
advocates of these positions were important figures in the Progressive
movement.

Finally, most historians recognize that Progressivism was an endorsement of capitalism, entrepreneurship, and middle class ambition. While the *excesses* of industrial capitalism were deplored in the muckraking press and addressed by new laws and agencies — in fact, by a whole new acceptance of government activism — it appears that the Progressives had little intention of attacking the foundations of the system. For the Progressives, "the route to social amelioration lay in adjusting the people to fit the new productive order, not the reverse" (Nasaw 1979, 100). The unprecedented concentrations of corporate wealth and power did not mean that capitalism should be questioned, only that certain mechanisms should be set up to make the competition more fair. In sum, the "venturous conservatives" continued to resist any fundamental change in the social order.

American education was deeply affected by this conservative, scientistic Progressivism. However, we need to be very careful about the term, because "progressive education" has been used to refer to a conflicting variety of educational approaches. There was a more liberal wing of the Progressive movement, represented by John Dewey and Jane Addams, which, while not radically critical of American culture, seemed to have a more genuine, humane interest in the lives of individuals and the plight of ethnic minorities. Later followers of this wing launched a child-centered education movement in the 1920s and (with Dewey) evolved toward a radical social critique in the 1930s. We will explore these more holistic and democratic progressive movements in Chapter Six. The important point is that they were clearly in the minority, and deeply at odds with the mainstream Progressivism that would impose a conservative "social efficiency" approach on American education for half a century.

Under the influence of mainstream Progressivism, the field of education became thoroughly enchanted by the spell of professionalism. Specialized training and credentials took on greater importance, beginning a trend of increasing bureaucracy in education that would continue throughout the twentieth century. "Normal schools" multiplied and then gave way to graduate colleges, creating an entrenched educational establishment with its own professional interests. Teachers began to specialize in grade levels and departments, and "special" education made its appearance in these years. Even more significantly, professionalism brought about the further centralization of school administration and its deliberate imitation of the business model of efficiency and "scientific management." Between the 1870s and 1910s, the school systems of every major American city were wrested from local neighborhood control by middle and upper class reformers (including university presidents like Butler and Eliot) who installed more "professional" (i.e., business-oriented) school boards and superintendents (Cronin 1973; Tyack 1974).

The business of running school systems became more of a specialty, increasingly isolated from educational issues. Raymond Callahan's *Education and the Cult of Efficiency* is the classic study of this phase of American educational history. Callahan asserts that educators were vulnerable to public criticism in an age of corporate power, middle class professionalism, and faith in science, and responded with an almost obsessive concern for cost effectiveness, factory-like efficiency, and public relations. He concludes that "the consequences for American education and American society were tragic," because the business mentality undermined truly pedagogical considerations (Callahan 1962, 244).

The rise of professionalism profoundly affected not only the structure, but the basic goals of public education. Intellectual and moral discipline were important goals of nineteenth century educators, supported by religious beliefs and a "faculty psychology" which saw the mind as a passive collection of abilities that needed to be exercised. This approach was challenged by scientific approaches to psychology and pedagogy, advocated by Herbert Spencer, William James, G. Stanley Hall, and others. The curriculum became more practical in content and purpose; traditional subjects like ancient languages and religious moralizing were phased out. This could have been a liberating step, a recognition of individual differences in learning and life goals, but the conservative culture had another task in mind: In a scientific, industrial society the major role of education came to be a process of selecting qualified young people for professional careers and fitting the rest for the labor pool. Educational psychology became a specialty in its own right, a "scientific" tool for assessing the individual's place in the well-managed industrial order. The new intelligence tests and college board exams were used with enthusiasm — and often supported class, nativist, and racial biases.

Professionalism and Progressivism were vehicles for middle class advancement; education for the immigrant and black working class was defined in increasingly condescending and authoritarian terms. Even the rhetoric of "common" schooling was abandoned, as leading educators — to use Eliot's phrase — sought to prepare children for their "probable destinies" in the social order (Nasaw 1979, 130-132). Although Americans would not adopt the European practice of thoroughly separating vocational and academic schooling, they made a major effort from the 1880s on to channel working class youth into "industrial" education. This effort was justified by self-righteous nativism. A Boston school committee member announced in 1889 that

> Many of these [immigrant] children come from homes of vice and crime. In their blood are generations of iniquity.... They hate restraint or any obedience to law. They know nothing of the feelings which are inherited by those who were born on our shores. (in Lazerson 1971, 33)

Since these supposedly inferior people could hardly be expected to rise into the aspiring middle class, it would be dangerous for education to arouse their hopes. "Know that it is a crime for any teacher, white or black, to educate the negro for positions which are not open to him," declared one Progressive businessman (in Church & Sedlak 1976, 211).

William Torrey Harris, as superintendent of schools in St. Louis and later the U.S. Commissioner of Education, was the most influential American educator of the late nineteenth century. He vigorously advocated the view that the purpose of schooling is to support the established industrial social order. A staunchly conservative Hegelian, Harris asserted that the individual "is totally depraved; that is, he is a mere animal, and governed by animal impulses and desires" unless disciplined by social institutions (in McCluskey 1958, 120). The mission of the school, to Harris, was to instill in children a subservience to authority and social order. The pupil

> must be taught first and foremost to conform his behavior to a general standard.... [He] must have his lessons ready at the appointed time, must rise at the tap of the bell, move to the line, return; in short, go through all the evolutions with equal precision.... Great stress is laid upon (1) punctuality, (2) regularity, (3) attention, and (4) silence, as habits necessary through life for successful combination with one's fellow-men in an industrial and commercial civilization. (in Tyack 1974, 43, 50)

Early in the twentieth century, this approach was enthusiastically adopted, with the trappings of scientific methodology, in the "social efficiency" movement. Colin Scott, head of the Boston Normal School, made this bald statement of the social efficiency approach in his book *Social Education* (1908):

> It is not primarily for his own individual good that the child is taken from his free and wandering life of play. It is for what society can get out of him, whether of a material or a spiritual kind, that he is sent to school. (in Spring 1972, 56-57)

This is probably the clearest, most undisguised confession of this educational approach that we are likely to encounter. It is precisely this attitude which separates most traditional educational approaches from the holistic view.

In the early years of the twentieth century, many leading educators expressed similarly authoritarian and undemocratic ideas. Textbooks such as William Bagley's popular *Classroom Management* (1907) advised teachers to enforce a "mechanical routine" in order to teach the child to sacrifice "his own pleasure when this interferes with the productive efforts of his fellows." This routine bade the child to sit "head erect, eyes turned toward the teacher, hands or arms folded ... feet flat on the floor" (in Spring 1972, 46, 47). Bagley called for "unquestioned obedience" because the school situation was "entirely analogous to that in any other organization or system — the army, the navy, governmental, great business enterprises (or small business enterprises, for that matter)" (in Callahan 1962, 7).

Such discipline, historians recognize, was directed primarily at the immigrant underclass. Immigration as well as violent labor confrontation reached a crescendo during these years, and the alarmed elite took control of the urban schools to enforce social order. It is clear that educators increasingly defined their role in these terms; the Portland, Oregon, superintendent of schools said in 1888 that the true aim of the public school must be "to teach and guide, and if need be compel, its youth to be law-respecting and law-abiding citizens" (in Welter 1962, 158). In 1902 a New York high school principal added that "ignorance is the mother of anarchy, poverty and crime. The nation has a right to demand intelligence and virtue of every citizen, and to obtain these by force if necessary" (in Tyack 1974, 232). The key words here are "compel," "demand," and "force"; surely their use is an ominous sign for a society (and its educational system) that supposes itself to be democratic and free.

Indeed, some Americans, around the time of the First World War, expressed their concern and opposition to these trends in American culture — but their protests were silenced by harassment and censorship, the Espionage and Sedition Acts, the Palmer Raids, and deportations which accompanied "the war to make the world safe for democracy." In truth, the culture of professionalism, and its manifestation in the Progressive movement, represented a large step toward centralized, bureaucratic control of society, with the professionally disciplined upper middle class imposing a moralistic discipline on the rest of society. The early twentieth century saw American society take a large step backward from its democratic ideals, a step in which education played a major role.

Expansion of Education: 1920s–1980s

In the nineteenth century public education had been assigned the task of safeguarding American culture. When the rise of urban industrialism posed new and serious threats to that culture, the schools adapted to meet the challenge. In addition to abandoning the "common school" rhetoric (which had been largely symbolic anyway) for the role of sorting people into their "probable destinies," public education responded to urban industrialism by expanding dramatically in scope. With mandatory attendance and child labor laws, the great majority of young people now went to school, and they stayed in it much longer. The junior high school was introduced to assist in vocational guidance before high school. Secondary and even college education came to be seen as essential to personal success and the achievement of national goals. By the 1960s, it was asserted that the "knowledge industry" was now "the focal point for national growth," taking the place the railroads had held in the nineteenth century (in Ravitch 1983, 185). Or, as Clarence Karier explained it, the "educational frontier" had replaced the western frontier "as the chief arena in which opportunities are gained" — and thus became "the battleground upon which the most significant social conflict would take place in the twentieth century" (Karier 1986, 78).

Indeed, one of the two major facts about public education in modern times is its massive expansion, in both its sheer size and its political significance. Public education at all levels has engaged the concern of corporations and foundations, influential teacher-training institutions, testing services and textbook publishers, national organizations promoting a variety of causes, powerful teachers' unions, and most significantly, all three branches of the federal government. This convergence of social forces and interest groups on a national level was uncommon in the nineteenth century, but has come to define the scope of public education in the twentieth.

The second major fact is the rapid acceleration of social, political, and technological change in this century. The problems of modern industrialism, of international relations in the nuclear age, of uncertainty about the future have simply overwhelmed the schools. Compared to these tasks, it was relatively simple to train agrarian workers to conform to industrial discipline, or to mold immigrants into American citizens; despite some resistance, there was a widely shared social consensus that these were necessary and desirable goals. But in the twentieth century, having experienced the Depression, the rise of fascism and the Second World War, the Cold War and the national security establishment, the civil rights movement, the women's movement, campus unrest and the counterculture, and a resurgence of religious fundamentalism — all against a background of breathtaking developments in science, technology, and communications, there is no longer a secure consensus on the direction of the future. While public education is receiving unprecedented attention and resources on a national scale, it is not because the nation is united in pursuit of social goals but because education has become the focal point for the intense cultural conflicts of our age.

The central educational question of the late twentieth century is whether the traditional themes of American culture can adapt to the demands of the post-industrial age that is apparently emerging. Behind the political and pedagogical conflicts in contemporary education there looms a major struggle between these themes and a new, unfamiliar world. For its part, American culture is persistent — as R. Freeman Butts observes,

> throughout the course of the middle decades of the twentieth century, recurrent waves of national chauvinism, nativism, business assertiveness, and religious authoritarianism swept through state legislatures and the Congress (Butts 1978, 271)

— suggesting that each of the themes of American culture has survived intact into our time. Indeed, recent social history suggests this as well.

Even in the modern, scientific twentieth century, conservative Protestantism has continued to play a large part in American society. Religious fundamentalism was a major movement in the 1920s and has become so again in the 1970s and 1980s. This movement is in many ways a renewal of traditional Puritanism; it holds an utter mistrust for human nature and undisciplined human impulses, and calls for strict moral authority to keep these impulses in check. Any reliance on human judgment without Biblical authority (such as scientific naturalism), or approaches that welcome self-awareness and self-expression, it terms "secular humanism" — and this blanket condemnation has had smothering effects on school curricula and books.

Many states, particularly in the south, have outlawed the teaching of evolution or mandated the teaching of "creation science." The Scopes trial of 1925 was of course the landmark case but by no means the end of the conflict: the biology teacher Scopes lost the case and the state of Tennessee kept its anti-evolution law on the books for years; the issue persists to this day in many states. In recent years, a variety of educational innovations, from sex education to values clarification, have been furiously attacked by conservative religious groups and often purged from the curriculum. Book censorship and occasionally the burning of books still occur in some communities.

While orthodoxy itself has become a minority position, American culture has largely retained its severe Protestant moralism in combination, as we have seen, with a new faith in scientific professionalism. This moralistic elitism was clearly in evidence earlier in the century, in the persisting belief of many Americans that only northern European-derived Protestants can sustain a moral republic. The 1920s saw the peak of the Ku Klux Klan and passage of the National Origins Act, which permanently stemmed the tide of immigration and was especially effective in excluding southern European Catholics. In these years, the citizens of Oregon (encouraged by the Klan) passed a referendum virtually outlawing private (i.e., parochial) schools and requiring public (i.e., wholesome American) school attendance. Other states restricted the use and teaching of foreign languages. The Supreme Court overturned both efforts, but nativism lingered. In the late 1940s, as the federal government began to consider aid to education, the separation of church and state became a heated issue because parochial schools wanted aid for their students. The rhetoric was not as vicious as a century before, when the Know-Nothing party was formed to oppose Catholic influence, but the controversy did stir up intense emotions and ultimately wound up in the courts.

Probably the most blatant expression of American chauvinism in this century has been the anti-Communist crusade. The Red Scare of the early 1920s was a preview of what was in store thirty years later. The Depression understandably generated interest, among many intellectuals, in communism and the Soviet experiment. Capitalism seemed impotent, and some thoughtful Americans were impressed by what they perceived as Russia's sense of purpose and cooperative community effort. Some actually joined the Communist Party, and others sympathized with its aims. Although most soon became disillusioned and disgusted by Stalin's reign of terror and pact with Hitler, their association with communism would come to haunt them. In the 1930s, and then especially after the Second World War, as tensions mounted between the Soviet Union and the United States, Americans launched an obsessive witchhunt for subversive "Reds."

The McCarthy hearings were but the tip of a very cold iceberg; intellectuals and educators who even dared to suggest that American society should place more emphasis on community values, and less on individualistic economic competition, could be branded as Reds by right-wing patriots. Laws were passed requiring loyalty oaths of teachers or dismissing them outright if they were found to be communists. Textbooks were screened and censored. Citizen watchdog groups like the National Council for American Education and publications like the *Educational Reviewer* newsletter alerted religiously patriotic parents to the undermining influence of "reducation" — which was the supposed attempt by communism to weaken the moral and intellectual fiber of the U.S. Any textbook which did not herald the superiority of capitalism or the American government was subject to these attacks.

The roots of this nationalist hysteria, as we have seen, were planted well before the Cold War. Throughout American history, times of cultural stress have brought out ugly expressions of nativism, bigotry, and mob violence. In 1940, for example, when the Supreme Court ruled that children of Jehovah's Witnesses could not exempt themselves from saluting the flag because "national feeling and unity" took precedence over individual conscience, the response by local communities was typical of defensive American nationalism at its worst:

> Within one week after the decision was made, hundreds of Jehovah's Witnesses — men, women, and children — were physically attacked and abused in most inhumane ways. Jehovah's Witnesses' meeting places were burned and their leaders driven out of town, usually with the law enforcement agency of the community leading the way. For example, "... a local judge warned a group of Witnesses that unless they compelled their children to salute the flag he would take the children away from them and place them in an institution where they would be taught to understand what Americanism is." (Karier 1986, 383-384)

During the Cold War, it became clear that "Americanism" meant fighting communism, no matter what methods needed to be used. A revealing point is made by Diane Ravitch: while most educators and scholars, even those who were themselves anti-communist, were deeply concerned about the assault on academic freedom and the constraint of free discussion of ideas, "the public did not perceive ... that basic liberties were in peril" (Ravitch 1983, 104). Communism, it appears, so threatened the core values of American culture that even this extreme nationalist hysteria seemed justifiable.

The witchhunts ended by the mid-1950s, but the Cold War continued. In fact, as Joel Spring has argued, the national educational policy that evolved after the Second World War, which brought the federal government into education with tremendous effect, was preoccupied by economic and technological competition with the Soviet Union (Spring 1976). A coalition of corporation-sponsored foundations (notably the Carnegie Corporation), universities, scientists, and the military establishment sought to mold America's youth into an efficient technocratic social order. The most visible figure in this effort was James Conant, a scientist for the military, president of Harvard University, and author of highly influential reports on public education (*Education in a Divided World* [1948]; *The American High School Today* [1959]; *Slums and Suburbs* [1961]). Another important figure was Admiral H.G. Rickover (*Education and Freedom* [1959]).

The main purpose of this effort was to train as many talented scientists and technologists as the American population could produce. The schools, it was argued, must develop science and math skills if the U.S. were to keep ahead of the Soviet Union. According to Edward Teller, the physicist who helped develop the hydrogen bomb, the Soviets "drive them [students] on in a really merciless manner" (in Spring 1976, 113). The implication is that, in order to win the Cold War, American educators must do the same. In the 1950s, this mentality was fostered by an expanding network of corporate foundations, organizations, and government activities (which Karier [1986] calls an "interlocking directorate" with close links to the CIA): The Committee on the Present Danger, the National Manpower Council, the Educational Testing Service, the National Science Foundation (and its offshoots, the Physical Science Study Committee and School Mathematics Study Group), the Selective Service Act, and the landmark National Defense Education Act of 1958, which brought the federal government into educational financing and policy making. The launching of Sputnik by the Soviet Union in 1957 has become a symbol of the Cold War technology race, and indeed it was a catalyst for renewed concern about the quality of American education, but educators had already been under pressure from Cold War patriots for a decade previously.

Clearly, then, American culture has made a strenuous effort to preserve itself amidst the challenges of the twentieth century. The significant introduction of the federal government into education can be seen as an act of desperation: the guardians of culture, fearing the dissolution of moral and social consensus, enlisted the most powerful agency available in order to enforce their worldview. As I argued before in reference to the onset of the industrial age, Americans made a *cultural choice* in the face of the nuclear age; Spring asks why the country created a National *Science* Foundation rather than a National *Peace* Foundation. What made it so important to train children to be scientists and mathematicians? The answer is found in the persistent themes of American culture. This Protestant-capitalist nation, its moral self-righteousness and national pride threatened by the rise of communism, called upon its faith in scientific positivism and professional expertise to fight the evil enemy.

The culturally defensive atmosphere of the 1950s provided the setting for what has been called "the great debate" over American education. Public education came under intense attack from a variety of critics — scholars, business leaders, and enthusiastic patriots — who feared that the nation's schools were failing to turn out properly educated citizens. Most of their ire was directed at "progressive education," and in fact they virtually succeeded in discrediting the term. Yet, as I have indicated, "progressive education" covered several, very different, educational movements, one of which was an important expression of the holistic tradition. For this reason we need to take a closer look at the issues involved in the "great debate."

The mission of the mainstream Progressive movement had been the efficient management of industrial society, the fitting of people into the social and economic positions for which their talents (often related to their racial and class background) were suited. One of the educational challenges of the urban industrial age was the dramatic rise in school attendance, especially at the secondary level. Millions of young people from every background, many of whom would not previously have entered high school, did so. Arguing that only a small portion of these students were fit for, or could benefit from, a highly intellectual training, many of the leading figures in the professional education establishment, such as E.P. Cubberley, Franklin Bobbitt, David Snedden and W.W. Charters, to name a few, endorsed the social efficiency approach. They claimed that the primary goal of education is the smooth adaptation of youth to the existing social order; for the majority of youth, the curriculum should emphasize vocational and life skills.

The 1918 Kingsley Report of the National Education Association was a major statement of this approach, and a stream of important reports in the late 1930s and early 1940s, with titles like *Education for All American Youth* and *That All May Learn*, argued that the majority of students do not need intellectual discipline, but practical skills that would help them adapt to American society. In 1945 a government committee headed by Charles Prosser, a veteran advocate of vocational training for the mass of students, launched the "life adjustment" movement which found a great deal of support among educators. By the late 1940s, high school curricula were apparently giving more and more attention to home economics and family life, grooming and dating, drivers' education, fire prevention, and purely vocational courses, at the expense of traditional academic subjects. By this time, many intellectuals, concerned citizens, and educators were aroused, and between the late 1940s and early 1960s they launched a heated attack on "progressive" education.

As early as 1938, a group of these educators had gathered to discuss trends in American schooling; in 1943 I.L. Kandel attacked progressive education in *The Cult of Uncertainty*. After the war, with the rise of the life adjustment movement, the Cold War, and the renewed perception by intellectuals that American society was hostile to the life of the mind, the criticism mounted. In 1949 Mortimer Smith published *And Madly Teach*, and 1953 saw the publication of major critiques by Arthur Bestor (*Educational Wastelands*), Robert M. Hutchins (*The Conflict in Education in a Democratic Society*), and Albert Lynd (*Quackery in the Public Schools*); in 1954 Smith put out *The Diminished Mind* and in 1955 Bestor published *The Restoration of Learning*. Other important critics included Mortimer Adler, Bernard Iddings Bell, Jacques Maritain, John Keats, Stringfellow Barr, Mark Van Doren, Harold Clapp, Douglas Bush, Max Rafferty and the Cold War educators Conant and Rickover. The Council for Basic Education was formed in 1956, and three years later one of its leading figures, James D. Koerner, came out with *The Case for Basic Education*.

How do the major themes of this literature fit into the history of

American culture and education? To begin with, these critics represented a highly conservative conception of education. Karier (1986) discusses this "neohumanist" movement and its literary, philosophical, and religious expressions; Wingo (1965) describes the conservative educational doctrines of *essentialism* and *perennialism* which fueled the Cold War-era criticism of "progressive" education. Basically, these doctrines hold that the primary purpose of education is intellectual and moral discipline, that established academic fields (and, for the perennialists, the "Great Books") are the best means of developing rational and intelligent judgment, and that all citizens should be so educated. Clearly this view is deeply at odds with the social efficiency approach. The critics were outraged that schools were being used for training in vocational and social skills instead of "transmitting the heritage of the race from generation to generation" (Smith 1949, 36). They argued that "adjustment" means *mediocrity*, that academically gifted children were actively discouraged rather than given the intellectual stimulation they needed, while the rest of the students were denied the opportunity even to learn about the Western intellectual heritage. Bestor was particularly eloquent in calling for the extension of a well-rounded liberal education to all youths, no matter what their "probable destinies."

Another major complaint of this group was the arrogant pretentiousness of professional "educationists." The critics ridiculed the training of teachers in pedagogical methods with little subject matter, the petty and intellectually weak research which passed for doctoral studies, and above all the entrenched system of credentials, qualifications, and promotions which serve to keep the academic "educationists" in power. The critics argued that the educational system was fundamentally undemocratic because this self-appointed and self-perpetuating group of professionals were autocratically making decisions about the lives of the nation's youth. The vast majority of Americans, they said, would not knowingly approve of the tenets of "progressive" education if they were given a choice.

In an important sense these arguments were right on the mark. In criticizing both the social efficiency approach and the self-justifying professionalism of the education establishment, these writers were responding to very real undemocratic trends in American education, which I have already described. Because both of these trends were instigated by the *mainstream* Progressive movement earlier in the twentieth century, the critics were in a certain way justified in their hostility toward "progressive" education — toward this one meaning of the term. Unfortunately, they went much further than this.

Almost all of these critics blamed the problems of "progressive" education on the work of John Dewey, and some reached further back to criticize the influence of Rousseau and Pestalozzi (important figures in holistic education, as we will see). The critics admitted that perhaps the educational methods of the previous century had been overly rigid, but they utterly rejected not only the conservative social efficiency approach but also the *liberal* progressive call to educate "the whole child." The essentialist critics, in my view, rejected the holistic approach *in the name of saving American culture from fundamental change*. What they attacked in Dewey and his followers was their willingness to rethink some of the core values of American culture. The works of these critics are permeated with unabashed nationalism, especially in relation to the Cold War. The opening statement of Rafferty's *Suffer, Little Children* clearly expressed their overriding concern: "Education's first duty is to make possible the survival of our country" (Rafferty 1962).

Several of the critics were fond of recalling Dewey's marginal association with communism; for example, Rickover observed that the early Soviet Union adopted Dewey's approach in its schools, and

> a glance at the Marxist version of familiar progressive ideas helps us realize just what can happen when schools are turned from their traditional concern with developing young minds to the progressive objective of conditioning the 'whole child' — something very close to propagandizing your children. (Rickover 1959, 173)

Similarly, some of the critics charged that public educators sought to impose Dewey's atheistic values on the nation's youth, undermining family values in the process. (Conservative religious groups continue this argument today with their assault on "secular humanism" in public education.)

It is true that Dewey and many of his followers seriously discussed naturalistic values, socialist ideals, and a loosening of traditional discipline in the classroom. But the essentialist critics did not, for the most part, offer serious rebuttals to Dewey's philosophy. In fact, several of them admitted (as I will myself in Chapter Six) that Dewey's work is highly sophisticated and subtle, and difficult to grasp completely. Rather than try to do so, they merely asserted (a) that the "educationist" establishment had imposed Dewey's ideas onto American education, and (b) that since most Americans were for family values, patriotism, and intellectual discipline, this was undemocratic.

The first point is simply wrong. It appears, as Dewey himself realized, that many of the "educationists" failed to understand his work! The social efficiency/life adjustment movement was the antithesis of liberal progressivism, yet the critics linked it with Dewey's teachings. And they made much of William H. Kilpatrick ("the Grand Master of the cult" according to Albert Lynd) who supposedly imparted Deweyan "progressive" education to thousands of teachers at Columbia University, without critically examining just what Kilpatrick taught and, more importantly, how his students interpreted and applied it. One thoughtful contemporary, writing of the criticism, said that

> much of the controversy is based upon what is actually observed in the contemporary public schools, and the great majority of these schools are not and never have been progressive in any sense.... (Woodring 1953, 50).

My point is that the critics made liberal progressive education (the more holistic child-centered followers of Dewey) into a scapegoat for the sins of the social efficiency approach (the *conservative* Progressivism I described above). For Rickover to equate holistic education with Marxist indoctrination shows a complete — and possibly deliberate — misunderstanding of Dewey's ideas and influence. We will explore Dewey's work and *holistic* progressive education in Chapter Six.

For now, let us look more carefully at the second point of Dewey's essentialist critics: the self-righteous assertions that Dewey's philosophy (and by extension all of liberal progressive education) is out of step with American values. The essentialists' determined, man-the-barricades defense of American culture is an important clue to their underlying purposes. There is far more to the essentialist/perennialist/neohumanist agenda than Rickover's simple formula of "developing young minds." The deeper question is, developing them for what? What are schools for? In fact, despite their sharply different choice of methods, most of the Cold War-era critics aimed for the same kind of moral and cultural discipline which the social efficiency educators sought. The ultimate purpose, for both groups, was to ensure that the next generation would see the world according to the "consensus consciousness" of the dominant culture. Pedagogical conservatism (essentialism and perennialism) asserts that this is best accomplished through strict intellectual discipline. While some of these critics (Bestor, for example) do seem genuinely concerned about critical, careful thinking, the conservative educational tradition places definite cultural limits on such thinking.

Essentialism assumes that Western culture is stable, healthy, and conducive to human growth, that it is, in fact, superior to non-Western cultures as well as to worldviews as yet unrealized. This is a haughty assumption, to say the least — and it is flawed. To argue that schools should only address intellectual discipline assumes that other social institutions are fundamentally sound: that our families are intact and nurturing, that our religious practices give fulfilling meaning to life and are not just programmed rituals. But since this is no longer the case in the late twentieth century, essentialism is a limited and obsolete approach to education.

In guarding the infallible wisdom of the established academic disciplines, the scientific method, or (in the case of perennialism) the "Great Books", the attackers of progressive education did not leave room for any penetrating critique of our worldview; almost any effort to change the curriculum may be rejected as "anti-intellectual," "non-rational," "mystical," "romantic," or "soft-headed." The stubborn insistence that certain authoritative writings are essential to clear thinking and accurate knowledge of the universe does not discriminate between thoughtless fads and truly revolutionary ways of educating — both are to be condemned. (For Kandel, any educational approach not centered around the "racial heritage" is anti-intellectual.) There is little distinction between approaches which clearly *are* anti-intellectual, such as social efficiency, and approaches (like the holistic approaches) which offer alternative conceptions of intellect and

reason — conceptions which are broader, more truly spiritual, and poten-
tially liberating and empowering. These are not merely historical considerations; holistic education today continues to face the resistance of the essentially conservative and ethnocentric "cultural literacy" movement.

It is no accident that educators who dwell on the "basics" and the
classics (for example, former Education Secretary William Bennett) are
welcomed by those with a conservative political agenda (for example, the
Reagan administration). Just as the classical, exclusively intellectual curriculum is the unalterable standard of reason, the present social order and
established beliefs about it (the cultural themes of capitalism, nationalism,
and the rest) are the unalterable standard of social values. As long as we
celebrate the "racial heritage," our attention is conveniently diverted from
racism and ethnocentrism and cultural imperialism — which need to be
confronted in the present.

The critics in the Cold War period left most of this unsaid. They
generally did not answer the social and cultural criticism made by liberal
progressive education so much as ridicule and dismiss it. They assumed
that the existing worldview is sound and that the existing social order is just
— and therefore assumed that something must be wrong with those who
would question either one! Their works contain many *ad hominem* arguments such as Lynd dismissing Rousseau's ideas because he was an
"unbalanced romantic" and Smith saying of Bronson Alcott, the holistic
Transcendentalist educator, that he "was something of a pompous old
windbag, and I can't discover that he ever said anything else of importance...." (Lynd 1953, 170; Smith 1949, 49). But who was pompous? Rafferty's
Suffer, Little Children compared progressive education to the child sacrifices
of the ancient Carthaginians, referred to the Soviet people as peasants and
"faceless masses ... of the Asian steppes," and shamelessly gushed with page
after page of irrelevant literary and historical allusions, meant, I suppose, to
demonstrate his mastery of the classical curriculum. Meanwhile, his argument, like many of the Cold War critics', utterly failed to address the cultural
criticism raised by liberal progressive educators.

The "great debate" succeeded in shaking up the "progressive" public
school establishment, and by the 1960s the schools were largely free of the
"life adjustment" movement. But the result was not some lofty classical
education that developed clear-thinking rational citizens; instead, the
schools became subjected to the far more ominous interest in social efficiency on the part of the federal government and powerful pressure groups.
The "great debate" ended where it began, by endorsing the role that public
education has played since colonial times: the schools were to serve
national and social interests first, and personal development (intellectual or
otherwise) secondarily, if at all.

Yet in the 1960s it became increasingly difficult to determine the actual
content of national and social interests. In the absence of consensus,
whoever had control of the political process, now on a national level, would

determine what those interests would be. It was inevitable that the schools would become virtual battlegrounds (Arons 1983). This is exactly what happened; as the nation moved out of the culturally defensive 1950s, a cascade of technological and social developments challenged traditional beliefs and lifestyles. Among these were television, computers, contraceptives, jet-age travel, missiles and space exploration, highways and suburbia, fast foods and labor saving gadgets, the rising divorce rate, crime, environmental crises and the ecology movement, and civil rights movements for many groups traditionally denied equal opportunities — African and Native Americans, Hispanics, women, homosexuals, and many others. The 1960s saw a youth rebellion of unprecedented scope, the emergence of the counterculture and the "Age of Aquarius," and a wave of critical thinking called *revisionism* in many academic fields. Thus, the second half of the twentieth century has raised a profound and troubling question for educators: What is the role of the public schools in an age of severe social stress, conflict, and change?

The civil rights movement provided the most visible and dramatic of these conflicts. The NAACP had begun challenging racial segregation in education before World War II, and in 1954 the Supreme Court ruled in the epic *Brown v. Board of Education* decision that racially segregated schools could no longer be tolerated. For the next thirty years, the public schools were embroiled in controversies over integration, busing, and equal opportunity. Ugly passions were aroused, resulting in frequent violence. An enduring image of this period is one of federal troops escorting black students into previously all-white schools. Massive federal involvement in education was initiated by the Civil Rights Act of 1964 and the Elementary and Secondary Education Act of 1965.

There are several underlying issues here. One, of course, is the persistence of racial injustice in American culture. A century after the Civil War, it still required legal and military force to give black people equal access to public institutions (in the North as well as the South). Another issue is the nationalist motivation of the federal role in civil rights. Revisionist scholars argue that postwar political leaders would not have supported the civil rights movement for fear of alienating the powerful southern white constituency, except that the Cold War made the persistence of racism a heavy burden on American foreign policy: As long as communists could point to these blatant injustices of American society, our self-serving mythology of liberty and equality was compromised. Furthermore, according to the radical analysis, the U.S. needed still more scientists and trained workers, as well as more consumers to keep the economy strong; it was inefficient to keep excluding a large portion of the population from social and economic life.

While this interpretation is arguable, it points to the possibility that humanitarian idealism was not the only — or even the primary — concern of the nation's leaders. We can discern a familiar trend in the growing federal involvement in education in the 1950s and 1960s: once again, school reform (this time along with civil rights legislation and the "war on poverty") was used as an acceptable substitute for more substantial cultural change. Certainly some progress was made, and in some ways the racial climate may be better today than before the 1960s; but the civil rights reforms, like the Progressive response to corporate industrialism, sought to soften the worst excesses of the system rather than fundamentally challenge cultural beliefs or social institutions. The United States continues to tolerate racism and poverty in the midst of unprecedented affluence; in the 1980s poverty and homelessness have not only persisted but increased. Americans continue to rely on education rather than examine cultural beliefs; if we provide equal opportunities to engage in the competition for social and economic status, it is believed, then the competition must be fair. Talented and well-disciplined people succeed, and those who fall behind must deserve their fate. This faith in education dissolves severe social criticism, such as that which erupted in the 1960s, because the trust in meritocracy is so deeply ingrained in American culture.

Given this belief, education in the late twentieth century has continued to be defined almost exclusively in economic and social terms; its value to society is that it enhances national strength, economic prosperity, and social order. The "summit" meeting on education between President Bush and the nation's governors in 1989 addressed the failing *methods* of public education, not at all its fundamental *purposes*; the politicians remained concerned with productivity, competitiveness, and higher national standards. Educational issues continue to be linked to the interests of business leaders, as they were during the original "common school" movement in the 1840s and the Progressive Era of the early 1900s. Some school districts now offer written guarantees that their graduates can perform the simple mental tasks that entry-level employees need. As one business publication reported,

> The small businessperson actually is looking at the finished product of education, not what is actually going in. He wants the product to be someone who can read, who can listen, who is punctual, who can take instruction, who has the work ethic....

One businessman interviewed in this article wanted

> students trained from an early age to adopt an entrepreneurial attitude — to understand that their skills are a product, and that the world is a vast marketplace where they should be prepared to compete, to create a demand and eventually to sell for the best offer. (Conn 1986, 32)

I can hardly make a better case for the influence of cultural limits on education than do these shamelessly blunt statements. As so well expressed by these narrow-minded capitalists, our culture does not so much care about the individual human person who is "actually going in" to school, as about the "product" that is coming out — a "product" that has no soul, no inherent dignity, but only an economic value determined by the marketplace! It is no wonder, no wonder at all, that the public schools have become the monstrous, inhuman bureaucracies that they are. As they become the pawns of ever more powerful political and cultural forces, every facet of education — administration, the teaching profession, and the curriculum itself — have become more homogenized by massive, bureaucratic entities. There are more laws and more certification requirements. There are powerful unions and a new crop of teacher strikes each year. Textbooks are produced by a few large corporations, and whole curricula are produced by national commissions.

It is time to pause and take a look at what our education has become. Is *this* what schools are for?

Certainly on any given day, in thousands of classrooms across the country, there are warm human interactions between teachers and students. Many children become excited about learning, and may even enjoy school. There are many important achievements: doors are opened to careers and personal success, and a sense of national and social loyalty — a sense of community — is, to a large extent, nourished. This study does not seek to diminish any of these authentic and commonplace experiences.

But we have seen that looming behind the public schools there is a worldview, a way of thinking and interpreting experience, which seeks to channel the educational endeavor in ways that diminish self-understanding and human development. I am thus suggesting an answer to the first fundamental question that opened this book: Who determines the purposes and goals of education in a society as diverse as ours? I argue that education is wholly guided by a dominant culture, a worldview, a particular "consensus consciousness" which dictates what are and what are not appropriate and acceptable ways of thinking and living. This worldview may be characterized by five themes — conservative Protestantism, scientific reductionism, restrained democratic ideals, capitalism, and nationalism — which together forge very definite limits on the individual's personal and spiritual aspirations. American education serves this worldview, and therefore serves to maintain these limits.

Let us now turn to the second fundamental question: *Should* the preservation of this worldview — or any established worldview, for that matter — be the consuming goal of education? There are some educators who argue that it should not. They argue that the goals of social efficiency, economic advancement, and technological superiority are profoundly inhumane. They argue that if Americans truly want a society that is democratic and life-affirming, then it is time to question these cultural goals. These dissident educators are the holistic educators, and I believe that it *is* time to address their questions.

The Holistic Paradigm in Education

CHAPTER 4

A major paradigm shift is taking place. The chances are that by the year 2000 we will have a vastly different system for educating our children. If this is to occur, however, we must explore both the old and the new assumptions relating to every facet of the educational process. Only then can we determine those which are most appropriate to the needs of young people who will spend most of their lives in the twenty-first century.

— Edward T. Clark, Jr. (1988)

In the context of American culture, the holistic paradigm is a distinctly countercultural movement. The history of holistic education is the story of an ongoing conflict between certain core themes of American culture (described in the previous chapters) and a small but determined group of dissidents who have opposed these cultural themes. For two hundred years, mainstream American culture has successfully ignored or suppressed the holistic vision. But there are growing indications that it may not be able to do so very much longer.

During the 1960s, the social institutions and accepted values of American culture came under their most severe and sustained criticism in our history. In the twenty years since, the mainstream worldview has appeared to rebound dramatically. The activism of the 1960s has been repudiated, and America has gone back to its business of economic prosperity and leadership of the free world. Ronald Reagan assured us that "It's morning again in America."

But the conservative political tide of the 1970s and 1980s is an incomplete picture of American society in recent years. A grassroots social movement (which has been called, among other things, "The Third Great Awakening," the "Third Wave," or the "Aquarian Conspiracy") has brought forth an unprecedented flowering of holistic approaches in medicine, psychotherapy, family and community life, work and leisure, spirituality, and education. Often, these movements are dismissed (as holistic education has been for two centuries) as sentimental and "romantic," but I suggest another interpretation: Quite possibly the discontent of the 1960s was not an aberrant and temporary phase in American culture but *the dawning realization that the traditional themes of American culture cannot satisfy the psychological, moral, and spiritual needs of a global, post-industrial age.*

This countercultural ferment has often been termed, by its enthusiasts as well as its critics, the "New Age" movement. In a sense this is accurate, because the culture that is now emerging promises to be as new and different from the industrial age as this period is from the feudal-agricultural age that preceded it. But the term "New Age" is not satisfactory because it has too often (especially in the mainstream media) been used as a label for the most blatantly commercial, celebrity-worshipping, and trivial elements of the movement, such as trance channeling and UFOs. In addition, the term has become a lightning rod for the hostility of conservatives and orthodox religious groups. The *holistic paradigm*, far from being a superficial fad or an idolatrous heresy, is in truth a fertile, imaginative, and highly diverse worldview which draws upon serious scholarship, authentic mystical traditions, radical politics, and, above all, a genuine search for personal wholeness and a culture that would truly nurture human potentials.

Many serious and insightful thinkers of the twentieth century have prepared the ground for this new paradigm, including Aldous Huxley and Teilhard de Chardin, Henri Bergson and Jan Christiaan Smuts (who coined the term *holism* in his book *Holism and Evolution*), Gregory Bateson and Carl Jung, Joseph Campbell and Abraham Maslow, E.F. Schumacher and Owen Barfield, Rudolf Steiner and G.I. Gurdjieff. A new generation of scholars and observers has described it from a number of perspectives and disciplines; among them are Theodore Roszak, Jeremy Rifkin, Jean Houston, Morris Berman, Fritjof Capra, Willis Harman, Marilyn Ferguson, Ken Wilber, David Bohm, Matthew Fox, Rupert Sheldrake, Barbara Marx Hubbard, Alvin Toffler, Robert Theobald, John Naisbett, and many, many others. (See bibliography for detailed references.) It is not possible here to attain the depth that is provided by their works, but in order to understand the significance of holistic education, we need to consider the outlines of this emerging worldview.

Most fundamentally, the holistic worldview is essentially spiritual rather than materialistic. In the broadest terms, this means that inner human qualities, such as mind, emotion, creativity, imagination, compassion, a sense of wonder and reverence, and the urge for self-realization, are recognized as vital aspects of human existence. A spiritual worldview treasures the more subtle, deeply personal qualities that are potential in all persons, and which are essential for true personal fulfillment and social harmony. Spirituality is the recognition that our lives have a purpose, a direction, a meaning, a goal that transcends our particular physical and cultural conditioning. It is the recognition that we are *connected*, at deep and profound levels, to the continuing evolution of life and the universe. Spirituality may or may not involve religious language, concepts, and rituals; it may or may not involve belief in a personal God. The essential feature of a spiritual perspective is that it sees the human being as creatively unfolding from within, rather than as a passive victim of biological, economic, or ideological forces. *A spiritual worldview is a reverence for life* — for the life that mysteriously and spontaneously arises from deep within each of us.

In contrast, the materialistic worldview which dominates our culture is more exclusively concerned with manipulating the outer environment (both physical and social), and it applies only *objective* standards (such as IQ, grades, income, gross national product) for measuring its success. Lacking a deep reverence for life, it leads instead to competition and a selfish consumerism; its sense of community identity is based on moralistic control rather than compassion or a feeling of inherent connectedness. According to holistic thinkers, the industrial age has almost completely obscured the central importance of the spiritual qualities and possibilities of human life.

The holistic paradigm dissolves the traditional dichotomies between mind and body, between spirit and matter. The central tenet of the holistic worldview — and this is the basis for the term *holistic* — is its emphasis on the *integration* of the inner qualities of human life with the outer physical, social world. The holistic paradigm opposes the overly materialistic, rational, technocratic, and hierarchical tendencies of the industrial age in order to achieve a greater *balance* between individuality and community, creativity and tradition, intuition and reason, inner peace and objective success.

The holistic paradigm does not reject the scientific method per se, but it strongly criticizes the one-sided reductionism of scientistic thinking; that is, its tendency to accept only mechanistic, cause-and-effect explanations of reality. In fact, many scientists are coming to realize that reductionism does not adequately describe the universe. The findings of quantum mechanics, the "uncertainty principle" and pathbreaking research in neuroscience are shattering the Cartesian/Newtonian worldview. In his writings, physicist Fritjof Capra has observed that the holistic paradigm is bringing science into alignment with ancient Oriental philosophies, in recognizing the basic interconnectedness of all existence.

Holistic science, then, is essentially an ecological approach. No phenomenon, physical or mental, can be adequately studied apart from its whole context. Nature — including human nature — is not a random assortment of matter blindly following mechanistic laws of cause and effect; holistic science refers to "systems," "fields," and other concepts that underscore the intricate connections among matter and energy. The emerging philosophy of deep ecology emphasizes that human life is embedded in nature and cannot be elevated above the rest of creation without doing severe violence both to the environment and to ourselves. In fact, the "Gaia hypothesis" holds that the Earth itself is not simply a large chunk of rock but a self-regulating — and therefore in a sense a *living* — system.

Another important theme in the holistic literature (well developed in Ken Wilber's writings, for example) is that human consciousness is engaged in a process of purposeful evolution. The human species has not yet achieved its potentials; our violent history is not the sum of our possibilities. The high moral and spiritual ideals envisioned by saints and prophets of the past are not unattainable dreams but a blueprint for developing our own latent qualities. What we call mystical or psychic powers are more highly refined qualities of consciousness, which have lain dormant in most people but which may yet be developed. The important educational implication of this view is that each new generation may be expected to surpass the level of consciousness of its parents, rather than merely to replicate it.

Several holistic writers have pursued Carl Jung's exploration of the mythologies of various civilizations, believing that they provide important insights into the ongoing evolution of consciousness. One of these insights is that the materialistic worldview is to a great extent the masculine archetype run amok; the urge to dominate nature, to compete for social and economic supremacy, and to keep emotional and spiritual expression under control are largely "masculine" qualities. The feminine archetype — nurturing, organic, connected to nature — has largely been repressed in this culture, not only during the industrial age, but for centuries. In a provocative study, Riane Eisler (1987) has drawn upon new archeological evidence as well as feminist theory to argue that before the advent of violent, patriarchical, "dominator"-model Western cultures, there existed for centuries far more peaceful, life-affirming "partnership"-model cultures. She contends that a major cultural transformation is now underway which seeks to return to this earlier and more balanced model. Indeed, one of the elements within the holistic movement is a revival of ancient Goddess traditions. This is a concrete example of how the holistic paradigm values the whole of human experience: to elevate the masculine and degrade the feminine is a destructive imbalance. An emphasis on rational, utilitarian intelligence, competition for success, and satisfaction of material desires while neglecting compassion, love, justice, and peace cannot be a humane way of life.

In the area of economic, political, and social theory, holistic thinkers have been among the first to recognize that industrialism has run its course and is in decline. It is becoming apparent that the ravenous use of fossil fuels and nuclear power, the proliferation of petrochemicals and other toxic substances, as well as the increasing bureaucratization of society and the centralization of political and economic power cannot be sustained much longer if we desire a humane civilization. This is not a leftist critique of capitalism, but a holistic confrontation with the inhuman scale and ecological recklessness of modern industrial society. Huge, powerful corporations, the massive military and national security establishment, and bureaucratic social service agencies (including education) do not truly serve the needs of human development.

What would take the place of industrialism is not entirely clear. There are visions of an "information society" using sophisticated electronic technology, as well as back-to-the-land dreams of traditional craftsmanship, communal celebrations, and small scale food and energy production — probably the post-industrial age will be some combination of these elements. The crucial goal of most holistic writers is the *decentralization* of economic and political power. The Green political movement, which began coalescing in the United States in the mid-1980s, clearly expresses the connection between a holistic, spiritual image of humanity and a radically democratic social philosophy (Capra & Spretnak 1986; Spretnak 1986; Satin 1979).

In essence, the holistic paradigm asserts that the materialistic worldview of the scientific-industrial age is a tragic narrowing of human possibilities. There is such greater depth to human experience, and such deeper meaning in existence, than is allowed by the reductionistic and utilitarian tendencies of our culture. Western civilization has lost the sense of reverence and mystery, the sense of belonging to the cosmos, which characterized traditional cultures (Huxley calls this the "perennial philosophy"). We have become alienated from nature and from our own human nature. Out of greed, technocratic *hubris* and reckless stupidity, we are now on the verge of destroying the ecosystem entirely. This is the realization that emerged in the 1960s, and its influence is growing. Obviously, this new worldview promises a fundamental transformation of education.

Education for Human Potential

Many of the more esoteric and intellectually specialized aspects of the holistic movement are still far removed from the public dialogue. But one expression of the new paradigm has touched the lives of millions of people: the "human potential" movement. This multi-faceted assortment of unorthodox therapies, growth centers, workshops, publications, professional associations, and training centers has been ridiculed (especially by moralistic conservative intellectuals) for encouraging narcissism and bringing about the so-called "Me Decade." While there truly have been some strange and trivial aspects to the human potential movement, to focus on them is to miss its critical cultural significance: this is a serious attempt to radically expand our culture's limited conception of human nature. It is based upon an emerging human science found in the pioneering work of Carl Jung, Roberto Assagioli, Carl Rogers, Abraham Maslow, Frederick Perls, Rollo May, Erich Fromm, Charles Tart, and many other creative theorists in "humanistic" psychology. Arthur W. Combs, a psychologist who has been instrumental in applying this work to education, sums up its importance by saying "We are living in a world today with new ideas about the nature of human capacity, about what is possible for human beings" (in Roberts 1975, 296).

One of the earliest expressions of this humanistic education was *Education and Ecstasy* (1968) by George Leonard, a journalist who was involved (and still is) in the human potential movement. Although his educational theory was relatively unsophisticated (he was oblivious to the already 200-year-old holistic tradition in education), Leonard passionately described the emerging view of expanded human possibilities and insisted that it be the basis for a new view of education. During the 1970s, this new view indeed blossomed, in an holistic approach variously called "humanistic," "affective," "integrative," and "confluent" education.

The "humanistic" education approach has sought to balance intellectual (cognitive) development with emotional (affective) development,
hence the "integration" or "confluence" of experience. These educators
have argued that a purely intellectual education involves only the external
material world. Reading, writing and counting, familiarity with subject
matter, knowledge of scientific (or academic interpretive) techniques enable
a person to deal more effectively with the natural environment and social
convention. And this is useful. But what of the Socratic imperative to
"Know thyself"? Where in a traditional academic education does a person
learn about the organic and emotional sources of one's own attitudes and
perceptions? How does one establish meaning and values? Humanistic
educators argue that education must give the student the opportunity —
and the skills — to integrate academic learning with personal meaning and
purpose. In the humanistic approach, education is not an attempt to mold
children's thought and behavior, but involves a deep

> concern for students as persons — for their mental health and self-
> development, for their interpersonal skills and potential roles in society, and
> for their joy in learning.... (Allender 1982)

These educators specifically assert that the primary purpose of education must be to activate and develop the latent potentials of each person,
not to prepare the individual for a limited set of tasks as determined by the
culture. One of the leading humanistic educators, George I. Brown, wrote:

> We believe that the uniqueness of the individual is a precious commodity and
> that for the state or any institution of the state to repress, inhibit, or distort the
> enormous potential of each individual for learning to do for himself and for his
> society is evil and wasteful. (Brown 1971, 236-237)

As we will see, this "humanistic" belief is a consistent theme in the literature
of holistic education. It is, in fact, a defining characteristic of this tradition.

Another key theme of holistic education is a basic trust in human
nature. Humanistic educators have asserted that natural human development aims toward growth and harmony and goodness. Evil, they have said,
is not a spontaneous expression of human nature but results from deprivation and repression of organic human qualities. The growing child, they argue,
has an urgent need for self-esteem and emotional security, and when this is
threatened by regimentation, competition and fear of failure, optimum
human development is thwarted. One of the most eloquent exponents of
this view was Abraham Maslow.

> We speak then of a self, a kind of intrinsic nature which is very subtle, which is
> not necessarily conscious, which has to be sought for, and which has to be
> uncovered and then built upon, actualized, taught, educated.... [A teacher
> should] help a person find out what's already in him rather than to reinforce
> him or shape him or teach him into a prearranged form, which someone else
> has decided upon in advance, *a priori*. (in Roberts 1975, 37)

Maslow argued that human nature is intrinsically good, or at least
neutral, and that self-actualization (the attainment of one's highest mental,
moral, and spiritual potentials) is the ultimate goal of human development.
In explaining why the majority of people not only fail to reach this level, but

indeed seem mired in neurotic, destructive, or anti-social behavior, Maslow postulated a hierarchy of developmental needs; he observed that as long as people are struggling for physical or *emotional* survival, they cannot be concerned with self-actualization or high ideals. (The work of Piaget and Lawrence Kohlberg on children's moral development strongly supports this view.)

Humanistic educators, then, strive to provide the social and emotional security that is necessary for healthy human development. It is becoming increasingly clear that in a time of cultural upheaval, traditional education is no longer able to attain even its own goals of academic and behavioral discipline. The alienation, cynicism, and violence which have been increasing dramatically among American youth in recent years will not be solved by greater discipline and a "back-to-basics" approach. In the humanistic view, it is not a lack of discipline, but the deprivation of emotional and spiritual needs, that are at the root of anti-social and self-destructive behavior (see, for example, Gordon 1989).

Carl Rogers, who pioneered "client-centered" psychotherapy and was perhaps the leading figure in the human potential movement, was an important influence on the humanistic education movement, especially with his book *Freedom to Learn* (1969). Rogers expressed the central themes of holistic education: True learning involves the whole person (including feelings, personal concerns, and creativity); the human being aspires toward growth and integration, but needs an emotionally supportive environment that encourages exploration and self-discovery; every student, and every teacher, ought to be respected as a unique and precious person and not be forced into role-bound behavior by rigid and extrinsic goals. For Rogers, these themes were extensions of his own central principles of client-centered therapy: trust and unconditional acceptance, empathic understanding, and personal authenticity and integrity.

Rogers confirmed that ultimately, the holistic approach represents a certain conception of human nature.

> It would be most unlikely that one could hold the ... attitudes I have described, or could commit himself to being a facilitator of learning, unless he has come to have a profound trust in the human organism and its potentialities. If I distrust the human being then I *must* cram him with information of my own choosing, lest he go his own mistaken way. (Rogers 1969, 114)

This simple observation cuts to the root of traditional education in American culture. As we have seen, the dominant worldview is based on a fundamental *mis*trust of the undisciplined human being. It is exactly this that is the underlying source of the hierarchical, authoritarian and controlling educational bureaucracy our society has fashioned. Rogers strongly questioned conventional educational assumptions.

> If our society is to meet the challenges of the dizzying changes in science, technology, communications, and social relationships, we cannot rest on the *answers* provided in the past, but must put our trust in the *processes* by which new problems are met.... This implies not only new techniques for education but ... a new goal. (Rogers 1969, 303, 304)

In the nuclear age, Rogers warned,

> unless individuals, groups, and nations can imagine, construct, and creatively revise new ways of relating to these complex changes, the lights will go out. (in Roberts 1975, 342)

In other words, with powerful new technologies available, the materialistic, nationalistic worldview of the industrial age may eventually destroy life on Earth. Rogers suggested that the humanistic approach, that is, a reverence for life and respect for life's unfolding manifestation in each person, was necessary for the very survival of humankind.

Transpersonal Approaches

The positive image of human nature advocated by humanistic and affective educators was an important break from mainstream culture. The techniques introduced by these educators, such as sensitivity and encounter groups and exercises for "values clarification," have been fiercely opposed by conservative (especially religious conservative) elements. Yet in some ways the early humanistic approaches were cautious. Their emphasis on the integrity of the individual person and their concern for a more open society were genuinely progressive ideas, but what is often missing in these writings is a sense of *transcendence*, a way of seeing human powers as expressions of something more vast and more mysterious than individual personality or social custom.

Implicit in the new psychology, however, especially in the work of Assagioli, Maslow, and Jung, was a glimpse of the "farther reaches of human nature" (the title of one of Maslow's books). While humanistic psychology and education are concerned with personal and interpersonal issues, a *trans*personal psychology explores the realms of mystical and religious experience, intuition and clairvoyance, dreams and hypnosis, the collective unconscious, and the fullest integration of human possibilities. The transpersonal approach has drawn upon ancient oriental teachings as well as Western research into psychic phenomena and states of consciousness, and has incorporated yoga, meditation, T'ai chi, and other Asian disciplines along with biofeedback, guided imagery and fantasy, and dance. A small transpersonal education movement emerged in the mid-1970s.

Transpersonal theory clearly exemplifies the holistic effort to integrate the spiritual and the empirical. Applied to education, this approach emphatically directs our efforts away from cultural programming toward the cultivation of human potentials. "Learning is not geared to the acquisition or transmission of knowledge, but to participation in the process of unfolding from within" (Frances Clark, in Roberts 1975, 499). On the face of it, this approach seems blatantly anti-intellectual, inviting the scorn of traditional educators. But after interviewing almost sixty holistic educators in various schools around the country, I found no teacher who rejected intellectual development, academic skills, or careful thinking as important educational goals. Rather, they argue that academic learning must not be the *sole* concern of education; I was told repeatedly that, in their experience, when children's natural unfolding is respected and their emotional and psychological needs addressed, then far *more* learning takes place with far less effort. With holistic education, it is possible to have both achievement and joy in learning.

But there is another way to address the charge of anti-intellectualism, and that is to expand our conception of learning and knowledge. Education defined in holistic terms is in fact "trans-intellectual." Rational analytical intellect is useful and necessary as far as it goes, but, as shown by research into states of consciousness, *it does not go far enough.* Just about every human civilization, with the exception of the Western materialist worldview, has recognized that the unfolding of the cosmos, both within and beyond direct human experience, is far deeper and more mysterious than is revealed by its surface appearances. The emphasis in Western education on intellect is not, as we are led to believe, the crowning pinnacle of human wisdom but a cultural prejudice. The assertion that other ways of knowing are "anti-intellectual" is an attempt to protect the materialist worldview from the deeper insights that are possible from a more spiritual point of view. Michael Murphy, the founder of Esalen, observed that

> the still dominant intellectual attitude in the Western world does not esteem transcendence as other cultures have. Instead, recent Western culture has prized science, social order and control of the natural world. In America it seems that we would rather conquer the moon than explore the worlds of subjective experience and personal relationship. Nowhere is this attitude more obvious than in our educational system. (in Roberts 1975, 439)

"Intellect," as it has come to be defined and applied in our culture, is one-dimensional and limited, oriented to manipulation rather than insight; and a social order based upon it often rewards those people who are most ruthless in its application. This is the true source of the "culture of professionalism" described in the last chapter.

In the past decade, the transpersonal approach has increasingly been applied to education. A growing number of educators, supported by an expanding network of organizations and publishers, are using yoga, meditation, imagery, and the arts to call forth the deeper potentials of their students. Some of these educators are affiliated with particular religious traditions — yogic or Sufi, for example — while many others have been influenced by Western research in neuroscience and learning.The recognition of the divergent functions of the left and right hemispheres of the brain, theories of "triarchic" and multiple intelligences, studies of learning styles, and research on "superlearning," "mind-mapping," and other techniques provide powerful empirical support to the holistic paradigm in education. This literature is growing rapidly and points the way toward a massive transformation of education in the near future.

Nevertheless, I want to emphasize strongly that the holistic paradigm is more than a collection of scientific findings; it is a comprehensive moral critique of modern culture. Holistic educational philosophy has been evolving for two hundred years, and it is a major purpose of this book to trace that development. In recent years, the holistic approach has found fresh expression in several emerging educational movements (the most widely known of which is the Whole Language approach, based upon a "child-centered" and "meaning-centered" pedagogy). Even more significantly, a number of serious scholars of culture and education have begun to recognize that industrial-age models of education have, in the late twentieth century, become obsolete.

Recent Works in Holistic Education

John P. Miller is affiliated with the Ontario Institute for Studies in Education and wrote on humanistic education in the 1970s. In *The Holistic Curriculum* (1988), Miller carefully describes the philosophical, psychological, and social contexts of holistic thought. He explains the influence of many of the earlier educators in the holistic tradition, and then describes specific approaches and methods that are in use or can be applied to education today. Miller's analysis of educational theory distinguishes between the "transmission" (conventional, academic), "transaction" (progressive, humanistic) and "transformation" (radical personal and social change) models of education, and makes a convincing case that the "transformation" model is essential to meet the needs of the emerging culture.

More recently, David Purpel of the University of North Carolina/ Greensboro has written *The Moral and Spiritual Crisis in Education* (1989). Interestingly, Purpel does not come out of the holistic tradition that I present in this book. Instead, he has been influenced by the "critical pedagogy" movement (Freire, Giroux, Apple, etc., whose approach John P. Miller does consider transformational) and has infused their left-leaning political analysis with a strong moral critique of American culture. The result is a provocative educational philosophy that is unquestionably spiritual, ecological, and global in orientation; in other words, it is holistic. Purpel argues that contemporary culture is today facing a severe crisis of meaning, which is only worsened by the technocratic reforms being proposed in education. He calls instead for educators to reaffirm, with a new "prophetic voice," our highest values of democracy, equality, justice, compassion, and peace.

I completely endorse Miller's and Purpel's views and highly recommend their books. I have not incorporated their work into this study, however, because my approach will take a parallel but largely original course. Here, though, I would like to review the work of three other writers who have articulated the holistic approach in education and explored its relationship to American culture: Joseph Chilton Pearce, Douglas Sloan, and Theodore Roszak. Understanding their work will prepare the ground for the chapters that follow.

In *The Crack in the Cosmic Egg* (1973), Joseph Chilton Pearce argues that the Western conception of reality is inadequate. He explores the fact (which is central to this study) that worldviews are *arbitrary constructs* which purport to describe "reality" but actually *shape* it according to a culture's preconceptions. The human mind, says Pearce, is "an open system of synthesis"; our conceptions and preconceptions are self-verifying: we perceive largely what we expect to perceive (Pearce 1973, 147, 78). Most significantly, Pearce argues that this is as true of Western science as of "primitive" or "superstitious" worldviews — that science is not a privileged path to truth but simply has an "aesthetic" appeal to the Western materialist mentality. Modern Western culture has rigidly classified reality into the *natural* (that which is material and measurable, which follows known laws) and the *supernatural* (that which is supposedly of divine origin, the spiritual and transcendent). Bound by this dichotomy, the Western mind must choose between an empiricist or scientific view that identifies any desire for transcendence as "superstition," and an idealist or theological interpretation that sees the material world as illusory or "fallen."

But Pearce, in holistic fashion, rejects this rigid dichotomy. "There is no supernatural," he states, "but there are an infinite number of possible natures" (Pearce 1973, 60). This is a tremendously important concept! It means that the struggle between scientific, secular humanism and dogmatic religious fundamentalism misses the point. It means that reality, and therefore human experience, is fluid, evolving, and capable of transformation. Ultimately, it means that each person is responsible for gaining awareness of the cultural preconceptions that limit our potentials. Pearce declares that

> life has created the means for a conscious directing of potential and we are the means, aware of it or not.... Every man needs the personal adventure of finding the true depths of himself. (Pearce 1973, 152, 157)

In later books, Pearce has explored the implications of the materialist worldview — and the promise of a holistic approach — for child rearing. *Magical Child* (1980) is a passionate defense of the innate intelligences and self-directing forces within the growing human being. He opens by announcing that

> The human mind-brain system is designed for functions radically different from and broader than its current uses. An astonishing capacity for creative power is built into our genes, ready to unfold. Our innate capacities of mind are nothing less than miraculous, and we are born with a driving intent to express this capacity. (Pearce 1980, 3)

Pearce asserts that the materialist worldview does not recognize or respect the innate organic wisdom that seeks to express itself in the unfolding personality of the child. *Magical Child* is a scathing critique of scientific reductionism and the culture of professionalism:

> How do we believe that we can predict and control the natural forces of the universe? Through clever intellectual manipulation and tool usage.... Our real criterion of value becomes the culture's body of knowledge offering or promising enhanced tool production, possible domination of nature, and so some security.... The training and education of children is designed to lead to better tool invention, production, consumption, and handling. (Pearce 1980, 39-40)

In striving to manipulate and control nature through sheer intellect, materialist culture has utterly lost the sense of participation with nature: the awareness that human existence, on levels far deeper than intellect, is intimately related to the evolution of the universe. We are cut off from nature, cut off from vital, active engagement with the world. Our tools and machines, our bureaucratic social institutions and omnivorous nation-states, have become our masters. Raw intellect and social efficiency determine our cultural and personal values. This, says Pearce, is a "monstrous" waste of human possibilities.

Drawing upon research by a variety of psychologists, Pearce argues that the human being begins learning in the womb, that we are born with an intense desire to comprehend and establish bonds with the world, but that we need physical security and emotional nurturance in order to actualize this inner drive. The materialist desire to control nature and human nature frustrates these basic needs — starting with birth itself. Pearce bitterly condemns the techno-medical birthing practices of "the age of professionalism." Reviewing cross-cultural and developmental research, Pearce argues that the technological approach to birthing, with its drugs, surgical instruments, bright lights, and ruthlessly efficient handling of newborns, has devastating consequences for the alertness, intelligence, and happiness of the young child. He calls modern birthing practices a "time bomb" because the personality effects resulting from such a brutal introduction to the world may smolder for years before fully revealing themselves. He contrasts the medical approach with a more natural, spontaneous, and loving way of birthing, which he claims gives the child the emotional security and the experience of bonding that healthy human development demands.

The technological approach to birth is the single most invasive and dramatic distortion of natural human development, but Pearce goes on to show how the materialist mentality frustrates innate human potentials throughout development. The child who feels secure and nurtured has an "open intelligence" and whole-heartedly explores new experiences and new phenomena, while the child ridden by anxiety (this means most children in modern society) has defined the world as a fearsome and dangerous place. He has lost any deep personal connection to the world, and thus the reliance on tools and cold calculation is reinforced. For example, Pearce explains "primary perceptions" — extrasensory and clairvoyant perceptions often reported by young children — as fully natural ways of "bonding to the earth" which are repressed by the socialization and education of this culture. The seven-year-old child, awakening to his or her separate identity, needs active engagement with the world; a "period of intensive and ecstatic play." But instead, "we slap the child into the anxiety-ridden and frightful experience of schooling" (Pearce 1980, 207). Pearce claims that this mistreatment of the child has led to our severe social problems:

> Each generation produced under schooling proves more shocked, crippled, violent, aggressive, hostile, confused, defiant, despairing, and the social body crumbles faster and faster. And increasingly, our reflexive, conditioned

answer is to inflict the tragedy on the child sooner and sooner. (Pearce 1980, 207-208)

This is a radical attack on scientific-industrial culture, but in a more recent book, *Magical Child Matures* (1986), Pearce's critique is even more explosive. This work reflects Pearce's own spiritual journey and discovery (he had become a disciple of a yoga master), and he asserts that the organic unfolding which he described in his earlier book is merely a preparation for "post-biological" or spiritual development which emerges around adolescence; this spiritual awakening is "a power of consciousness related to possibility rather than to what has already been created." By spirituality, Pearce means

the exuberant, explosive creative power bubbling up from our hearts in adolescence, when we manifest the first inkling of our identities with the creative power bringing our universe into being. (Pearce 1986, 24)

Although Pearce goes on to describe yogic teachings in some detail, using Sanskrit terms and warm personal reflections on his guru, his conception of spiritual development is in keeping with the holistic paradigm: At a level deeper than intellect, he is arguing, the human spirit is intimately engaged with the creative force of the universe. Whether this be described as divine or "God," archetype or self-actualization, or "Shiva" and "Shakti," the point is that the obsessively intellectual, economic, materialistic concerns of Western industrial culture suppress and distort our awareness of this pervading unity and meaning. The highest levels of human experience are reached through self-disciplined *imagination*, not through academic and behavioral discipline alone — through intuition as much as intellect.

In *Magical Child Matures*, Pearce argues that our materialistic goals — our narrow concern with intellectual and technological achievements — cannot produce true contentment or fulfillment. Spiritual unfolding — attainment of the higher Self — is the true aim of human development, and gives meaning to all organic, mental, and social unfolding which leads up to it. Pearce, in fact, claims that *culture itself* is a "counterfeit model of development [pointing] us back to the physical, sensory-motor realm as our only possibility" (Pearce 1986, 160, 147). This claim is similar to Ken Wilber's assertion that the human spirit desires *atman* (re-unification with its source), but is distracted by cultural beliefs and institutions which provide a false sense of meaning — what Wilber calls the "atman project" (Wilber 1981). Culture, Pearce says, is "the antipathy of spirit" (Pearce 1986, 152).

This is a radical position and it is well beyond my intention (or ability) to assess whether or not it is ultimately correct. But I think it is important to contend with this perspective, and find where it leads us. In our present culture, such an attitude is considered to be merely "romantic" and is dismissed as sentimental and unrealistic. Perhaps it is. But perhaps it points the way toward a vital realm of experience that we have all but lost. The holistic paradigm takes this possibility seriously.

Douglas Sloan is another contemporary holistic writer. He is a scholar at Teachers College, Columbia University, and has edited the prestigious *Teachers College Record*. He holds impressive credentials, yet he is, like Pearce, highly critical of the dominant materialism of our culture. In his excellent book *Insight-Imagination* (1983), Sloan examines the scientism, positivism, and "technicism" of the industrial age and concludes that our culture imposes a terribly narrow definition of reason and knowledge. Instead of wonder, mystery, and vision, we are only permitted to explain our experience in utilitarian, mechanistic terms. This has led, he says, to a callous disregard of ecology, human community, and true individuality.

Like Pearce, Sloan argues that human consciousness participates in creating our reality, that *imagination* — knowledge of one's inner world — is "the foundation of all thinking that is alive, creative, and rational" (Sloan 1983, 86).* Thought patterns that are imposed by culture — especially a scientistic and materialistic culture — inhibit the realization of true insight and wisdom. Sloan expresses the holistic theme of the evolution of consciousness; as he puts it, in the contemporary age the experience of self in relation to the world has expanded, and this "individuation has brought with it capacities for creative action also hitherto unavailable" (Sloan 1983, 56). Unlike many "New Age" enthusiasts, however, he warns against "cultural strip mining," the practice of borrowing esoteric and spiritual techniques to satisfy goals that remain utilitarian and materialistic. This is an important reminder that the holistic paradigm is an integrated worldview that cannot simply be grafted onto our present culture without being trivialized.

Given an expanded understanding of thought and knowledge, our definition of education must be expanded accordingly.

> An adequate conception of education, an education of imagination, will always strive for that way of knowing which springs from the participation of the person as a total willing, feeling, valuing, thinking being — a way of knowing that leads to the wisdom in living that makes personal life truly possible and worthy. It will have as its prime purpose, as its ground and aim, the complete, harmonious realization of the full capacities and potential of the individual as a whole person. (Sloan 1983, 193)

Yet traditional education is interested only in the child's intellectual potential,

> while other capacities and aptitudes, personal, social, moral, aesthetic, go unattended. The deep wisdom inherent in the body and in the emotions is neglected. Indeed, the natural energies and passions of the child become problems to be dealt with (Sloan 1983, 194)

Furthermore, children who do not attain intellectual achievements according to the established schedule are considered failures no matter what their other qualities and sensitivities.

Sloan explicitly addresses the social and political implications of this narrowed definition of human potential. In our society, he says, public policy is concerned with efficiency, cost-benefit analysis, and maintenance

---

*Note: Quotations from *Insight-Imagination* are reprinted with the permission of the publisher, Greenwood Press, under the auspices of the Charles F. Kettering Foundation.

of institutions — not with serving actual human needs. This preoccupation with the "material elements of society, and with their manipulation, management and control" leads to "cultural impoverishment." In such a society, those who "display the requisite intellectual skills" become the leaders and elite class, even though their moral and aesthetic sensitivities may be underdeveloped or quite lacking (Sloan 1983, 196, 197, 198). Sloan calls for a "cultural transformation" starting with a rejection of our limited view of human nature.

> A thoroughgoing utilitarianism does not aim for the liberation of the human spirit: It provides individuals with no inner resources for a self-directed life, no basis for distance from enmeshment in the immediate social circumstances, no channels for the creative expression of their own vital energies and insights, no inner resistance to the low-level enticements and sedatives of an entertainment-consumer culture, no capacity for rational criticism of the society or of its leaders. It fits individuals to the given social arrangements. It is not an education for citizens, it is an education for servants. (Sloan 1983, 200)

This is a strong critique, indicating that the holistic approach is far more than a sentimental withdrawal from the world, much less a batch of techniques for brightening up a traditional classroom. Holistic education is radical.

This critique is shared by Theodore Roszak, who is, I believe, one of the finest observers of the emerging holistic paradigm. His several books offer a well-balanced historical, sociological, and philosophical perspective on the holistic movement — along with a passionate concern for the realization of human potentials. In *Person/Planet* (1978) he presents an excellent discussion of holistic education, blending theory with his own experience with the limitations of traditional schooling.

Roszak asserts that all people bring into life and to school

> a wholly unexplored, radically unpredictable identity. To educate is to unfold that identity — to unfold it with the utmost delicacy.... First of all, we must want children to teach us *who they are*. We should think of our meeting with them as a glad encounter with the unexpected, believing that somewhere in these young humans there is a calling which wants to be found and named.... It is the task of the educator to champion that right of self-discovery against all the forces of the world that see in our children only so much raw material for more of the same, the established, the "successful." (Roszak 1978, 182, 183)

Roszak, too, criticizes the social hierarchy based on intellectual achievement.

> And we see the bright academics clamber on up the social ladder to become doctors, lawyers, junior executives; we see the nonacademics take jobs as plumbers, mechanics, typists.... But now go back, all the way to the beginning. Suppose back there in kindergarten, in the first years of school, we could have known, before we turned them into what they became, that it was in these unexplored and unformed young to become very different human beings. This one an Emily Dickinson, this one a Nijinsky, this one a St. Francis.... What would our "excellence" have gained us that was worth such a loss? (Roszak 1978, 184)

This is a frequent claim of holistic educators: that all people contain seeds of genius in one calling or another, which are utterly neglected by the goals and practices of conventional education. Of course the question arises: Who, then, would do the plumbing, fixing and typing? The question itself assumes the existence of a hierarchical social order and meaningless, alienating industrial styles of work. The holistic approach does not seek to turn all children into respectable and prosperous professionals, but questions the very basis of the social order itself. Why is most work in materialist, industrial culture so unfulfilling and dreary? What happened to the pride and joy of craftsmanship? And why do we so casually accept a hierarchical social structure which gives *some* people the opportunity to pursue self-development while forcing most people to toil at uncreative jobs and pacifying them with the banality of popular entertainment and consumer goods? In the context of American culture, it is assumed that this is a natural hierarchy, a meritocracy; those who obtain professional status have deserved it in an open competition. But the competition is not open. In this culture, success depends a great deal on what kind of home a child grows up in, and a great deal more on whether or not the child has an aptitude for linear, academic thinking. Many — if not most — young people in this culture confront these barriers from the beginning of their lives. Some overcome them; many do not.

Roszak argues that school has become a ritualized performance — "complete assignments, take tests, get grades" — geared to career success, and that this falls far short of what education ought to be.

> In that "great leap forward" by which one generation transcends the expectations of the last, we glimpse the awesome powers of innovation that reside within us — and perhaps a glimmer of our destiny as a species. (Roszak 1978, 187)

This is a theme that has been expressed by many holistic educators, who claim that the highest purpose of education is not to make the young generation an obedient copy of its parents, but to draw forth the transcendent creative powers that are inherent in human nature. Roszak likes the Socratic equation of the teacher with a *midwife* — "one who brings forth what is already there, waiting to be born: the hidden splendors of self-knowledge" (Roszak 1978, 187).

In his chapter on education, Roszak makes one of the earliest attempts to identify the ongoing tradition of holistic (or, in his term, "personalist") education. He classifies holistic educators into the more radical cultural-political group, which he calls the libertarian tradition, and a group that is more concerned with human development and affective education. His rationale for assigning educators to one class or another is not altogether precise, and I disagree with a few of his judgments. Nevertheless, he makes an important attempt to establish that true educational transformation requires *both* approaches: a critique of a repressive culture as well as a holistic, spiritual conception of human nature.

Roszak concludes the chapter with a brilliant proposal for a pact between teacher and students, in which the teacher pledges to respect the individuality, autonomy, and inherent creativity of each person.

> You and I are members of a remarkable species possessed (perhaps) of limitless potentialities. I will help you explore the full size of your humanity,

rejecting no talent or trouble we find there as outside the boundaries of true education. For *you* are my subject matter and constant study.... I will at all times keep you aware of the difference between those things that are merely of social usefulness and those that are humanly fulfilling.... You (and now the "you" becomes singular, no longer plural) come to me as the person no one else can be, a unique event in the universe. Somewhere in you there is a special destiny waiting to be discovered. I will watch carefully for the moment of its awakening, because that is the crown and the summit of my calling. (Roszak 1978, 203, 204)

Holistic education, in all its forms, despite its various styles and appearances, is precisely described in this statement, as we will see in the chapters that follow.

Pioneers of Holistic Education

CHAPTER 5

The roots of holistic education are far deeper than the human potential movement or the 1960s counterculture; they extend back over two centuries through the work of several innovative, dissident educators. Mainstream scholarship in educational history has not considered this group of educators as a cohesive philosophical movement, but only as a loose collection of child-centered romantics. I believe, however, that the holistic paradigm which is now emerging provides a strong conceptual framework for understanding the worldview that these educators, despite their differences in technique and emphasis, have held in common.

In *The Philosophy of American Education* (1965), G. Max Wingo expressed a position similar to my own: that mainstream education is fundamentally conservative, i.e., that the ruling purpose of public schooling is to maintain American cultural values (of which his list is quite similar to mine). To describe the dissenting approaches, Wingo used the term "liberal" education. The core of their belief, he wrote, is that

> no set of ideals, no constellation of institutions, is so hallowed by tradition that it should stand outside the possibility of critical scrutiny, and if necessary, substantial alteration. Institutions exist to serve human welfare, and when they fail to do so they should be changed or abolished.... The real test of their worth is how they serve human beings. (Wingo 1965, 200)

The word "liberal" seems appropriate here, because it aligns this approach with the liberal democratic, Jeffersonian tradition, which tends to welcome social change for the benefit of human welfare. Yet the educational radicals I will be considering have a set of beliefs more specific than the usual meaning of "liberal education." And although the term *humanistic* is currently popular in describing such person-centered approaches, this word also has too many other connotations. (These educators must not, for example, be confused with "secular humanists," and certainly not with the conservative "neohumanists" of the early twentieth century.) In a sense, the label "romantic" is an accurate way to describe the underlying worldview of these educators; like Blake and Coleridge and Goethe, they emphasize the organic, emotional, spiritual, mythical and intuitive aspects of human experience, in opposition to a culture they perceive as overly rigid, intellectual, materialistic, reductionistic, and technological. But for many modern Americans "romantic" means inherently sentimental, unrealistic, and childish; *these* educators, on the contrary, comprise a very serious and, I believe, attractive alternative to mainstream culture.

To describe these educators, who are indeed liberal, humanistic, and romantic, I have chosen the term *holistic*. The word itself is of rather recent origin; very few of the educators described here have actually used it. But it fits them all. What they have in common is their conviction that the whole personality of each child must be considered in education. All facets of human experience — not just rational intellect and the responsibilities of vocation and citizenship, but also the innate physical, emotional, social, esthetic, creative, intuitive, and spiritual aspects of our nature — are precious gifts which must be honored and cultivated if they are not to be lost and wasted. To return to Wingo's characterization, these educators insist that social institutions must "serve human beings," that *a culture must serve the highest potentials of human development,* rather than force the growing child to conform to the prejudices of the adult culture.

This attitude is what I defined in Chapter Four as the holistic world-view: it is the conviction that the ultimate value of life is at once more profound and more subtle than the materialistic goals of modern culture. Holistic education, then, is an expression of the "perennial philosophy" described by Aldous Huxley; its roots are as ancient as recorded history. In modern Western culture, it emerged as the countercultural "romantic" movement, and the one figure who most represents its influence in education is Jean-Jacques Rousseau.

Rousseau

The significance of Rousseau (1712–1778) is in his resistance to the materialist worldview which was gaining ascendence in the eighteenth century. He warned that a society becoming so thoroughly based on scientific reason, conventional roles, and urban life would snuff out vital human qualities which need emotional expression, freedom, and natural surroundings in order to thrive. In *Emile* (1762), Rousseau argued that education, rather than ruthlessly instilling intellectual and social discipline, should seek a harmony between the organic needs of human development and the rational requirements of the "social contract." He observed that child development proceeds at its own natural pace, which, he argued, must be respected because "the first impulses of nature are always right; there is no original sin in the human heart" (Rousseau [1762] 1911, 56). This statement is the core of the romantic, or what I call the holistic, approach. It is the belief that *human development unfolds according to an inherent order, direction, and wisdom that transcend our cultural and ideological prejudices.* Human welfare and happiness can only be achieved if we remain in harmony with this organic development. Education must start by understanding and respecting the nature of this unfolding, rather than with a cultural program to be instilled at all costs. For the cost in personal happiness and spiritual fulfillment is tragically high.

What is the source of the unfolding human personality? For Rousseau, as for many holistic educators since, it is the creative power of the universe itself; that is, God. Yet the romantic/holistic religious faith is distinct from more traditional sects in that holistic spirituality sees each person as a direct expression or manifestation of the divine creative source. Spiritual truth may be revealed directly to human beings, without the dogmatic authority of churches, texts, and ministers.

> What God will have a man do, He does not leave to the words of another man, He speaks Himself; His words are written in the secret heart. (Rousseau [1762] 1911, 173)

Clearly this faith shatters the orthodox Protestant separation of human and divine. The holistic spiritual approach, then, opposes not only the scientistic materialism of modern culture, but also the "Fall/Redemption" theology that has dominated mainstream religious thought. It is equally foreign to "secular humanism" and religious orthodoxy. It is deeply spiritual and yet mistrustful of theology. Consequently, it has never been more than a small, dissenting movement in American culture; serious romanticism, such as that advocated by Rousseau, has always been treated with suspicion if not outright contempt by mainstream American culture.

Some strands of the holistic tradition, especially in the more secular twentieth century, have used a nonreligious language to describe the mysterious inner unfolding of human personality. The insights of Jungian and humanistic psychology, for example, are often used today in place of religious conceptions. But the central theme has remained the same: our highest value must be the organic, spontaneous energies of the growing child, and then we must attempt to design an education *and a society* that nurture and encourage these energies. This is truly the essence of holistic education.

Pestalozzi

The first important educator to apply Rousseau's ideas was the Swiss reformer Johann Heinrich Pestalozzi (1746–1827). An almost exact contemporary of Jefferson (1743–1826), Pestalozzi shared the new empirical spirit of the Enlightenment, rejecting the Calvinist doctrine of innate depravity. He believed in the innate goodness and wisdom of the human being, maintaining that it is only a repressive environment or inhumane society that corrupts human nature. Thus, Pestalozzi sought to provide an environment that would nurture the organic needs of human development. He established residential schools on working farms for orphans and paupers, the most influential of which was at Yverdon from 1805 to 1825. He also wrote several books, including *Leonard and Gertrude* (1781), *Inquiry Into the Course of Nature in the Development of the Human Race* (1797), and *How Gertrude Teaches Her Children* (1801). Pestalozzi's life and work are well described by several authors; I will only summarize the main tenets of his philosophy, as these comprise the foundation for the holistic tradition in American education.

Essentially, Pestalozzi "turned the traditional method of teaching upside down" (Silber 1965, 116). He was more concerned with the needs and characteristics of the learner than with the requirements of the subject matter.

> The reading, writing, and arithmetic are not, after all, what they most need; it is all well and good for them to learn something, but the really important thing is for them to *be* something, — for them to become what they are meant to be....
> (in Barlow 1977, 17)

For Pestalozzi, education was not primarily the handing down of facts or cultural practices. The human nature of each person, which Pestalozzi saw as more fundamental, more essential than societal obligations, must be the true concern of education. In his New Year "address to the House" (Yverdon) in 1809, he proclaimed

> God's nature which is in you is held sacred in this House. We do not hem it in; we try to develop it. Nor do we impose on you our own natures. It is far from our intention to make of you men such as we are. It is equally far from our intention to make of you such men as are the majority of men in our time. Under our guidance you should become men such as your natures — the divine and sacred in your nature — require you to be. (in Silber 1965, 213)

Here is a concise statement of the holistic approach. The contrast between this emphasis on human qualities which transcend cultural prejudices, and the underlying purposes of mainstream education, is striking.

According to Pestalozzi, the essence of education is love. He sought to provide a home-like environment in which every child felt genuinely cherished. In his schools, he cultivated an intimate, friendly, supportive relationship between the teachers and students. Emotional security, he felt, was necessary for personal development and learning. Pestalozzi discouraged the use of coercion and corporal punishment and rejected the traditional methods of rote memorization and recitation.

A fundamental part of Pestalozzi's approach was his insistence that the teacher respect the child's own experience. Begin with what is already familiar to the child, said Pestalozzi, and allow him or her to gradually discover increasing complexity through the evidence of one's own senses. Pestalozzi's "object method" sought to educate by means of real objects from the child's own world. "Life itself educates," he believed; language and books must follow concrete experience and self-directed activity. In such a learning environment, the intrinsic joy of discovery would make extrinsic rewards — praise, prizes, grades — unnecessary.

Pestalozzi sought to cultivate the balanced development of his students' personal qualities: intellectual abilities, moral (or spiritual) sensitivity, emotional security, physical and manual skills, as well as the capability for leading a productive life in society. It is this comprehensive view of child development that makes the romantic approach *holistic*.

Pestalozzi's ideas have had a significant, but complex, influence on modern education. As the Enlightenment spread the canons of scientific empiricism, the old pedagogical methods were becoming obsolete. A more naturalistic view of the child was replacing the theological. Mainstream educators adopted Pestalozzian techniques as a step toward a science of education. The schools of Prussia became world famous for their Pestalozzian innovations, and visitors brought the word back to other nations, especially the United States. In 1823 John Griscom published *Year in Europe,* which Henry Barnard considered one of the major catalysts of the public school movement. Barnard himself spread Pestalozzi's ideas through his encyclopedic *American Journal of Education* and a book, *Pestalozzi and Pestalozzianism* (1862). Horace Mann's Seventh Report (1843) was an enthusiastic description of the Prussian schools, which he had visited that year. In the 1860s, Edward A. Sheldon popularized the object method at his highly influential Oswego (N.Y.) Normal School. In a sense, Pestalozzi can be considered the "father of modern pedagogy" (Downs 1975; Barlow 1977).

But the Pestalozzianism adopted by Prussian and American educators was a selective version of Pestalozzi's work. What has taken place in the classrooms of modern school systems bears little resemblance to the home-like community at Yverdon. It is apparent that Pestalozzi's cultivation of a loving, deeply respectful attitude toward the personality and growth of the individual child runs counter to mainstream education's purpose of instilling cultural values: "It is far from our intention to make of you men such as we are." However fully Pestalozzi could actually practice such a benign neutrality, this was his aim. The missionary zeal of Protestantism, scientism, capitalism, and nationalism leaves little room for such tolerance. The object method, without Pestalozzi's spirit of respect and love for the individual student, was a mere mechanical routine, a way of *more efficiently* inculcating the educators' goals of social and intellectual discipline.

The spirit of Pestalozzi is found, instead, in alternative school movements propagated by critics of American culture. The first such social/educational critic was William Maclure (1763-1840). He was born in Scotland and emigrated to the U.S. after amassing a fortune in commerce. He was a gentleman scientist whose extensive research has led some authors to call him "the father of American geology." He was also extremely interested in democratic social change; he saw society as being divided into a large mass of productive people who needed a useful education, and a small leisure class, which exploited them, that sought a classical, merely ornamental education to distinguish itself. Maclure thus became an early advocate of educational reform and visited Yverdon in 1805. He was so impressed that he asked Pestalozzi to come back to the States with him. Pestalozzi declined, but recommended one of his associates, Joseph Neef (1770–1854). Maclure offered to underwrite Neef's emigration and educational work in America. He was convinced that Pestalozzian ideas would find a better reception there than in Napoleonic Europe; Neef agreed and went with Maclure to Philadelphia.

In 1808, after teaching himself English, Neef was ready to embark on his educational work. He published a book, as a prospectus for his school, which described his Pestalozzian educational philosophy. *Sketch of a Plan and Method of Education* remains one of the classic expositions of the holistic educational approach. "Education," wrote Neef, "is nothing else than the gradual unfolding of the faculties and powers which Providence chuses [sic] to bestow on the noblest work of this sublunary creation, man" (Neef [1808] 1969, 6). The arts and sciences are "accessory things": Pestalozzian teaching does not aim to pour subject matter into the student, but to develop abilities already latent in the person.

> My way is not the way of *learned* men. These sublime truths my pupils will not learn from me; they will ... *discover them of themselves*.... My whole task will consist in aiding them to unfold, to develop their own ideas.... (Neef [1808] 1969, 77)

Like Pestalozzi, Neef argued that concrete experience and empirical evidence must be the means of education.

> My pupils shall pry into no book ... till they are able not only to comprehend what they are to read, but also to distinguish perfectly well, good from bad; truth from falsehood, reality from chimera; and probabilities from absurdities.... My pupils shall never believe what I tell them because I tell it to them, but because their own senses and understandings convince them that it is true. (Neef [1808] 1969, 15, 77)

Neef was a thoroughgoing empiricist who mistrusted intellectual authority as well as religion (he did not share Pestalozzi's spiritual beliefs). He would provide no "dogmatical instruction" but did teach a rational morality based on the golden rule. He did not see himself as an authority figure but as his students' "friend and guide, their school fellow, play fellow, and messmate." He expected them to correct his mistakes; in fact, his teaching method included making false or ridiculous claims in order for students to present their case for the truth (Neef [1808] 1969, 165).

In *Sketch*, Neef is critical, to the point of sarcasm, of traditional teaching methods. He observes that children's curiosity can be annoying and embarrassing, but that school and schoolbooks can be a remedy:

> Send him thither, place him under the care and inspection of your eminent teachers, and I warrant you, that in a few years hence, all this desire of knowing, all this teasing curiosity ... will abate if it be not wholly annihilated! (Neef [1808] 1969, 98)

Elsewhere he claims that children in a traditional school are trained to think, speak, and act like parrots.

In 1809 Neef opened his school near Philadelphia. He gathered seventy-five or a hundred students (the historical accounts differ) and took them on frequent field trips to the countryside. In later years, his former students recalled the informal relationship between them and their teacher, which was highly unusual — if not unique — for that period. In fact, his unorthodox educational, religious, and social views seem to have alienated the community; the school moved further out of the city in 1812, and only a year later, Neef left the area entirely and went to Louisville, Kentucky. He had little success there and retired to farming until 1826. His patron Maclure began to realize that American society was not as receptive to Pestalozzian egalitarianism as he had hoped (Gutek 1978, 29). Still, he brought two more of Pestalozzi's teachers, Marie Fretageot and Phiquepal d'Arusmont, to Philadelphia in the early 1820s.

Robert Owen's founding of the New Harmony community in Indiana in 1825 gave new life to the radical idealism of Maclure and his Pestalozzian educators. In 1826 they settled at New Harmony and attempted to create a model educational community that was clearly alternative to American cultural values. A German visitor commented that Neef (like his New Harmony colleagues)

> is still full of the maxims and principles of the French Revolution; captivated with the system of equality; talks of the emancipation of the negroes, and openly proclaims himself as an ATHEIST. (in Gutek 1978, 50)

Given these beliefs, it is not surprising that American culture would turn a deaf ear to the ideals of New Harmony. The Indiana Senate refused to incorporate the community for fear of encouraging atheism. Torn by internal dissention, New Harmony collapsed by 1827; but even had it prospered, it could have had very little influence on American culture. Two of its young, energetic supporters — Robert Dale Owen (son of the founder) and Frances Wright — took the message of social equality and intellectual freedom to the major cities, but had little more impact than did the utopian community. At Maclure's death, a eulogist said

> His educational plans, it is true, were repeatedly inoperative, not because he did too little but because he expected more than could be realized in the social institutions by which he was surrounded. (in Monroe 1969, 55)

This is a perceptive observation about the reluctance of American culture to accept the sort of educational ideas we are considering here. Although Pestalozzi is credited with modernizing education, the true spirit of his work expanded beyond the bounds of American culture. What mainstream educators such as Mann, Barnard, and Sheldon adopted was, as Gutek puts it, only a "pale version" of his holistic approach. This is a theme that would recur repeatedly over the next century and a half.

Froebel

While he is more commonly known as the founder of the kindergarten, Friedrich Froebel (1782-1852) also contributed to the holistic literature. After working with Pestalozzi from 1808 to 1810, Froebel began his own schools in central Europe. In 1826 he wrote *The Education of Man*, a somewhat rambling religious-idealist treatise which nevertheless contains many authentic holistic passages. Essentially, Froebel held a romantic spirituality similar to Pestalozzi's and important in the holistic tradition; he "completely rejected the notion ... of inherited sin" (Downs 1978, 53) and asserted that through education

> the divine essence of man should be unfolded, brought out, lifted into consciousness, and man himself raised into free, conscious obedience to the divine principle that lives in him.... (Froebel [1826] 1893, 4-5)

Such holistic spirituality opposes the essentialist belief that education should be limited to intellectual and moral discipline. For Froebel,

> the end of education is not reason per se, but rather the happy, unified man who need not keep his instincts and impulses chained down, for they are functionally a part of the integrated man at peace with himself, his universe, and his God. (Karier 1986, 227)

If human development is an expression of a divine principle, then its unfolding is a spontaneous, natural, and inherently salutary process which needs to be respected. Froebel asserted that young human beings, like other growing living things, should be nurtured according to their inherent nature. Just as a gardener must not attempt to force plants to violate the laws of their own development, neither should the educator force the child. Thus the school for the young child is called the kindergarten, the "children's garden." He also observed that growth occurs in distinct stages, each with its own special contribution to the personality of the individual, and hence to be respected. Play, for example, is of vital importance to early development, not to be suppressed by adult demands for accelerated learning.

Moreover, the unfolding of the divine within is a *creative* process, emanating from a source which is beyond the present understanding of most adults and certainly beyond the intellectual and moral constraints of the established culture. The adult must not attempt to determine the limits to the child's potential growth:

> It is unspeakably pernicious to look upon the development of humanity as stationary and completed, and to see in its present phases simply repetitions and greater generalizations of itself. For the child, as well as every successive generation, becomes thereby exclusively imitative, an external dead copy.... (Froebel [1826] 1893, 17)

All of these ideas — the divine unfolding within the person, the spontaneous and essentially creative nature of this unfolding, and the cultivation of an educational environment which respects the fullness and natural stages of this unfolding — are central holistic themes. For mainstream education, Froebel's influence has not extended much beyond the kindergarten. According to Karier,

> Froebel had instituted a radical child-centered reform movement which, if not contained at the kindergarten level, could have serious implications for the elementary school.... The educational time bomb which Froebel so neatly planted at the base of the educational system, set to go off whenever men realized that the true aim of education was to follow the nature of the child and not the rationalized interests of society, was effectively dismissed at that point when the kindergarten became incorporated into American education as a play school which prepared the young for schoolwork. (Karier 1986, 229)

Karier observes that it was William T. Harris, the leading conservative educator of Victorian age America, who was most responsible for this diluting of Froebel's thought. But Froebel's ideas were influential on later holistic educators, including Francis W. Parker and Maria Montessori.

The Transcendentalists

In the 1830s America produced its first home-grown movement of radical social criticism: New England Transcendentalism. This was a many-faceted movement that addressed literary, philosophical, religious, and political issues; it was a conflict between generations and a romantic response to industrialization. In sum, it was a comprehensive critique of American culture itself: a true countercultural movement. Historian Perry Miller has called Transcendentalism "a highly sensitized awareness of the plight of American culture in the 1830s ... a protest of the human spirit against emotional starvation" (Miller 1960, 7-8). This is a significant characterization, suggesting that Transcendentalism went beyond any economic or political ideology and was a deeply felt *yearning for personal wholeness*. These young critics claimed that the American worldview, despite its democratic veneer, is not conducive to genuine personal integration or spiritual freedom. Theirs was, indeed, a holistic critique.

The central teaching of the Transcendentalists was the primacy of individuality and personal spiritual development. Consequently, they found themselves in opposition to social institutions —government, churches, traditional schooling, and even many reform movements — which they perceived as hostile to individual spiritual growth. They were in significant disagreement with all of the cultural themes described in the previous chapters, and opposed the social and moral discipline that American culture sought to impose.* Maxine Greene has commented that

> only a Transcendentalist or a Utopian in those days could put his trust in spontaneity. Those who assented to Trade and Manifest Destiny were those who believed in character training as discipline, in knowledge as the power to control. A Bronson Alcott [the leading Transcendentalist educator] — like a Robert Owen — could not make himself heard by those subjecting a continent to their will while a McGuffey (and a Mann) spoke a language familiar to thousands.... (Greene 1965, 56)

This statement expresses my thesis well. The holistic worldview, with its trust in the spontaneous energies of the human being, is threatening — at least, it is unintelligible — to those who remain bound by the "consensus consciousness" of American culture. Transcendentalism, then, was destined to fail.

But for several years in the 1830s, the Transcendentalists were a stimulating and lively group of young scholars who spread their views through masterful writings, popular lectures, pulpit sermons (most were Unitarian ministers), and other gatherings. There were ten to fifteen leading figures active in the group; in this study I will focus on two major thinkers — William Ellery Channing and Ralph Waldo Emerson — and then on three

---

*Note: Mainstream scholarship had been critical of this anti-institutional orientation, but the revisionism that emerged in the 1960s reflected a new attitude toward the individual's place in American society. Miller's interpretation of Transcendentalism as a serious countercultural movement has been joined by several recent works, including Anne C. Rose, *Transcendentalism as a Social Movement 1830-1850* (New Haven: Yale, 1981); Catherine L. Albanese, *Corresponding Motion: Transcendental Religion and the New America* (Philadelphia: Temple University Press, 1977); and others cited below.

Transcendentalist educators — Henry David Thoreau, George Ripley, and A. Bronson Alcott.

William Ellery Channing

William Ellery Channing (1780–1842) has been called "The Great Awakener" of antebellum philanthropy, social reform, and Transcendentalist idealism. Although he was trained as a traditional Congregational minister, he shed the Calvinist theology and conservative social philosophy of his youth, and between 1813 and 1819 emerged as the spiritual leader of the Unitarian movement. This philosophical shift — like Pestalozzi's — consisted essentially of Channing's rejecting the pessimistic Calvinist view of human nature, and his growing conviction that every person contains within oneself the potential for spiritual realization. While the Unitarian movement as a whole, reflecting the interests of the Boston elite, remained politically conservative, Channing's thought grew increasingly democratic during the last thirty years of his life. Apparently Jefferson, Tocqueville, and others believed that Channing's teaching "was the true religion of American democracy" (Arieli 1964, 265). Since, in my view, Channing was an important ancestor of the holistic paradigm, we will consider his ideas rather extensively here.

Channing is best described as a religious humanist.

> All our inquiries in morals, religion, and politics must begin with human nature.... No book can be written wisely, no plan wisely formed for the improvement of mankind, which has not its origin in just reverence of the powers of the human spirit. (in W. H. Channing 1880, 437, 438)

Human experience, human powers of reason, observation, feeling, and moral judgment were to Channing the immediate source of ultimate truth. In other words, no abstract ideology or sectarian dogma should overrule the claims of the life experience of individual persons. This was not a *secular* humanist view, however; Channing retained a deep religious faith. Where he differed from mainstream American Protestantism was in his teaching that every individual has direct access, through one's distinctly human qualities, to spiritual truth. He asserted that "in comprehending man, we comprehend God." Starting from this belief, Channing preached insistently on behalf of the inherent dignity of all people:

> It is because the human being has moral powers, because he carries a law in his own breast, and was made to govern himself, that I cannot endure to see him taken out of his own hands and fashioned into a tool by another's avarice or pride....
>
> Indeed every man, in every condition, is great.... A man is great as a man, be he where or what he may.... His powers of intellect, of conscience, of love, of knowing God, of perceiving the beautiful, of acting on his own mind, on outward nature, and on his fellow-creatures — these are glorious prerogatives. (Channing 1900, 7-8, 12)

An especially important aspect of Channing's thought was his recognition, like Froebel's, that human experience is spontaneously creative and continually unfolding.

> There is an infinity of resource in the human soul.... We can never say that our nature is exhausted. It breaks out suddenly into new and most unexpected forms.... We were made to grow. Our faculties are germs, and given for an expansion to which nothing authorizes us to set bounds. (in W.H. Channing 1880, 520, 416, 346-347)

> The greatest minds admit no biography. They are determined from within. Their works spring from unfathomed depths in their own souls.... A man should look to his own soul to learn what makes him happiest, and so decide when he is conscious of acting most in *harmony with his whole nature*. (in Arieli 1964, 272)

This spiritual conception of human nature and development is the basis for Channing's moral and social thought. It led to his serious criticism of some of the central themes of American culture, including capitalism, nationalism, and the conservative limits on democracy. The individual, he asserted,

> has a value, not as belonging to a community, and contributing to a general good which is distinct from himself, but on his own account. He is not a mere part of a machine.... He is not simply a means, but an end, and exists for his own sake, for the unfolding of his nature, for his own virtue and happiness. I would maintain that the individual is not made for the state so much as the state for the individual.... Rulers have called the private man the property of the state, meaning generally themselves, and thus the many have been immolated to the few.... (Channing 1900, 49, 176)

But Channing's individualism was most assuredly not the meritocratic competition sanctioned by capitalism. Although his congregation was comprised of some of Boston's wealthiest elite, he regularly preached against the materialistic excesses of capitalism. A narrow striving for material status, he warned, deadened one's spiritual sensitivity.

> No man has a right to seek property in order that he may enjoy, may lead a life of indulgence, may throw all toil on another class of society. The saddest aspect of the age, to me, is that which undoubtedly contributes to social order. It is the absorption of the multitude of men in outward, material interests; it is the selfish prudence which is never tired of the labor of accumulation, and which keeps men steady, regular, respectable drudges from morning to night.... (in W.H. Channing 1880, 510)

> It is a sad thought, that the infinite energies of the soul have no higher end than to cover the back, and fill the belly, and keep caste in society. (Channing 1900, 170)

This is radical criticism of American culture. Yet Channing was a "reluctant radical" (Mendelssohn 1971). He opposed reform movements which swept people into ideological conflict, and called instead for the moral and spiritual renewal of society.

> All slavery, all oppressive institutions, all social abuses, spring from or involve contempt of human nature.... The inappreciable worth of every human being, and the derivation of his rights ... from his spiritual and immortal nature ... are the truths which are to renovate society. (in W. H. Channing 1880, 568)

It is this "spiritual and immortal nature" inherent in every person, not ideological or political positions, that social reformers must advocate. In a sense, of course, this approach appears to follow the traditional Protestant tendency of substituting moralizing and education for needed changes in social institutions, and Channing was criticized by activists of his day (and later by some historians) for being an opponent of social reform and a pillar of the Boston Whig establishment. But there was something deeper to his message: an insistence that the "spiritual and immortal nature" of human beings demands dignity and justice. Channing did not oppose social reform, only the mass psychology of most political and social movements.

In fact, Channing was revered by a whole generation of reformers (including Horace Mann, Dorothea Dix, Samuel J. May, Elizabeth Palmer Peabody, and some of the Transcendentalists themselves), who credited him with inspiring their desire to improve the conditions of their fellow men and women. His sermons called upon them to recognize and nurture the highest possibilities of human nature. Channing frequently preached about education, and his conception of education was clearly holistic.

> The strongest argument for education is found in the nobleness of the human faculties.... Such a being is not to be viewed as an inferior animal, or as important only because he can perform certain labors for the community. He is valuable when considered as an *individual*.... He has a nature which, for its own sake, deserves to be developed.

> To educate a man is to unfold his faculties, to give him the free and full use of his powers, and especially of his best powers. (in W.H. Channing 1880, 261-262, 488)

Channing, like Rousseau, Pestalozzi, and Froebel, asserted that education must start with the child's nature rather than with the educator's preconceptions.

> We begin, perhaps, with ascribing a kind of omnipotence to education, and think that we can turn out a human mind, such as we wish it, almost as surely as a mechanic can turn out from his machinery a good piece of work. But ... the human mind is more complex and delicate in nature, and especially more independent and self-active, than we had imagined. Free-will ... belongs to the child as truly as to the man .... It is well that no mind is put into the hands of another to be moulded at pleasure.... (in W.H. Channing 1880, 656-657)

> Of all the discoveries which men need to make, the most important ... is that of the self-forming power treasured up in themselves. (Channing 1900, 15)

Channing is a fascinating figure in American intellectual history. He can be seen as a spokesman of the "true American religion" or as a radical critic of American culture, as a Protestant moralist or the "first of the Transcendentalists" (Tyler 1962, 66). There is a discrepancy between his own personal background, temperament, and social position — which remained rooted in the mainstream culture — and the profound implications of his ideas, which were radically holistic. Middle class reformers (like Horace Mann), while inspired by Channing's call for human dignity, retained their own Protestant/moralistic cultural biases, as perhaps Channing did himself. On the other hand, the Transcendentalists were inspired by the more radical implications of his views, and out of these they fashioned a holistic cultural critique.

Ralph Waldo Emerson

Ralph Waldo Emerson (1803–1882) was the leading figure in the Transcendentalist circle. Although much of his thought can be traced to European romantic and idealist writers, there is little doubt that he was

stimulated by Channing's humanism as well. Originally a Unitarian minister, Emerson came to believe that ritual and doctrine, even Channing's
liberalized Christianity, were barriers to true spiritual experience. "The
relations of the soul to the divine spirit are so pure, that it is profane to seek
to interpose helps," he wrote in "Self-Reliance" (1841) — this is the most
concise statement of Transcendentalism. Emerson developed his philosophy in a series of essays and addresses, beginning in 1836 with "Nature,"
where he asked,

> Why should not we also enjoy an original relation to the universe? Why should
> not we have a poetry and philosophy of insight and not of tradition, and a
> religion by revelation to us, and not the history of theirs? (Emerson 1965, 186)

This trust in "insight" and "revelation" is the romantic/holistic faith in
the self-creative powers of the human spirit. Just as Emerson questioned the
authority of established religion, he rejected the narrow worldview of
scientism.

> Empirical science is apt to cloud the sight.... It is not so pertinent to man to
> know all the individuals of the animal kingdom, as it is to know whence and
> whereto is this tyrannizing unity in his constitution, which evermore sepa-
> rates and classifies things, endeavoring to reduce the most diverse to one
> form. (Emerson 1965, 218)

This critique of reductionism is an explicit statement of the holistic worldview — almost a century before the term *holistic* was first actually used.

Emerson was critical of the other themes of American culture as well
and felt that conservative republicanism, nationalism, and capitalism stifled
the spiritual development of the individual. In "Politics" (1844), he observed
that government is based on the defense of property and commented that
"every actual State is corrupt"; it is not government but free individual
effort that advances the progress of humanity.

> The antidote to this abuse of formal government is the influence of private
> character, the growth of the individual.... The appearance of character makes
> the State unnecessary. (Emerson 1965, 357)

Emerson proposed an alternative: "The power of love, as the basis of a State,
has never been tried.... Society can be maintained without artificial restraints, as well as the solar system." Emerson's anarchism was based on his
radical humanism: persons are always more essential than institutions
(Emerson 1965, 358, 359).

Emerson's views on education reflect this humanism. He deplored the
traditional conception of education as the handing down of cultural and
intellectual traditions. In "The American Scholar" (1837), he claimed that

> the book, the college, the school of art, the institution of any kind, stop with
> some past utterance of genius.... They pin me down. They look backward and
> not forward. (Emerson 1965, 228)

Emerson believed that true education must come from first-hand experience, from an active engagement of the soul with the lessons of Nature.
"Only so much do I know, as I have lived," he wrote, and he lamented that
"meek young men grow up in libraries" instead (Emerson 1965, 230, 227).

While Channing remained rooted enough in mainstream society to
encourage Horace Mann's vision of the public school system, Emerson's

criticism was more penetrating. After attending one of Mann's local conventions, he wrote in his journal that

> we are shut up in schools and college recitation rooms for ten or fifteen years and come out at last with a belly full of words and do not know a thing. We cannot use our hands, or our legs, or our eyes, or our arms. (in Messerli 1972, 347)

Emerson's main criticism of education was that it impedes the inward development of the individual. In "The Divinity School Address" (1838), he asserted:

> Truly speaking, it is not instruction, but provocation, that I can receive from another soul. What he announces, I must find true in me, or wholly reject. (Emerson 1965, 244-245)

This is a radical reversal of the very foundation of traditional education, but Emerson was not simply being dramatic; his faith in the self-forming power of the individual was genuine. In his essay on "Education," published thirty-five years later, he returned to the same theme.

> The secret of Education lies in respecting the pupil. It is not for you to choose what he shall know, what he shall do. It is chosen and foreordained, and he only holds the key to his own secret. By your tampering and thwarting and too much governing he may be hindered from his end. (Emerson 1965, 430)

This is an important holistic theme: the direction of the young person's life is "chosen and foreordained" by a transcendent creative power, and it is the task of the adult culture to provide the conditions for its unfolding.

The cultural legacy of Emerson is as ambiguous as that of Pestalozzi and Channing. A watered-down version of Emersonian individualism became a popular theme in the self-help and personal success literature of the late nineteenth and mid-twentieth centuries. But Emerson's rigorous, spiritually attuned self-development, which is a major philosophical basis of a holistic educational approach, was clearly contrary to the American worldview. He challenged social institutions "so fundamentally and so irrevocably" that anything short of a serious cultural change would constitute a rejection of his ideas (Welter 1962, 123). Indeed, "Emerson was among the greatest failures of all the reformers. Only a handful of Americans ever shared his transcendentalist ideals and vision..." (Griffin 1967, 66).

Henry David Thoreau

One American who not only shared his vision but took it even further was Henry David Thoreau (1817–1862). Although he is more famous for his two-year experiment at Walden Pond, and for his anarchist political writings, Thoreau was for several years an educator with a generally holistic approach. During the winter of 1835-1836, while a student at Harvard, Thoreau taught in Canton, Massachusetts, and boarded with Orestes Brownson (1803-1876), the mercurial left-wing Transcendentalist who was at the time a Unitarian minister. It is difficult to determine the extent of Brownson's influence on the young Thoreau, but upon graduating from college in 1837, Thoreau wrote to him to seek a permanent teaching position, expressing ideas which few Americans of the time, except for the followers of Channing and Emerson, would have held:

> I would make education a pleasant thing both to the teacher and the scholar. This discipline, which we allow to be the end of life, should not be one thing in the schoolroom and another in the street. We should seek to be fellow students with the pupil, and we should learn of, as well as with him, if we would be most helpful to him. (in Harding 1982, 55)

Thoreau's pedagogy was not child-centered sentimentality, but was grounded in a radical critique of social institutions. Continuing in the same letter, he realized that his educational approach

> supposes a degree of freedom which rarely exists. It hath not entered into the heart of man to conceive the full import of that word — Freedom — not a paltry Republican freedom, with a *posse comitatus* at his heels to administer it in doses as to a sick child — but a freedom proportionate to the dignity of his nature. (in Metzger & Harding 1962, 37)

In many of his works, Thoreau made this Transcendentalist argument that American culture does not offer sufficient personal freedom for true inner spiritual development. Thoreau's educational approach, like his social philosophy, sought to abolish artificial cultural restraints on self-realization.

Thoreau began teaching in his native Concord in the fall of 1837. After two weeks, a school committee member came by and, finding discipline too lax for his taste, instructed Thoreau to administer corporal punishment. In an act of sarcastic disobedience, Thoreau promptly chose a few students at random, flogged them, and resigned. He later began teaching boys in his mother's boarding house and, in September 1838, took over the unused Concord Academy. His brother John joined him early in 1839, and together they ran a school which "was one of the first in our educational history to operate on the principle of 'learning by doing'" (Harding 1982, 84). Although they apparently were demanding instructors and maintained effective discipline (without corporal punishment), there were frequent field trips and much hands-on experience. The relationship between teachers and students was reportedly warm and intimate. The school was successful but closed in April, 1841, because of John's failing health.

Henry tutored occasionally, but his heart was no longer in teaching, and in 1845 he went to live at Walden Pond. In his writings, he returned, from time to time, to the subject of education. He consistently stressed that true learning arises from one's direct experience of nature. In *Walden* he said

> If I wished a boy to know something about the arts and sciences ... I would not pursue the common course, which is merely to send him into the neighborhood of some professor, where anything is professed and practiced but the art of life. (Thoreau 1950, 84)

Like Channing and Emerson, Thoreau had profound respect for the creative potential of the individual, and resented the limitations of social institutions. In his journal he complained that schooling "makes a straight-cut ditch of a free, meandering brook." Education should, he wrote, be "the bringing-out or development of that which is in man"; he called this "wisdom" or "genius" or "manhood" — a true knowledge of one's powers and one's place in nature. He admired the spontaneous education of Indians, and the unschooled abolitionist radical John Brown. Scholarly accomplishments — and Thoreau was an accomplished scholar — must complement, never substitute for, self-knowledge (Salomon 1962; Willson 1962).

George Ripley

Another Transcendentalist scholar concerned with education was George Ripley (1802-1880). While Thoreau chose a solitary alternative to American culture, Ripley founded a communal one: Brook Farm. Ripley was a student of Channing (he was a Unitarian minister) and an admirer of Pestalozzi. The "Brook Farm Institute for Agriculture and Education" reflected the influence of both men. In 1840 Ripley wrote to Emerson that his goals were to

> insure a more natural union between intellectual and manual labor than now exists; to combine the thinker and the worker, as far as possible, in the same individual; to guarantee the highest mental freedom; ... and thus to prepare a society of liberal, intelligent, and cultivated persons, whose relations with each other would permit a more simple and wholesome life, than can be led amidst the pressure of our competitive institutions. (in Rose 1981, 133)

As head teacher at the Brook Farm School, Ripley combined a rigorous academic program (a few families even sent their sons to be prepared for Harvard) with a variety of hands-on experiences, including field trips, work on the farm, and participation in the social life of the commune, which included music, art, dances, and conversations with visiting celebrities. Again, a distinguishing feature of the school was the close relationship between the adults and children; personal involvement and responsibility rather than punishment were used to maintain order, and inquiry and critical thought were encouraged. One early historian of Brook Farm commented that "for this very reason the school could never have been popular" (Swift 1904, 74). But it did attract enough students — girls as well as boys — to bring income into the commune, and lasted until Brook Farm itself closed in 1847.

A. Bronson Alcott

Finally, we come to A. Bronson Alcott (1799-1888), by far the most radical Transcendentalist educator. Alcott was a religious pilgrim who eventually took the idea of spiritual freedom into a personal mysticism that was well beyond Channing's ideas. He did not turn his spiritual restlessness into cogent social criticism as did the other Transcendentalists; rather, he embarked on a personal religious odyssey, of which his educational work was an essential element. He saw children — as yet uncorrupted by "custom and convention" — as his teachers.

Alcott was neither a minister nor a college-trained scholar. After growing up in a pious Connecticut farm family, he became a traveling peddlar in the southern states, and apparently a visit to a Quaker community in North Carolina reawakened his religious search. In 1823 he returned to Connecticut and began teaching in rural schools. At this point, with his spiritual quest in its early stages, Alcott was a holistic educator in the Pestalozzian tradition. He seems to have been intuitively sensitive to children's learning and thinking styles, and introduced a variety of child-oriented innovations: comfortable desks, slates, and real objects to handle and count. He taught through conversations, journal writing, and physical activities, and encouraged imagination and self-expression. He maintained order (reportedly very effectively) by cultivating students' sense of responsibility rather than through corporal punishment. He wrote in his journal that

> the province of the instructor should be simple, awakening, invigorating, directing, rather than the forcing of the child's faculties upon prescribed and exclusive courses of thought. He should look to the child to see what is to be done, rather than to his book or his system. The Child is the Book.... Let him follow out the impulses, the thoughts, the volitions, of the child's mind and heart ... and his training will be what God designed it to be — an aid to prepare the child to aid himself. (Alcott 1938, 12)

Alcott apparently came to these conclusions on his own, but soon discovered how his ideas were aligned with the ideas of Pestalozzi, Neef, and Owen and the school at New Harmony. By 1826 he was calling his school "Pestalozzian" and late in his life he wrote that Pestalozzi had had the most influence on his own educational work. He began writing articles for the new education journals, and his work attracted favorable attention from early school reformers. Samuel J. May, a Unitarian minister in Connecticut and head of the Society for Improvement of the Common Schools, said of Alcott's method that it served

> to invite rather than to compel attention; to awaken thought rather than to load the memory; and in one word to develop the whole mind and heart, rather than a few of the properties of either. (in McCuskey 1969, 49)

In other words, Alcott's approach was holistic.

However, although Alcott received much praise from afar (several Boston newspapers had called Alcott's school one of the finest in the country, and he himself was termed "the American Pestalozzi"), and despite the fact that the children enjoyed school so much that they visited Alcott in the evenings for tutoring and storytelling, the parents were alarmed. As one biographer has pointed out, Alcott's respect for the child was contrary to the prevailing Calvinist belief in innate depravity. To most parents of the time, schooling was supposed to involve discipline and "book larnin'" — not, as Alcott proclaimed, "the production, and original exercise of thought." Parents forced Alcott out of town schools on several occasions, at least once by simply opening a competing school (McCuskey 1969, 25, 32).

In 1828, encouraged by Samuel May (whose sister Abigail would soon become Alcott's wife), Bronson Alcott went to Boston. He continued his holistic teaching in "infant" and Sunday schools, and continued to attract the attention of reformers, particularly William Russell, editor of the *American Journal of Education*. Alcott became more familiar with the intellectual and educational trends of the day (he pronounced the Lancasterian system "an engine of orthodoxy") and became acquainted with leading social reformers and thinkers. Among these, the most important influence on Alcott's thought was William Ellery Channing, who encouraged Alcott's educational work and his spiritual exploration.

For the next few years, Alcott remained open to a variety of intellectual influences. He was involved in Garrison's radical abolitionism, and was invited — although he declined — to instruct the children of "free enquir-ers," the atheist followers of Frances Wright and Robert Dale Owen. He wrote articles on Pestalozzi and "infant" (early childhood) education which are forceful expressions of the holistic approach.

> The animal nature, the affections, the conscience, and the intellect, present their united claims for distinct and systematic attention. The whole being of the child asks for expansion and guidance. The child is essentially an active being.... The quickening instinct of his nature urges him to the exertion of all its functions....
>
> ... Taught to look within for the dictates of duty, they will be led to the exercise of self-knowledge, and of self-control — the safeguards of virtue and happi-ness.... Few laws are, therefore, required, and few punishments and rewards. The child becomes a law to himself. (Alcott 1960, 4, 5, 21, 22)

For Alcott, "the mere communication of knowledge" was not the essential purpose of education. Instead, education must nurture the full develop-ment of the human powers of each child. While Alcott was in Boston, this meant a truly holistic approach.

But late in 1830, Alcott and William Russell were invited to conduct a school in Germantown, Pennsylvania. Encouraged by Russell, Alcott's attention during the next four years turned increasingly to idealist, roman-tic, and Platonist philosophy. Especially after reading Coleridge's *Aids to Reflection*, Alcott moved away from the empirical, humanistic approach he had shared with Pestalozzi and Channing. From about 1832 until the end of his life, Alcott upheld a firm conviction that the material world is only a pale manifestation of the realm of spirit (Dahlstrand 1982).

> Talk to him of outward nature as long as we will, he remains unconscious of God, save by communion with his own spirit. (in McCuskey 1969, 79)

Alcott returned to Boston in 1834 as the first, and most otherworldly, of the Transcendentalists.

In September Alcott began a school in rooms at the Masonic Temple: the Temple School. With Channing's endorsement, it attracted several of the leading families of the city — thirty students in all. Channing's secretary, Elizabeth Palmer Peabody, assisted Alcott and taught Latin. (She later had an illustrious career of her own as an educator, as a founder of the kinder-garten movement in the U.S.) During the next several months the school thrived. In 1835 Peabody published *Record of a School*, her diary of daily events in the classroom. It was well received, for it portrayed Alcott as a conscientious teacher who achieved extraordinary results in intellectual and moral discipline.

But a close reading of *Record of a School* shows that in his pursuit of spiritual purity, Alcott had become less holistic as an educator. Now the "full development" of a child's powers seemed to be narrowed to "the process of making children aware of their inner spiritual nature" according to Alcott's own conception of it (Dahlstrand 1981, 102, 113). He presumed that the correct development of each child must lead to lofty religious and moral sentiments, and the child who strayed from this path was no longer seen as "a law to himself."

> I believe that those who cannot conceive of spirit without body, existing in God before it comes out upon earth, are the very ones who have required the most discipline and punishment, and have the least love of obedience. (Peabody 1969, 116, 123-124)

Alcott resorted to moralizing, peer pressure, and at times criticism bordering on ridicule. He now justified corporal punishment on the grounds that physical suffering could cultivate moral sentiment! He continued to teach through conversation and journal writing, but his ostensibly Socratic questioning was bristling with leading questions and some which appear incredibly inappropriate for young children. In order to teach the meaning of love, for example, he asked one girl if she would be willing to die in her mother's place; and when the little girl hesitated to say yes, he pressured her to answer correctly!

By setting himself up as the moral authority, Alcott actually contradicted the primary teaching of Transcendentalism. He did not give his students real freedom to make their own decisions. At one point in the *Record*, he asks whether anyone wishes to leave the room rather than stay for the lesson. Eight children respond that they would like to leave.

> He stopped them, and asked them if they thought it right to go? And having called up many reasons why they should not, by asking them questions, so that some concluded they would prefer to stay, the rest went. When they had been gone a little while, he went out and called them all in. (Peabody 1969, 146)

Nevertheless, Alcott's approach was still very different from the traditional method of rote memorization and outright coercion. Peabody inserted several passages which expressed Alcott's longstanding beliefs, if not his everyday practice.

> A teacher should never forget that the mind he is directing, may be on a larger scale than his own; that its sensibilities may be deeper, tenderer, wider; that its imagination may be infinitely more rapid ... and he should ever have the humility to feel himself at times in the place of the child, and the magnanimity to teach him how to defend himself against his own (i.e., the teacher's) influence. (Peabody 1969, 22)

Enough of Alcott's radical views emerged to attract the attention of Emerson. In 1835 they met for the first time, and began a friendship that lasted a lifetime. In 1836, the "Transcendental club" began to meet, and its members poured out a barrage of social, moral, and educational criticism, including Emerson's "Nature" and Alcott's *Conversations With Children on the Gospels*.

The two volumes of *Conversations*, published in December 1836 and February 1837, ruined Alcott's career as a schoolmaster. His patrons, along with the Boston religious establishment and press, finally realized that their children were being taught by a man who believed that churches and ministers were unnecessary hindrances. Furthermore, his discourses on the conception and birth of Jesus were considered obscene. Even Channing criticized *Conversations*, which alienated Alcott from his mentor. But it was Channing who maintained a holistic educational philosophy. He observed that "the strong passion of the young for the outward is an indication of

Nature to be respected. Spirituality may be too exclusive for its own good" (in Tyler 1944, 248). Alcott, in becoming so enraptured with Idealist philosophy, had lost much of his humanistic openness to children's experience.*

Aside from these criticisms, I find the alarmed response by the community to be very revealing. Alcott was attacked by the establishment ostensibly because he "threatened to sap the religious sentiment of the community." But there was more to the opposition than this. Samuel May observed that

> the worldly, the great, the wise, the prudent will sneer at it [*Conversations*] because its tendency is not to make good merchants, or lawyers, or civil engineers, or manufacturing agents. (in Dahlstrand 1981, 141)

Alcott's educational approach was opposed by parents throughout his career, and I suspect that even had he conducted Temple School according to the more holistic ideals of his earlier years, the combined opposition of conservative Protestantism and middle class economic self-interest would have eventually forced him out. The virulent attacks made on Alcott in the press, and the almost total exodus of families from his school, indicate that his insistence on individual spiritual development was intrinsically unacceptable to defenders of American culture.

Temple School failed in 1838. Alcott soon began another school, serving a less affluent population. But again he offended the sensitivities of his culture. When he admitted a black girl into the school, and refused to dismiss her when the white parents complained, they took their children out. Alcott was left with five pupils: the black girl, a child of William Russell, and Alcott's three daughters, including six-year-old Louisa May. By June 1839, Alcott's teaching career was over.

Assessing Alcott's pedagogical approach as a whole, the distinctive feature is its profound respect for the untapped potentials of the human spirit. In an introduction to *Conversations* called "The Doctrine and Discipline of Human Culture," Alcott complained that

> we estimate man too low to hope for bright manifestations. And our views create the imperfection that mocks us.... To work worthily, man must aspire worthily. His theory of human attainment must be lofty. It must ever be lifting him above the low plain of custom and convention, in which the senses confine him, into the high mount of vision, and of renovating ideas. (Alcott 1972, xl, xlii)

To Alcott, education was the primary means of awakening each person to one's highest aspirations; this is what he meant by "human culture." Despite the growing insularity of his spiritual odyssey, Alcott's educational career was an unceasing struggle on behalf of the individual against the limitations of a restricted worldview.

> Education should not be regarded as a process instituted on the human being, to fit him for a specific employment, by the installation of a given amount of

---

*Note: It is significant that William T. Harris, the major spokesman for conservatism in education, was first inspired to pursue his Idealist philosophy as a student, when he heard Alcott speak at Yale. In his later years, Alcott admired Harris and even collaborated with him. Yet Alcott's early educational ideas had been the very antithesis of Harris's approach!

knowledge into his intellect; but *as the complete development of human nature*.... (in McCuskey 1969, 163)

It is obvious that Alcott would have little influence on mainstream schooling. In fact, in 1847, Alcott attended a Teachers' Institute which Horace Mann was holding in Concord. Alcott recorded the event in his journal.

> But I learned little from teachers, or the teachers' teachers, on education. The time was passed in exhibition of methods, with the least reference to the principles of the mind or the philosophy of culture.... The Secretary of Education deemed it unsafe to introduce me to the teachers, and, on pressing my desire to give them the benefit of my experience as an educator, I was informed that my political opinions were esteemed hostile to the existence of the State, and that I could not aid the cause of popular culture. (Alcott 1938, 195)

According to Maxine Greene, Alcott "disclosed dimensions of experience which could not yet be encompassed by the rhetoric of the schools" (Greene 1965, 45). This is truly the heart of the matter. The dominant American worldview is threatened by "dimensions of experience" beyond its control. To encourage the continuing growth of the individual, to the extent advocated by holistic educators, is to be "hostile to the existence of the State" in its current form. Bronson Alcott challenged this worldview, but it prevailed.

Like Alcott, Transcendentalism as a whole failed as a radical reform movement. By the end of the 1840s, it was evident that Manifest Destiny was a more stimulating national purpose than "human culture." The nation would become preoccupied with slavery and the Civil War and would enter a "Gilded Age" of industrial capitalism. There would be only one major advocate of holistic education during the sixty years between the Transcendentalists and the rise of progressive education.

Francis W. Parker

Francis W. Parker (1837–1902) was an unusual holistic educator, in that his career took place in public schools. After serving many years as a classroom teacher, he became Superintendent of the Quincy, Massachusetts, schools in 1875, and was head of the Cook County (Illinois) Normal School from 1883 to 1899. Apparently his service in the Civil War (where he attained the rank of Colonel) aroused Parker's misgivings about regimentation in schools, and in 1872 he went to Germany where he studied the ideas of Pestalozzi and Froebel. His holistic reforms became known as "the Quincy system" and "the new education" (Curti 1968, 376). Unlike the Transcendentalists, Parker had a widespread influence on American educators, directly through the thousands of teachers he trained and public lectures he gave, as well as indirectly through the visitors and journal articles that spoke of his work. But the more radically holistic of his ideas were not widely applied.

Parker's major contribution to the holistic education literature was *Talks on Pedagogics* (1894). He subtitled this work, "An outline of the theory of concentration," and his central theme was that true education involves self-initiated activity that is focused and sustained. The book was essentially an argument against traditional teaching methods that view the teacher and textbook as authoritative and the pupil as passive. Like other holistic educators, Parker made this argument on the basis of a deeply held faith in human nature.

> First of all, we should recognize the great dignity of the child, the child's divine power and divine possibilities, and then we are to present the conditions for their complete outworking. (Parker 1969, 24)

Parker's faith, like Channing's, was a religious humanism: each person has dignity and deserves the opportunity to develop to his or her full potential, because that potential aspires to the transcendent.

> I shall take it for granted that the human being was created and designed for the exercise of the highest moral power; that in each individual there are germs of the divine; ... and that education consists entirely in the *presentation of conditions for the exercise and outworking of moral power*. (Parker 1969, 348)

For Parker, education ultimately meant spiritual growth; by gaining knowledge of the creation, he said, we may become closer to the Creator. Of course, conservative Protestantism explicitly denies this; significantly, Parker remarked that "the doctrine of total depravity is man's excuse for his ignorance of the divine nature of the child." Here is an indication that the legacy of Calvinist Protestantism remained alive in American culture at least into the 1890s, and that Parker perceived it as an obstacle to educational reform (Parker 1969, 26, 46, 372).

Supported by the assurance that human nature is essentially good, Parker argued that all aspects of humanness ought to be developed. Education is nothing less than "the realization of all the possibilities of human growth and development." *Talks on Pedagogics* was a comprehensive manual of holistic education. Intellectual work, said Parker, must not be detached from the other aspects of the person's life; knowledge is not gained for its own sake but in order to develop spiritual awareness. Moral training must not be indoctrination of dogma, but the cultivation of personal character.

> There is absolutely no separation of intellectual and moral power in education. Morality is the direction of mental power, is the movement of the being upward. (Parker 1969, 25, 349)

Parker pointed out that mental activity cannot be considered separately from the physical needs of the child, and insisted that true learning can only take place when the child is emotionally satisfied. "Without emotion man is nothing.... Life devoid of pleasure is worthless" (Parker 1969, 234, 359). He also emphasized the importance of artistic expression, manual skills, and vocational guidance, and discussed at length the moral and social awareness which children acquire by participating in the school community.

A central theme of Parker's approach is "unity of action." He argued that people, including children, act most wisely and learn most effectively when they are acting in harmony with their own highest purposes. It is an egregious error, he said, to try to develop particular skills or qualities in isolation from the motivating interests and desires of the person (Parker 1969, 266-268). He insisted that education must arise from "self-activity."

The traditional approach to education, he said, holds that children must be drilled in a variety of skills so that they can apply these skills when and if needed in later life. His approach, by contrast, maintained that skills "may be thoroughly acquired under the immediate impulses of intrinsic thought"; people want to learn what they need to know to carry out their purposes. The ultimate aim of education, then, is not the presentation of subject matter, but the refinement of motive; help young people develop their highest purposes, and they will learn, and act, accordingly (Parker 1969, 288, 227).

> "The truth shall make you free" means that, given the right conditions, the human soul will find that tentative truth which is best for itself.... Every step in personal development is through original inference and its practical application. No human being can find the truth for another.... (Parker 1969, 352-353)

Parker criticized traditional education on a number of points, first of all for ignoring the individuality of each student:

> You feel, as a teacher, that the child must see as you see, have the same action that you have, and you try to bring it about.... He cannot have the same action and when he becomes exhausted through futile efforts to attend, the product is disgust. (Parker 1969, 135)

Believing that learning should be a joyful experience, Parker challenged the traditional view that such "disgust" is a normal part of education. He argued that the best learning occurs spontaneously while the child is actively involved in personally meaningful pursuits. For Parker, "teaching has for its main function the cultivation of the creative power of the mind," and traditional methods of memorization and recitation are nothing but mindless drudgery (Parker 1969, 356, 269). Reading, he said, must be an extension of thought, not a mechanical skill. A wholly bookish education precludes personal observation and thought:

> Educators and authorities have clung tenaciously to the delusion that the greatest and most effective means of education consist in the study of books.... The greatest problem of the past, in which the paramount idea was "control of the many by the few," was how to make man believe he was educated, and at the same time deprive him of the power of original thinking. (Parker 1969, 149)

Parker's strongest criticism was directed against the methods of extrinsic motivation practiced in traditional schools: corporal punishment, grades, rankings, and rewards.

> Corporal punishment has for its basis the working hypothesis that children are bad by birth, by nature, and by tendency, and that this badness must be suppressed; that children do not like education or educative work; that it is necessary to discipline the mind through fear.... Corporal punishment is ... the living relic of dungeons, torture, police, standing armies, used to force human beings into unreasoning obedience and fixed beliefs; to suppress the divine aspirations of the human soul.... (Parker 1969, 366, 370)

But the use of rewards — the appeal to selfishness and avarice — "is infinitely worse."

> Bought at home, bought at school, with merits, percents, and prizes, bought in college and university by the offer of high places, the young man with a *finished* education stands in the world's market-place and cries: "I'm for sale; what will you give for me?" The cultivation of the reward system in our

> schools is the cultivation of inordinate ambition, the sinking of every other motive into the one of personal success. (Parker 1969, 367, 368, 370)

Because Parker saw education as self-motivated, and as an expansion of "moral" power, he was adamantly opposed to educational methods which discourage children from exploration and self-expression for fear of risking failure. He also pointed out that offering rewards based on achievement does not take into account that children differ in native abilities; inheritance, not effort, is recognized.

> I have no hesitation in saying that the development of fear by punishment and selfishness by reward is radically immoral.... Real, genuine educative work, real search for truth and its ethical application, needs no other stimulus. Drudgery must be driven by fear or the unnatural incentive of rewards; but work ... that best develops the whole being ... brings its own sweet, joyous reward. (Parker 1969, 371)

This is radical pedagogy. Certainly, "it can be said that he threw dynamite into self-satisfied educational circles" (Curti 1968, 394). Then how are we to explain his success as a public school administrator and trainer of public school teachers? It is true that he ran into some fierce opposition, but how could this clearly holistic educator have had any impact at all on mainstream education? Curiously, even William T. Harris approved of Parker's approach! Perhaps a clue is found in Harris's statement that Parker's movement was "a reform instead of a revolution." Apparently, this is how Parker himself considered his work. The closing chapter of *Talks on Pedagogics* — titled, like John Dewey's masterpiece of twenty years later, "Democracy and Education" — suggests that Parker did not see his work as fundamentally at odds with American culture, but as a continuation of the reform tradition within it.

Parker contrasted democracy (the principle that society can rule itself) with aristocracy (the rule of the many by the few based upon a mistrust of the common person). Parker despised aristocracy because, like traditional education, it thwarts human freedom and self-development. Democracy, for Parker, meant "mutual responsibility": each member of the community is concerned for the welfare of all.

> There is no religion or government worthy the name which does not give to each individual the means of self-effort, the means of self-support, the means of gaining food and a livelihood, happiness and freedom. (Parker 1969, 416)

In this passage, Parker's definition of democracy is extremely liberal, almost leaning toward socialism. Indeed, he was outraged when he once suggested to a nail manufacturer that he should provide his employees with "better opportunities for personal improvement," and the capitalist replied, "'But that would spoil them as laborers. I must have employees; there must be a class of workers.'" Parker commented, "This Christian gentleman was entirely willing to suppress human souls in the interest of nails" (Parker 1969, 439).

However, Parker did not step beyond moral indignation. He recognized that the United States has not lived up to its professed democratic ideals, but he failed to realize that the spirit of "aristocracy" was very much a part of American culture. He did not seem to recognize that American conservatism, nationalism, and capitalism might encourage values that are inherently hostile to the "personal improvement" of all individuals. Thus, even though he had shown how aristocratic societies deliberately use education to keep the population under control, he suggested that in the United States the use of "drudgery," corporal punishment, and extrinsic rewards were merely holdovers or "traditions" that are difficult to get rid of. He blamed the "indifference" of citizens, the nondemocratic traditions of immigrants and the corruption of urban bosses; and he was especially critical of traditional teaching methods. These were safe, Progressive criticisms to make.

Parker's faith in common schooling as "the one means for the preservation of the republic" and the antidote for all social ills is what defines him as a reformer in the mainstream American tradition, rather than a radical critic. He viewed Horace Mann as a "thorough democrat" and the common school system as having been "born of the people," which of course ignores the tensions raised by class and ethnic differences, centralized control, and industrialization (Parker 1969, 435-438).

Like most mainstream reformers, Parker was most disturbed by the *moral* failure of Americans to achieve their ideals.

> Why is it that the sordid nature of man is so highly developed in our country? Why is it that man looks upon his fellow man as a means to his own selfish ends? Why is it that we doubt almost every man who seeks for office — doubt whether he loves his country more than he does himself? (Parker 1969, 367)

Parker's answer was that selfishness is cultivated by the old-fashioned methods of the schools; once we institute a science of education, he implied, all will be well. There is not even a hint in this book that "looking upon his fellow man as a means to his own selfish ends" may be fostered by a materialist, capitalist worldview.

This raises an important issue. Even though Parker was a genuine holistic educator who seriously challenged the moral and civic indoctrination advocated by conservative educators, he did not (at least in his most important book) make the connection between a holistic education and a holistic critique of American culture. In this sense he was similar to Channing, but very different from Maclure and Neef, Emerson and Thoreau. We begin to see that there are two groups of holistic educators — two different temperaments, we might say. Although their ideas about education contain the same core themes, they have two different ways of dealing with the mainstream society. Some are more *accommodating*, either because they believe that American society is fundamentally democratic and will welcome their ideas — or because they are so absorbed in their work that they have not thought about cultural problems. Other holistic educators are more *radical*; they are countercultural rebels, consciously and often painfully at odds with mainstream society. This characterization of two types of holistic educators still applies and emerged clearly when I interviewed sixty educators around the country in the 1980s. It was a major issue in the progressive education movement, to which we now turn.

John Dewey and Progressive Education

CHAPTER 6

Any serious examination of American education must contend with the prolific work of John Dewey (1859-1952). He was a major intellectual figure whose educational ideas were only one aspect of his wide-ranging concern with social, cultural, and philosophical issues. It is impossible to adequately summarize, in a few pages, the tremendous depth and breadth of his thought, which evolved during sixty years of changing social conditions and intellectual movements. His criticisms of traditional education and American culture were not always holistic, but they were incisive, and twentieth century holistic educators have found much inspiration in his writings. In this chapter I will discuss a few of the major themes of Dewey's work and show their relevance to holistic education in American culture.

A central concern of Dewey's work is human *experience*. One brief statement of his position is found in his important book *Democracy and Education* (1916):

> An ounce of experience is better than a ton of theory simply because it is only in experience that any theory has vital and verifiable significance. (Dewey 1966a, 144)

Experience is real and alive; theory (or belief, ideology) is merely derivative and should not be considered primary. Dewey gave at least three reasons for holding experience as primary. First, experience is "habitual." By this, Dewey meant to include knowledge that is beneath immediate consciousness and prior to rational thought. A person's physical capacities, previous experience, and selective exposure to the world (by growing up in a particular culture, for example — a point Dewey especially emphasized) bring about a certain orientation to the world. Things are already charged with meaning — one sees some of their possible implications and not others — before the person even begins to deliberate on them. Dewey said that the intrinsic qualities of things cannot even be described adequately in words, but must be "had" directly. To summarize his position, I think the essential point is that if theory (or belief) is always grounded in habitual ways of perception and experience, then *it does not come from some realm of pure knowledge, logic, or truth*, but from the meaningful "situation" inhabited by the person; and to make any sense, it must refer back to this world-as-experienced (e.g., Dewey 1957, 30-33).

Second, experience is unsundered, whole, organic. All living organisms, including persons, are intimately related to their environment. Behavior, habits, desires, needs, and thoughts do not occur in isolation but always involve an interaction (or "transaction") between an organism and its surrounding physical and (in the case of humans) social conditions. Dewey's idea of experience opposes the reductionistic social science notion that a self-contained "stimulus" in the environment mechanically evokes a "response" in the organism. Objects or events in the environment are stimuli only as they awaken an impulse, need, or aim already attuned to them. In the language of the philosophical school of phenomenology (which parallels Dewey's approach), experience is "intentional"; it always reflects a meaningful connection between the individual and the world. Experience is essentially an ongoing relationship between inner and outer aspects of nature. Therefore, it is incorrect to arbitrarily separate person and world, individual and society, freedom and discipline, mind and body, natural and supernatural. Dewey criticized theory and belief systems, most of all, for their dualism; that is, their tendency to separate experience into opposing and mutually exclusive categories. For Dewey, experience that is *integrated* — that which attains the fullest possible meaning — is a primary goal of human activity.

A third characteristic of experience is that it is constantly evolving. Dewey placed great emphasis on the *reconstruction* of experience: New experience is not merely added onto past experience, but transforms how the past is perceived. Old meanings, although habitual and somewhat resistant to change, are nevertheless subject to enlargement and enrichment by subsequent experience. Life is growth, *an ongoing experiment*, a continuous process of learning in a world that is only relatively predictable and "stable" and in many ways quite indeterminate and "precarious." Of course, growth under these circumstances involves risk and the willingness to relinquish the authority of tradition. This is the importance of education: it should enable the person — as well as an entire society — to look critically at previously accepted beliefs in the light of new experience. Dewey strongly opposed what he called the "quest for certainty": the substitution of rigid, dogmatic theory for the ongoing discoveries of experience.

Consequently, Dewey has been recognized as the major liberal social philosopher of the twentieth century. In his view, unquestioning allegiance to traditional beliefs and institutions is futile; cultures must change, and the only issue is whether change will be violently induced or intelligently directed. For Dewey, democracy is the best type of social order because it allows for intelligent inquiry and reconstruction. True democracy avoids the extreme concentration of economic and political power and mass indoctrination that characterize totalitarian societies, and it encourages citizens to take an active role in addressing social problems.

> What does democracy mean save that the individual is to have a share in determining the conditions and the aims of his own work; and that, upon the

> whole, through the free and mutual harmonizing of different individuals, the
> work of the world is better done than when planned, arranged, and directed
> by a few...? (Dewey 1940, 66)

For Dewey, the contribution of individuals is vitally important for social
reconstruction because "only diversity makes change and progress.... Every
new idea, every conception of things differing from that authorized by
current belief, must have its origin in an individual" (Dewey 1966a, 90, 296).

Dewey was an important opponent of the conservative social efficiency movement in education. In an age when Jeffersonian ideals were
under attack by the forces of an elitist professionalism, Dewey advocated
the education of all persons for full participation in community life. Yet
because of his integrated view of the individual-in-society, democracy for
Dewey always meant a balance between this intellectual individualism and
a strong concern for the *common* values of the community. This latter
concern led him, especially in the years after the First World War, to explore
a democratic socialism; during the Depression he led a group of "social
reconstructionists" in an aggressive examination of *laissez-faire* capitalism.
Thus, while Dewey valued the individual, he was not an enthusiastic
libertarian as many holistic educators have been. On the other hand, while
he emphasized the importance of *social* intelligence and values, he was not
by any means a radical leftist. Because of this subtle blending of individualism and community interests in Dewey's thought, it fails to completely
satisfy the partisans of more extreme views — either radical or conservative.
From the holistic point of view, where Dewey emphasized individual
growth he has provided a welcome critique of traditional educational
practices, but where he emphasized social and scientific intelligence his
conclusions are somewhat troubling, as I will discuss below.

Dewey's work is an important contribution to holistic theory, for he
gave strong support to holistic educators' emphasis on the growing person.
To Dewey, as to the holistic tradition, the student must not be seen as an
empty mind waiting to be filled with an assortment of facts and the wisdom
of the ages, but must be respected as a person with characteristic needs,
interests, and goals. Dewey agreed with Parker that, to be truly *educative*, the
subject matter must evoke active inquiry and interaction; it must call to the
student's present experience. Education, Dewey said, is not preparation for
adulthood but the further integration of experience at the present level of
growth. Dewey asserted that there is no finished state of development; the
adult personality —like the established culture — is always subject to
further growth, unfolding and reconstruction. Education should nurture an
intellectual openness, a desire to continue learning in every situation; and
one's present experience or "habit" should be seen as an instrument for new
openings, for a still more inclusive integration (Dewey 1966a).

In Dewey's view, it is *intelligence* — an inquiring, experimental openness
to experience — that most successfully links the person to the larger world.
The mission of education is to develop "reflective habits," because intelli-

gent reflection on life's unfolding experience best enables a person to live fully and successfully. Dewey criticized the "quest for certainty" that leads the traditional educator to place excessive emphasis on a rigid, purely academic curriculum, learning by drill and rote, and the absolute authority of the teacher. However, he also warned his progressive followers that they would be mistaken to reject the authority of disciplined intelligence. Education must aim for the development of integrated experience; it must therefore recognize *both* the organization of subject matter (the "logical" element of experience) and the particular needs, interests, and current level of understanding of the learner (the "psychological").

Dewey recognized that natural impulses make the child an active, dynamic being. Learning is a *functional* relationship between the person and the environment; in one's attempts to solve the practical problems of daily life, intelligent thought is a vital ally. If there is no abstract realm of "truth" beyond our experience of it, then the purpose of education is not merely to impart an established body of knowledge, but to enable us to continually reconstruct our experience or grow toward an ever more inclusive understanding of the world. This openness comes naturally to the child, but traditional educational approaches repress it. Observing that the human infant is uniquely helpless and dependent, with a highly impressionable, plastic mind and character, Dewey lamented that this docility

> is looked upon not as ability to learn whatever the world has to teach, but as subjection to those instructions of others which reflect *their* current habits. To be truly docile is to be eager to learn all the lessons of active, inquiring, expanding experience. The inert, stupid quality of current customs perverts learning into a willingness to follow where others point the way, into conformity, constriction, surrender of skepticism and experiment.

He then went on to attack

> the insolent coercions, the insinuating briberies, the pedagogic solemnities by which the freshness of youth can be faded and its vivid curiosities dulled. Education becomes the art of taking advantage of the helplessness of the young; the forming of habits becomes a guarantee for the maintenance of hedges of custom. (Dewey 1957, 64)

Dewey supported the observation of earlier holistic educators that strict intellectual discipline is inappropriate for young children.

> There is every reason to suppose that a premature demand upon the abstract intellectual capacity stands in its own way. It cripples rather than furthers later intellectual development. (Dewey 1940, 26)

Dewey argued (as had Joseph Neef ninety years before) that reading should not be taught until the child can understand what he or she is reading. A premature emphasis on "basics" makes them into nothing more than mere mechanical skills, and thus, said Dewey, even as an adult the person would have little sense of discrimination between meaningful literature and sensationalist trash.

> What avail is it to win prescribed amounts of information,... to win ability to read and write, if in the process the individual loses his own soul: loses his appreciation of things worth while, of the values to which things are relative, if he loses desire to apply what he has learned and, above all, loses the ability to extract meaning from his future experiences as they occur? ...Only by extract-

ing at each present time the full meaning of each present experience are we prepared for doing the same thing in the future. (Dewey 1938, 50, 51)

Dewey shared with holistic educators the belief that strictly academic learning must be seen as an enrichment of, rather than a substitute for, first-hand experience of the world; literacy is an extension of intelligence rather than its source. In his seminal writings around the turn of the century, Dewey emphasized that the traditional role of the school as a source of literary stimulation is obsolete in the modern urban world. He was one of the first to recognize that in this culture there is a surplus of *information* but far less opportunity for youth to participate actively in community activities and so to learn the social and ethical applications of information. He argued that without this ethical sensitivity, any amount of intellectual attainment is lifeless, mechanical, and ultimately dangerous. In *Freedom and Culture*, written in 1938 in response to the rise of fascism in Europe, he was especially concerned with the thoughtless, mass consumption of information in modern society; without intelligent reflection, citizens — even in a democracy — are prime subjects for propaganda. Fascism could happen here, he warned.

Dewey argued that critical inquiry and intelligence can only be developed when they are *actively used* in current, concrete, meaningful situations. The school curriculum devised at Dewey's Laboratory School at the University of Chicago and used by many progressive educators was centered on basic problems confronted by all human societies: the production and distribution of food, shelter, clothing. Through field trips, historical study, and hands-on "occupations," students would come to experience social problems as their own, at their own level of understanding.

It is a common but serious mistake to interpret Dewey's approach as "romantic," "sentimental," or "child-centered." As I have said, his philosophy was extremely well balanced, and the point of this curriculum was not to turn children loose on any projects that popped into their heads, but to engage them in *socially significant* activities. In many ways, despite Dewey's concern for the individual, his philosophy was more fully oriented to the development of society than to the inner needs of the individual person. In Dewey's work the ultimate significance of intelligence, and hence of education, is social rather than personal.

> Education implies the existence of social habits which constitute the standards and ideals for directing and determining the growth of the individual.... There are no such things as powers in the abstract. Power is the ability to do something, to accomplish something.... It involves, therefore, relation to the environment, to the conditions under which the work is to be done. (Dewey 1966b, 34, 88-89)

Intelligence is social, he said, because it is the social group, the culture, that determines how the various objects in the natural world may become "instruments" for dealing with the environment more effectively. While Dewey was aware of the danger of a conservative culture imposing outworn habits on the young, he did not see the curriculum or subject matter as being external to the child; it was a vital means by which the child enters a fuller relationship with the world. One's cultural heritage *is* important — vitally so — because it provides the instrumentalities (all the various arts and techniques) for dealing fruitfully with the world.

Thus, even though the extreme child-centered wing of the progressive education movement claimed Dewey as its inspiration, and conservative critics have blamed him for the decline of American education in the twentieth century, Dewey never advocated pedagogical anarchism; he would never have accepted Alcott's assertion, for example, that the child is "a law to himself." For Dewey, freedom in education is neither a "riotous loosening" of the child's impulses nor a "planless improvisation" on the teacher's part (Dewey 1940, 69; Dewey 1938, 18). Rather, true freedom requires disciplined intelligence, and while the student must be allowed to discover through experiment and trial-and-error, such inquiry must provide an enriched understanding, leading to better adaptation to the environment — or it is not education, but merely amusement. Dewey, like the holistic educators, believed that education must respect the child's experience; but for Dewey personal experience is always tied in some way to social meaning, and in order to be educative, experience must be subjected to the claims of social intelligence.

This emphasis on the social meaning of personality and intelligence requires a closer look. While Dewey's careful attempt to integrate individual and society is, on the surface, a balanced and "holistic" perspective, I believe he went a step too far — a step which the truly holistic approach does not take. In order to integrate the person fully into the natural and social environment, *Dewey consistently diminished the spiritual element of human experience*. He thoroughly rejected the romantic view that there is any transcendent, spiritual source, beyond society and culture, which guides the unfolding of human personality. In other words, aside from biological impulses, there is no unfolding from within the person. This emphasis on the social sources of personality, as well as Dewey's emphasis on the scientific method as the model of intelligence, place Dewey's work just outside the boundaries of the holistic tradition, as I am defining it here. Certainly Dewey was not a conservative opponent of the holistic approach, but his mistrust of the spiritual was simply too definitive. In looking more closely at this issue we can better understand the holistic emphasis on spirituality.

For Dewey, religious concepts (including romantic spirituality) represent the "quest for certainty"; they are attempts to escape from the risks and unpredictability of the natural world. They offer security and refuge in place of the rigorous demands of intelligence. According to Dewey's instrumentalist or experimentalist philosophy, an assertion must prove itself in action, in interaction with the natural or physical environment, in order to have validity. Assertions about spiritual experience are largely beyond such verification, which makes them immediately suspect. The scientific method, said Dewey, is the only authentic means at our command for getting at the significance of our everyday experiences of the world in which we live.

In violation of his own criticism of dualistic, either-or thinking, he asserted that educators must move

either backward to the intellectual and moral standards of a pre-scientific age or forward to ever greater utilization of scientific method. (Dewey 1938, 111, 113-114)

There is no recognition here that pre-scientific cultures might have anything of value for the enhancement of human life, no recognition that while the scientific method might be appropriate for many human activities, it might not be appropriate for *all*. In his hostility to religious dogmatism, Dewey became one of the founders of the twentieth century humanist movement: the "secular" humanism which has come under such intense criticism from social and religious conservatives. But even many of Dewey's more liberal critics have interpreted his experimentalism as a positivistic and scientistic approach that reduces human experience and values to a level of utilitarian calculation. In Dewey's work it is difficult to discover the *source* of our ideals beyond biological needs and their adaptation to the demands of the physical or social environment: Although there are references to "desired results" and "habits of decent and refined life" and a "life of excellence," the ultimate source and actual meaning of these values always seems relative and contingent. At one point he explicitly writes that "Means and ends are two names for the same reality" and argues that ends cannot be meaningfully established apart from means, which are established by practical intelligence (Dewey 1957, 21, 36). But this leaves us in an existential void. How does scientific method, by itself, tell us what is *worth* striving for, experimenting for, educating for? With other students of Dewey's work, I would ask, "Exactly where does the value element enter into our judgment?" (Bernstein 1966, 119); if nature "possesses no directive force (i.e., a guiding purpose) within itself, how can we account for its sudden emergence in man?" (Roth 1962, 138-139).

Dewey's defenders claim that he answered all this, by his emphasis on "esthetic" or consummatory experience: the spontaneous sense of wholeness and meaning which people may achieve at times of intense concentration or integrated activity (Geiger 1958; Kestenbaum 1977). There is nothing transcendent about this, according to Dewey; it is simply an experience which can only be "had" and does not involve intellectual or scientific inquiry. The "spiritual" aspect of experience is not a question of any overarching purpose in the universe but simply an exploration of how we are pre-reflectively and pre-consciously engaged with the world.

According to his supporters, Dewey relied on the scientific method because, unlike religion and much of philosophy, it is not a dogmatic approach but an *integration* of imagination, interest, and curiosity with disciplined intelligence and experimental activity. It is an experiential rather than theoretical way of understanding, and a cooperative rather than sectarian way of establishing truth. Dewey did not seek to impose scientific materialism on all layers of experience, and he did in fact highly value the integrated meaning of artistic endeavor, which he defined broadly.

To be sure, there is a lesson in Dewey's cautious approach to the spiritual. All too often, religious concepts are based on little more than rigidly held beliefs, backed up by authority rather than lived experience. As Dewey observed, religious institutions are almost always profoundly conservative social forces. When the spiritual quest — the search for life's ultimate meanings —becomes a quest for certainty of belief, then openness to experience, which is the essence of true spirituality, is lost. We have seen, for example, how this happened to Bronson Alcott when he became lost in his spiritual quest; it is a danger for so-called "New Age" seekers today as well.

Nevertheless, Dewey's concept of spirituality as esthetic experience cannot satisfy the genuine spiritual seeker and does not encompass the meaning of spirituality represented by the holistic paradigm. "Esthetic" experience refers only to the person's relationship to the physical and social environments. Dewey said that the term "religious" does not imply a distinctive kind of experience but describes a quality of any integrated experience of the "natural" world. But experience that is truly spiritual *is* distinctive; it *transcends* our relationship to physical and social conditions. According to one Quaker philosopher, "An ethical and spiritual being introduces a superfluous element, that is, something that goes beyond what is needed for survival purposes" (Jones 1931, 110). This is not to reintroduce a dualistic separation between the "natural" and the "supernatural," but to argue that *the human soul inhabits a spiritual environment which is as truly a part of nature as the physical and social environments*. It is useful here to recall Joseph Chilton Pearce's comment that "there is no supernatural but there are an infinite number of possible natures," depending on the quality of our perception (see page 67, above). Materialistic, scientific inquiry provides access only to one of many possible aspects of nature.

For all his brilliant insight into the integration of the organism into its environment, Dewey utterly neglected the spiritual context of human life. But those who have undertaken spiritual disciplines (as Dewey had not) regularly report their discovery of an "inner light" or "inner voice" — a "higher self" — which is some kind of direct link to the ongoing and meaningful evolution of the universe — and hence a source of abiding wisdom and guidance, the true source of our highest ends (*as* ends) and ideals. The difficulty is that this spiritual source of meaning and value is more subtle than the everyday world. While the natural environment is primarily experienced through the senses and the social environment through shared meanings, the spiritual environment can be experienced only through an inner searching by the person — for example, through meditation, or work with dream symbols, or rituals such as the Native American vision quest. Dewey dismissed these rituals as "hocus-pocus" and "magic," but he missed the essential point. Rituals often are not meant, as Dewey assumed they are, to magically alter the natural world, but to attune the person to his or her own inner spiritual development. Spiritual disciplines need not, and should not, replace intelligent inquiry as the most effective way of adapting to the physical and social environments, but they are essential for gaining insight into the inner spiritual environment.

The spiritual seeker is interested in the esoteric, or hidden, reality which human language and beliefs (even the most sophisticated philosophical thought) can only vaguely sketch. Until our century, this path only had traditional religious terms available to describe its insights: "God," "divine," "spirit," "soul"; but in the twentieth century many seekers have begun to adopt the language of depth psychology — "archetype," "collective unconscious," "authentic self," "individuation," "self-actualization" — in their attempt to describe experience that transcends rational intellectual analysis. Leading-edge thinkers in physics, too, are exploring a new language to describe the spontaneous, nonrational behavior of matter/energy; David Bohm's "implicate order" is a fine example. I believe that these more secular terms refer to the same "spiritual" reality as the older religious terms. Many holistic educators in the twentieth century (and a few in the nineteenth, like Joseph Neef) have held a profound respect for the spontaneously creative, transcendent, inner source of human personality even without using traditional religious concepts to describe this source.

Dewey, however, would not accept this trans-biological, trans-cultural source no matter what it was called. Because spiritual reality cannot be captured by pragmatic, scientific methods, Dewey dismissed spirituality as futile speculation, as "the optimism of romanticism, an optimism which is only the reverse side of pessimism about actualities" (Dewey 1957, 74). This is a blatantly uninformed and prejudiced statement; nowhere in my reading of Dewey could I find any serious attempt to address the Buddhist's *experience* of enlightenment or the Christian mystic's *experience* of divine presence, nor have I found where he seriously considered the mystical aspects of Jung's or Assagioli's work in psychology. It seems to me that despite Dewey's concern for art and esthetic experience, he has left out the most profoundly important of human experiences!

It is because he rejected a spiritual perspective that Dewey was forced to distance his work from his child-centered followers; Dewey was not so libertarian. But in holistic thought, the individual is considered to be a *self-unfolding personality*; holistic and spiritual approaches, while recognizing the importance of cultural and social influences on human development, assert that the cultivation of the "inner light" or "true self" (whether this is described in conventional religious or modern psychological terms) requires that a person free oneself from the social limitations of "consensus consciousness." This is evident in any of the world's contemplative traditions, and this is precisely what Emerson meant when he said that "the appearance of character makes the State unnecessary."

Consequently, holistic educators in some important ways see the child's natural development as a struggle against the demands and repressions of society — of any society which fails to honor spiritual development. But this is just what Dewey absolutely refused to accept. In his effort to dispel philosophical dualism, he argued that the development of personality is *essentially a social process.* Thus the holistic emphasis on the *inner* (nonbiological) sources of human development (such as Jung's concept of individuation or Maria Montessori's focus on the child as a "spiritual embryo" or Rudolf Steiner's detailed discussion of spiritual forces emerging through the individual's growth) are almost entirely discounted by the Deweyan approach. (Progressive educators, in fact, criticized Montessori's approach as too individualistic. See Chapter Seven for a fuller discussion of Montessori and Steiner).

In one of his very few criticisms of Dewey, George Geiger admitted that

> There is almost nothing in his writings of anxiety, loneliness, anguish. The distressing experiences of humans all seem socially determined and socially controllable. (Geiger 1958, 160)

Geiger says only that this "dates" Dewey and "itself is not a theoretical weakness," but I strongly disagree. The absence of these considerations is not due to Dewey's place in time; spiritual disciplines are ancient and Dewey had as much access to them as his contemporary, Jung. But more to the point, it is precisely these most poignant of human experiences — anxiety, loneliness, anguish, awareness of our mortality, or what Gautama Buddha described as "suffering" — which reveal the profound human need for spiritual unfolding, the soul's intense need for something more than intelligent adaptation to the physical world and social environment. Loneliness and anguish can be urgent reminders that the growth of human consciousness is a spiritual and hence an inner, personal, individual journey.

For Dewey the individual's originality stems from biological instincts or "impulses" which cry out when cultural habits become too restrictive of natural development. Yet it is difficult to see how these impulses can be anything but blind material forces — where is the *purpose*, the *creativity* in biological instinct? In fact, Dewey asserted that "there is no spontaneous germination in the mental life"; without the guidance of habit, impulses "are almost sure to be casual, sporadic and ultimately fatiguing, accompanied by nervous strain" (Dewey 1939, 624). Dewey argued that impulses are relatively weak compared to the inertia of culturally sanctioned habits, and hence intelligent action is necessary to effectively change person and society. But according to romantic spirituality, there *is* "spontaneous germination in the mental life," and cultivating this spontaneity is not fatiguing but deeply refreshing.

Furthermore, the inner life may be subtle but it is not weak; through spiritual discipline the person can directly affect, and transcend, social conditioning, habitual ways of thinking and perceiving, and "consensus consciousness." The spiritually awakened person simply cannot be described as a bundle of biological impulses interacting with its environment. Thus, while intelligent (i.e., socially effective) action has its place, in holistic approaches it is seen as a *means*; the *source* of our goals is a more direct insight or inspiration.

But Dewey insisted that both the individual and the school derive their purposes from the common aims of the social group. A fundamental task of education in a democracy is to encourage a "heightened emotional appreciation of common interests" (Dewey 1940, 142). Unfortunately, it was all too easy to twist this view, despite Dewey's other writings, into "life adjustment" education and mass indoctrination (Lasch 1965). Other educators, under the emblem of Deweyan "progressive education," were far less careful to uphold the balance between individual freedom and social responsibility, and gave Dewey's work a social efficiency orientation which he never intended. This is a misinterpretation from which holistic education, because of its steadfast emphasis on the inner unfolding of the person, is not in danger.

In summary, I argue that because of the central importance of spirituality in the holistic worldview, Dewey should not be counted as a *holistic* educational thinker. (Both Roszak [1978] and J. Miller [1988] tend to support this judgment.) Still, we should recognize that Dewey's critique of traditional educational assumptions — and of the culture that has produced them — remains an important contribution to the holistic paradigm. His sophisticated and insightful work signifies that criticism of this culture is not merely a "romantic" rebellion (for he was no romantic), but is a sound and vital reflection upon some very serious social problems. The progressive education movement which followed Dewey's work (and in important ways expanded upon it) became the most important reform movement American education had yet seen. Progressive education contained many classic holistic themes and deserves a thorough review in this study.

Progressive Education

There is considerable disagreement among scholars over the meaning of the term *progressive education*. A contemporary observer, Paul Woodring, decided that there were four different approaches using the name "progressive": one that was primarily conservative (the social efficiency approach), one comprised of Dewey and his closest followers, one that was politically radical (the social reconstructionists), and the "do-as-you-please variety or lunatic fringe" (Woodring 1953, 58). Indeed, Herbert Kliebard asserts in *The Struggle for the American Curriculum* (1986) that the term *progressive* was applied to so many different approaches that it is meaningless. And yet, in *The Transformation of the School* (1961), which remains the standard history of progressive education, Lawrence Cremin claims that the educational reforms attempted between the 1880s and 1950s were all essentially one prolonged expression of the larger cultural movement known as Progressivism. Although he recognizes that the educational reformers shifted their emphasis around the end of the First World War, Cremin maintains that the later phase, based on the same intellectual foundations, was fundamentally continuous with the earlier.

I do not find any of these interpretations helpful. Instead, I would argue, as has historian Patricia Albjerg Graham (1967), that there were essentially *two* distinct movements under the name "progressive." One was the Progressive movement in American politics and culture, which I described in Chapter Four as a movement to preserve American culture in the face of burgeoning industrialism, immigration, and urban crowding (including the crowding of schools in the wake of mandatory attendance laws). The Progressive Era extended roughly from the 1880s through the First World War, while the "social efficiency" approach which it spawned continues to influence educational policy in this country. The other movement, which I have called "liberal" progressive education, was in many ways a holistic movement. Although it had its roots in the Progressive Era (as Cremin observes), it really did not fully blossom until after the World War. It peaked in the mid-1930s, and steadily faded until its influence was negligible by the mid-1950s. This "progressive education" was based on the work of Francis Parker and John Dewey and other innovative educators.

This interpretation explains, more adequately than Cremin's, why the reforms of the earlier Progressives were largely — and permanently — adopted, while the ideas of the postwar progressive educators were ultimately rejected, often with stinging criticism. According to my thesis, it was not merely a matter of timing, but of a profound difference in how well they conformed to the themes of American culture. The prewar Progressive movement, which strove for scientific efficiency, centralization of authority, vocational provisions for the working class, and so on, was an expression of mainstream, middle class American culture. The postwar movement was a critical approach which raised serious questions about the relationship of the individual to accepted social institutions.

In the years just before World War I, bohemian circles such as that which flourished in New York's Greenwich Village were alive with wholly new areas of cultural exploration and self-expression. Pragmatism, psychoanalysis, modern art, anarchism, socialism, and new attitudes toward sexuality and womens' rights were among the challenges to the intellectual, artistic, and moral canons of the culture. A budding youth movement questioned the very basis of the American worldview — *including the Progressive views of their parents* (see Rosenstone 1975, 113). These countercultural trends found expression in the progressive education movement. Although the progressive educators were, on the whole, less politically radical or socially bohemian than many of the critics of the prewar years, there were strains of cultural criticism in progressive education which had not been expressed by educators since the Transcendentalists, eighty years before.

John Dewey's influence on this movement was important, though somewhat ambiguous. His Laboratory School at the University of Chicago, founded in 1896, was the prototype of the experimental progressive school. His writings stemming from this project —*The School and Society* (1899) and *The Child and the Curriculum* (1902) — were joined in 1915 by *Schools of Tomorrow*, a survey of other experimental schools around the country, and in 1916 by *Democracy and Education*, his most important work in educational philosophy. But during these years Dewey's social and political thinking was more aligned with Wilsonian liberalism than with the more radical cultural critics, and his support for America's entry into the World War was bitterly attacked by some of his youthful followers, particularly Randolph Bourne (1965, 191-203). As I have said, Dewey was no romantic. When some progressive educators, influenced by Freudian and Jungian theory, began to explore holistic themes in the 1920s, Dewey sought to temper such "child-centered" impulses. During the 1930s, Dewey's political thought became more radical and he participated in the social reconstructionist critique of American capitalism, but this movement in its turn moved away from the child-centered position. This tension between the personal and the political elements of progressive education is the subject of the discussion that follows.

The end of the war, which after months of unprecedented savagery had utterly failed to "make the world safe for democracy," gave the progressive education movement a significant boost. Mainstream Progressivism was largely discredited, and Americans anxiously searched for ways to reclaim a sense of cultural purpose (Nash 1970). One approach was to turn inward to the self, following the paths of psychoanalysis and expressive art rather than social reform. Margaret Naumburg, founder of the progressive Walden School in New York, wrote that

> any possibility of an immediate social or economic escape from the impasse of our civilization has become quite remote and rather absurd to me now.... Although one can do nothing directly with social and economic groups as they now exist, one can do something with individual youth.... (Naumburg 1928, 40)

Thus emerged the approach called "child-centered education," practiced by a group of experimental (mainly private) schools which formed, in 1919, the Progressive Education Association. As Horace Kallen later observed, the PEA was the first organized movement dedicated to "a discipline of freedom" (Kallen 1949, 264). Until then, the few educators who had advocated a similar approach had always worked alone or in small communities of dissenters. The PEA was different, and its leaders knew it. "We aimed at nothing short of reforming the entire school system of America," declared its founder, Stanwood Cobb (*Progressive Education* 1929, 68). But, as Naumburg's comment indicates, the child-centered educators were exclusively interested in *pedagogical* reform: schools must be changed for the sake of the child, not for social reform. The articles in their magazine, *Progressive Education*, rarely addressed social issues, and hardly seemed to recognize that education takes place in a cultural and social context.

The Depression alarmed many intellectuals, including some progres-

sive educators, out of this complacency. In 1932, George Counts electrified a
PEA convention with his address "Dare Progressive Education Be Progressive?", which was then published as *Dare the School Build a New Social Order?*
In 1933 a PEA committee headed by Counts issued *A Call to the Teachers of the
Nation*, and the influential progressive educator William Heard Kilpatrick
edited a volume of critical essays called *The Educational Frontier*. Like their
mentor Dewey, these social reconstructionists rejected *laissez-faire* capitalism and called for a program of deliberate social planning. In order to further
develop their views, they began a provocative journal, *The Social Frontier*, in
1934.

The bulk of the PEA membership never fully accepted the radical
criticisms of the reconstructionists, but from that time on, "progressive
education" was associated, in the public mind, with unacceptable radicalism. In the late 1930s, even with the continuing Depression, the public
became increasingly defensive of the "American Way of Life," as the rise of
fascism and Soviet communism in Europe became more threatening. The
PEA embarked on a campaign of "education for democracy" which turned
out to be an uninspiring compromise between the child-centered and
reconstructionist positions. Philosophically aimless, growing more professionally aloof, the PEA finally succumbed to the conservative climate which
followed the Second World War.

Such is the standard history of progressive education. But let us consider the movement as an ambitious — in fact, the most successful to that
point — holistic critique of education. When we consider the child-centered
and social reconstructionist wings as two essential elements of an integrated holistic approach, progressive education may be understood as a
provocative challenge to American education, rather than a picturesque but
outdated pedagogical fashion.

At the heart of the progressive philosophy was an expanded definition
of education. Education was no longer to be seen as merely the instilling of
mental, moral, and social discipline, but as a vital part of the total development of the person. Eugene R. Smith, one of the leaders of the PEA, declared
that

> education is concerned not with any one part or any one phase of childhood,
> but rather with the complete child and child life.... You cannot touch one side
> of child life without influencing other sides, and therefore ... the school must
> think in terms of the complete human being. (*Progressive Education* 1926, 199)

This theme runs consistently through the writings of the progressive educators. In his work, Harold Rugg emphasized that human action is the
response of the "total organism," not mind or body alone (Carbone 1977,
102), and Caroline Pratt declared that

> it is the whole child we must nurture, not just one part of him. It takes a whole
> man or woman to live capably in our complex civilization. (Pratt 1948, 48)

In emphasizing the "complete human being," the "total organism," and
(most commonly) the "whole child," these educators were expressing the
central holistic concept that human experience is a unified whole that

should not be broken up by arbitrary cultural definitions. In one article, William Heard Kilpatrick observed that traditional education

> chose school facts and skills and concerned itself with them. It ignored these other learnings that were none the less going on all the time ... the character effects, the personality effects, the emotional adjustments. (*Progressive Education* 1930, 385)

For the progressive educator, these aspects of experience were just as important as intellectual training. Naumburg asked a question which every holistic educator has raised:

> What can be the use of presenting any amount of subject matter, however well organized according to modern teaching methods, if the children's inner lives are not moving so as to allow the maximum of interest or attention? (Naumburg 1928, 117)

The child is not a disembodied intellect, but a *person* moved by physiological, emotional, moral, social, and self-expressive forces. To truly educate a person means to address each of these needs. Naumburg argued that

> specialization is really a lopsided development of an individual.... The real job of education ought to be to develop what is still buried or less evolved in our natures. . . . About 90 per cent of what we really are is pushed out of sight by the time we're seven years old! The standards of education and society force back below the surface the most living and essential parts of our natures. (Naumburg 1928, 311)

One corollary to this belief is that a whole new definition must be given to the concept of "intelligence." Abstract concepual thinking may or may not be relevant for a particular person in a given situation and should not be considered the only element of intelligence. To do so is a way of imposing limiting adult standards onto the life of the child. Naumburg observed that there are intuitive and emotional ways of knowing which are not measured by intelligence tests; to neglect them is to ignore the individuality of the person. In the 1980s, this view is receiving powerful empirical support in the work of Howard Gardner (1984), among others.

In order to allow the full range of the personality to be expressed and nurtured, the progressive educators placed a heavy emphasis on the creative arts. Music, drama, poetry, drawing, sculpture, and a variety of crafts were the outstanding features of many progressive schools, and the subject of many articles in *Progressive Education* magazine in the 1920s. In contrast to mainstream schools which set aside a few art periods per week where students execute assigned projects, in progressive schools the arts held a central and exalted place. It was through artistic expression that progressive educators addressed spiritual development. Art was seen as the direct expression of the unfolding life of the person, of the inner creative spark yearning to explore the world. Naumburg wrote that "there is in each child a life-force, a potential power, an essential urge" (1928, 116). Like most of the child-centered progressives, she did not use religious language but the new concepts of Freudian, Jungian, and gestalt psychology to argue that the primary need of human development is not socialization but individuation.

For the child-centered progressive educators, the focus of education was not so much subject matter as the personal development of the child. A truly holistic approach needs to consider both aspects, of course, and the child-centered educators, especially in some of their more polemical writings, appear extremely naive about the social aspect of human development (which was the basis for Dewey's criticism of them). Yet their emphasis on the unfolding life of the child was a desperately needed corrective to the overwhelming tide of the social efficiency movement, as well as an important addition to the Deweyan/reconstructionist emphasis on social development. At times the reconstructionist group grew too strident (George Counts for a time advocated explicit indoctrination in progressive social values), and the social critics needed the child-centered approach as much as the romantics needed a more sophisticated cultural awareness.

The child-centered approach emphasized learning more than teaching; if the educator is not attuned to the rhythm of the child's style of learning, then mastery of pedagogical techniques and materials is ultimately rather pointless. The first thing that the progressive educators, like other holistic educators, noticed about children is that they learn best through activity rather than passive reception. Moreover, they are naturally active and in search of learning. Caroline Pratt observed that the child

> is driven constantly by that little fire burning inside him, to do, to see, to learn. You will not find a child anywhere who will sit still and idle unless he is sick — or in a traditional classroom. (Pratt 1948, 10)

Like the Transcendentalists, Pratt and her colleagues believed that "education does not begin with books, but with life" (Pratt 1948, 201). The child wants to learn by engaging his or her environment through a personally fulfilling activity. Boyd Bode, a leading advocate of Deweyan thinking as an education professor at Ohio State, criticized the excesses of the child-centered approach, but endorsed this element of it.

> The traditional method consists in teaching each subject as though the pupils were to be trained to become research specialists in that particular subject. Teaching is thus made technical rather than human.... But it is rarely that a youngster wants to be a technical mathematician. He wants to learn more about this fascinating world in which he lives, and when this hope is disappointed the initial enthusiasm fades away into dull routine. (Bode 1927, 143-144)

It is significant that Bode uses the adjective "human" to indicate that the *whole person* is to be educated. Many of the holistic educators I interviewed around the country in the mid-1980s also emphasized the "human" potentials of their students and the natural "human" ways of learning. Passive memorization of facts may be effective for some limited purposes, but it does not allow for the full development of one's humanity.

Another aspect of the child-centered approach was its respect for individual differences. While some characteristics, such as the need for meaningful activity, are common to almost all children, it must be recognized that each student is a unique personality, with his or her own interests, motives, feelings, and style and rate of learning.

> The object of the new education is just the opposite of the old. It wishes to do away with the uniform product.... It seeks individual development by encouraging such differences in type and temperament as form the base of each personality. (Naumburg 1928, 15)

The purpose of education, then, is not to impose the values of the adult world onto children but to help them to grow toward their own personal potential.

In this emphasis on individuality, the child-centered educators were more influenced by Rousseau, Pestalozzi, Froebel, and Transcendentalism than by the social emphasis of Dewey (see Graham, 19). The romantic urge to break out of the dehumanizing constraints of modern life was clearly expressed by J. Milnor Dorey in 1930:

> We are tired of facts, persons in the mass, things, propaganda, social and economic classifications, standardization.... We are talking about the person as an end in himself, his individuality, not of an economic factor in society.

The author praised Emerson, who, he said,

> knew that thought proceeded from human interests, not the contrary.... This is the exact kernel of what we call today "progressive education." (*Progressive Education* 1930, 335, 336)

In all fairness, neither Dewey nor the reconstructionists advocated "persons in the mass, things, propaganda" and the like — far from it! But they insisted on a direct confrontation with the dehumanizing forces of society. They argued that disciplined intelligence, cooperative community effort, and a willingness to take a stand against entrenched interests even at personal risk were required to bring about social change. A hopeful faith in the hidden powers of the child would not be enough. In terms of my analysis of the holistic tradition, the reconstructionists would say that the "accommodating" temperament fails to address the moral, cultural, and institutional barriers to a more humane and democratic education. And I would agree with them.

The progressive education movement reflected Parker's and Dewey's concern with the advancement of democracy in education — although again, the child-centered and social reconstructionist groups offered different approaches to the problem. The former placed more emphasis on democratizing the classroom, while the latter sought greater democracy in American society itself, with education as an instrument. We can see how an integrated approach requires both elements. To begin with, it makes no sense to expect citizens to practice democracy as adults if they have been denied the experience of democracy as students (Washburne 1952, 40). And yet, as Kallen observed, the founders of the public school systems, for all their democratic rhetoric,

> did not think of the school as a self-governing community of free men. Teaching remained in their thought as an art of indoctrination by authority, learning a submission to discipline in the correct, the desirable ancient "liberal arts." (Kallen 1949, 129)

The result, as Harold Rugg pointed out, was that

> instead of constituting an informed thinking citizenry, cognizant of public questions and critically observant of the acts of their elected representatives, the youths turned out from our schools are merely fit subjects for systematic propaganda. (in Carbone 1977, 134)

The child-centered progressive educators sought to replace the authoritarian educational environment with a model of participatory democracy.

No longer should teachers, students, or parents think of school simply as a place to do what was laid out to be done.... The school should be a living social organism of which each student is a vital part.... To develop a sense of worth in each individual, to promote full participation by each one in the affairs of the school, and to lead everyone to think for himself would demand radical change in many aspects of the curriculum and ways of teaching. (Aikin 1942, 17, 19)

On the other hand, merely giving children greater freedom and initiative in school, without a guiding vision of how a democratic society ought to be constituted, only perpetuates the isolation of the school from the real problems of the society. In *Dare the School Build a New Social Order?*, Counts called progressive educators "romantic sentimentalists" who wanted to protect children from harsh realities. Instead, he called for educators to reclaim a "revolutionary" democratic temper, which would fight for the "moral equality of men" against the selfishness, exploitation, and privileges of capitalism. In asking teachers to attack capitalism directly, Counts was more radical than many of the reconstructionists, but they shared his view that education must be guided by a vision of greater democracy in society (Counts 1932).

Dewey sought to link the personal and the political. *"For the sake of individual development,"* he said,

education must promote some forms of association and community life and must work against others. Admit that education is concerned with a development of individual potentialities and you are committed to the conclusion that education cannot be neutral and indifferent as to the kind of social organization which exists. (Dewey 1940, 291)

Boyd Bode expanded on Dewey's ideas. He maintained that "democracy requires a sensitiveness to all manner of human interests" — i.e., to individual differences — because individual experience is the source of social progress" (Bode 1927, 236). To Dewey and his followers, democracy meant a progressive reconstruction of society. Educating for democracy meant educating people to take responsibility for guiding social change. One underlying premise of the progressive philosophy was that in modern industrial society, rapid change is inevitable; the prime educational question is whether social values and institutions will keep pace with technological innovations. The school can either serve to perpetuate an authoritarian social order, in which science and industry benefit an elite class, or it can stimulate critical thinking and personal initiative so that people can determine their own destinies.

Bode argued that any educational program which sought to fit individuals into predetermined places in society was "aristocratic."

The spirit of aristocracy may express itself in the doctrine of the divine right of kings or of the immutable perfection of the Constitution or in the demand for a differentiation between liberal and vocational education on the basis of the I.Q.... A truly democratic society regards its institutions and practices as instrumentalities that are to be modified or discarded with the growth of experience.... *The purpose of education is not to fit the individual for a place in society, but to enable him to make his own place.* (Bode 1927, 32, 79, 234-237; italics added)

We can see why conservative critics —essentialists and social efficiency advocates alike — attacked progressive education with such fury. Calling the progressive educators "anti-intellectual" or accusing them of retaining Communist sympathies in the 1950s was an indirect way of attacking their most truly subversive belief: that American culture must change significantly in order to adapt to the changed conditions of corporate industrialism. Progressive education, both the child-centered and reconstructionist branches, was based on a fundamental (if often implicit) critique of the major themes of American culture.

The progressive educators offered an alternative to the pessimistic, moralistic view of human nature characteristic of conservative American Protestantism. They recognized that an

> unconscious image of the child as a vessel of natural depravity still rules the classroom, and grounds the suppressions and the inhibitions on which the teaching tasks are postulated. (Kallen 1949, 62)

Although they did not often confront the conservative Protestant tradition this directly, the child-centered position was clearly based on a positive, even romantic/spiritual conception of human nature. The reconstructionists shared Dewey's faith in disciplined intelligence over all religious ideology.

The progressive educators were more explicit in their opposition to scientific reductionism. Kilpatrick pointed out that

> the wrong kind of science wishes us to study a child but forget his personality, wishes us to begin, not with "the whole" child, but with little pieces of knowledge, separate skills, separate habits, and the like. (*Progressive Education* 1930, 383)

This is just the criticism that the humanistic psychology movement would take up in the 1960s. Unfortunately, during the 1920s the mental testing movement was still going strong; social scientists and social efficiency educators (for example, E.L. Thorndike and Franklin Bobbitt) were confidently predicting that all educational tasks could eventually be quantified and measured. Progressive education was the front line against this scientistic reductionism.

> I remember how one expert's faith in the Binet intelligence tests declined when she found on the basis of her tests of the children from year to year that human intelligence is not after all fixed at birth, that it can grow if given the right kind of nourishment to grow on! (Pratt 1948, 58-59)

The progressive educators recognized that the experience — and intelligence — of the individual person is ever unfolding, exploring, adapting. The fluid quality of life cannot be adequately captured by fixed quantification.

Bode attacked scientism as a conservative social force. Science cannot substitute for moral choices, he said; it is only a technique for obtaining values we have already chosen. To claim that "science" can determine educational goals amounts to a tacit acceptance of the status quo, or moral choice by default. Bode insisted that education is a moral enterprise: "The most important thing about an educator is his social vision" (Bode 1927, 241).

The progressive ideal of democracy was far more liberal than mainstream American ideology. In a remarkably astute analysis, *The American Road to Culture* (1930), Counts observed that Americans believe firmly that the state should control the schools for the purpose of making good citizens; but they regard the good citizen as the man or woman who reveres the names of the founding fathers, accepts the American form of government as almost divinely ordered, and performs honestly and efficiently, but unimaginatively, the routine tasks of civic life. (Counts 1930, 28)

Even the far less radical Carleton Washburne, explaining resistance to progressive education, claimed that

many people, deep down, have little faith in democracy. They are afraid to let people see all sides of a question.... (Washburne 1952, 107)

The progressive educators came upon the same discovery made by holistic educators since Maclure and Neef: Despite the democratic rhetoric of the Declaration of Independence and history textbooks, there appears to be an entrenched resistance in American culture to a full expression of democratic values. It is not simply that an elite class subjugates the masses; rather, a majority of Americans of all classes appear to be suspicious of excessive self-determination — especially, as we have seen, in the case of mistrusted minorities such as blacks, immigrants, and children. Educators who have attempted to give students greater responsibility for their own learning have consistently had their ideas ignored, attacked, or diluted by public educational practice as well as parental resistance.

The progressive educators, even the child-centered group, were sensitized to the cultural theme of nationalism by the loyalty crusade and Red Scare that accompanied the First World War. They recognized nationalism as a potential enemy of both individual expression and social reconstruction, and offered a different view.

Our emphasis should be on the individual, utilizing his natural loyalty to his group to get him to help make his country always worthy of love, rather than on the country, toward which he must maintain an unvarying affection, no matter what its acts nor in whose interests it may be controlled.... Who is to decide what are American ideals?.... With the clever appeal which the handle "American" makes to nationalistic prejudice, the phrase ["American ideals"] becomes an agent of repression against real but disturbing idealists. (*Progressive Education* 1925, 212-213)

The fundamental problem with rabid nationalism is that patriotic slogans can be used to stifle dissent — any dissent — from the ruling ideology. This is what happened in the 1950s. The moderate Washburne, a public school superintendent, protested vigorously. The opponents of progressive education, he said,

march under the banner of Americanism.... Any digression by teachers or pupils from the points of view held by those conservatives ... is called by them "subversive" or "un-American." They fail to recognize that their own distrust of democracy, their own attempt to suppress free thought and free discussion, is the most dangerous subversion of American ideals. (Washburne 1952, 107-108).

And finally, progressive education offered a critique of capitalism, not only on abstract economic grounds but as a moral and ideological pillar of the American worldview. The progressive educators objected above all to the way industrial capitalism fosters a single-minded, selfish competitiveness. Harold Rugg observed that American culture is essentially *"a business*

civilization resting on the possession of money income" and that historically, the rush to conquer the continent (Manifest Destiny) rewarded acqui-
sitiveness and materialism at the expense of other qualities.

> While the individual was given free rein for conquest, self-cultivation was all
> but impossible; esthetic interests were at a low ebb. (Rugg 1939, 41, 128)

In 1930, *Progressive Education* ran an essay by Robert S. Lynd (co-author of the
Middletown studies), who argued that in American society, making money
had become "a self-justifying ritual, an end in itself" which narrowed
people's career choices and critical judgment (*Progressive Education* 1930, 171,
172). It is significant, in terms of my thesis, that he attributed the single-
minded pursuit of wealth to the influence of Protestant moralism.

Arguments such as these raise the question of whether capitalism is
truly "individualistic." Does the self-serving pursuit of wealth represent the
fullest development or assertion of one's individuality? Counts addressed
this issue directly:

> Concern over promoting individual success, and the organization of society
> about the principle of individualism, are two very different things. In fact the
> emphasis in America on individual *success*, since society must after all define
> the goals to be striven for and the standards by which individual performance
> is to be judged, constitutes a most emphatic denial of genuine individualism.
> Under such conditions, particularly if such ideals and standards are narrow, as
> they are in America ... the urge to success may prove to be the most austere
> and merciless of masters. (Counts 1930, 120-121)

The social reconstructionists, in criticizing "individualism," were rejecting
the capitalist emphasis on the single-minded competition for wealth and
status. They were not calling for some kind of social homogenization. It was
characteristic of progressive educators — reconstructionists as well as the
child-centered romantics — to point out how American culture frustrates
individual growth and self-expression. In this they clearly belonged to the
holistic tradition.

The social reconstructionists offered a radical perspective to holistic
theory. They echoed Tocqueville's warning that even in a relatively open
society where, theoretically, no one was to be excluded from the opportunity to compete, industrialism would lead to a new aristocracy. American
culture, they claimed, sanctions selfish competition by rewarding the successful with a disproportionate share of wealth and power and relegating
the rest to lives of drudgery, if not poverty. This is fundamentally wrong,
they argued. It is simply not democratic.

It should be obvious that the progressive education movement utterly
failed to inject its ideals into mainstream American education. Despite the
claims of conservatives in the 1950s, and even by many historians later, it is
clear to those scholars who understand the countercultural themes of
progressive education that American culture and mainstream education
decisively repudiated the progressive approach (Nash 1964; Williams 1963;
Zilversmit 1976). There is substantial evidence that most teacher-training
institutions retained their traditional approaches, and even contemporary

surveys (for example, the extensive Gulick Study of New York state schools in the mid-1930s) showed little innovation along progressive lines.

In fact, as we have already seen, there was determined opposition to progressive education from the guardians of American culture. For example, Harold Rugg introduced a series of social studies textbooks which, in true progressive fashion, encouraged critical reflection on American history and society. Reaction was severe. An official of the Daughters of the Colonial Wars wrote that these books sought

> to give the child an unbiased viewpoint instead of teaching him real Americanism. All the old histories taught my country right or wrong. That's the point of view we want our children to adopt. We can't afford to teach them to be unbiased and let them make up their own minds. (in Carbone 1977, 28)

This amazingly authoritarian outburst seems like a right-wing caricature rather than a true reflection of American culture. Perhaps it is, but similar criticism was voiced by the American Legion, the National Association of Manufacturers, the American Federation of Advertising, and *Forbes* magazine. Likewise, *The Social Frontier* magazine, according to another historian, was branded as "Red" or Marxist by some of these same critics (Gutek 1970, 75). We see once again that capitalism and conservative nationalism are in alliance against what is perceived as undisciplined thought and expression. Historian Peter Carbone surmises that Americans do not want schools to develop critical thinking or artistic sensitivity, that ideas such as Rugg's are "too direct, too much a threat to accepted values" (Carbone 1977, 168-171, 179). I completely agree.

Progressive education — the liberal, holistic progressive education — was thoroughly diluted before finding its way into the educational mainstream. Cosmetic changes, such as portable rather than fixed seating in classrooms, are about as near to progressive reform as most public schools have ventured. To actually conceive of the school as a laboratory where individuals may explore their lives' possibilities, or where the whole society may experiment with new values, would entail sweeping changes in the philosophy, curriculum, methods, and administration of the public schools. With the brief exception of the "education crisis" in the early 1970s (see Chapter Eight), American schools have yet to see such changes.

Imported Holistic Movements

CHAPTER 7

During the period (1910s–1950s) in which progressive education was the major representative of the holistic approach in America, several European educational movements were brought to this country and joined the holistic challenge to traditional educational thought. One of them, the "Modern School" movement, appealed mainly to anarchists and bohemians, and after a short peak of activity before the First World War, became virtually invisible. Two others — the Montessori method and the Waldorf schools of Rudolf Steiner — were slow to acquire influence, but since the 1960s have established themselves as significant alternatives to mainstream American education.

The Anarchists

At the turn of the century, many European societies were still dominated by monarchist governments, rigid class structures, and established churches. In opposition to this repressive social order, workers' movements were turning to socialism, anarchism, and anti-religious "rationalism," which were viewed as vehicles of progress and modernity. The anarchist movement, inspired by Kropotkin, Bakunin, and Tolstoy, found considerable support in Spain, one of the most conservative societies. Francisco Ferrer (1859–1909) was a well-known figure in the Spanish radical movement; he was ultimately convicted (on questionable evidence) of inciting destructive riots and was put to death. The last years of his life had been devoted to education; from 1901 to 1906 he ran the "Modern School" in Barcelona (until it was closed by the authorities) and thereafter wrote on the anarchist-rationalist theory of education.

Ferrer drew upon a libertarian educational tradition with its roots in Rousseau, Tolstoy, the British anarchist William Godwin, and French and Spanish anarchist educators. He argued that established educational systems — in Spain and elsewhere — were dominated by the interests of state, class, and church. The elite sought to control the population through schooling.

> The children must learn to obey, to believe, and to think according to the prevailing social dogmas.... There is no question of promoting the spontaneous

> development of the child's faculties, or encouraging it to seek freely the
> satisfaction of its physical, intellectual, and moral needs. There is question
> only of imposing ready-made ideas on it, of preventing it from ever thinking
> otherwise than is required for the maintenance of existing social institutions....
> (Ferrer 1913, 68)

At its heart, then, the anarchist approach shares with the holistic tradition a
romantic faith in "the spontaneous development of the child's faculties."
Essentially, anarchism is a critique of social institutions that distort or
repress this natural unfolding of human nature. The anarchists were atheists,
determined to overthrow the power of the clergy and "religious fiction,"
and so they conceived of human development in naturalistic rather than
overtly spiritual terms. Yet this was not a positivist faith in science but an
empirical approach, similar to that of Pestalozzi's disciple Joseph Neef. They
held that people should learn to trust their own observations and judgment
rather than blindly obey the authority of "consensus consciousness." Education, said Ferrer, should not be grounded in social beliefs but in independent thinking. Pedagogical methods should be empirical, based on the
psychological and physiological needs of the developing child. The student
should emerge from school freed from all prejudice and dogma, able to
determine his or her own beliefs and values based on intelligence and
experience. In short, education must serve the development of the person
rather than the institutions of society.

> We do not hesitate to say that we want men who will continue unceasingly to
> develop; men who are capable of constantly destroying and renewing their
> surroundings and renewing themselves.... Society fears such men; you cannot
> expect it to set up a system of education which will produce them. (Ferrer
> 1913, 71)

Ferrer was a holistic educator in another important sense: He argued
that the traditional definition of schooling as intellectual discipline and
book learning failed to address the full development of the human
personality.

> The education of a man does not consist merely in the training of his intelli-
> gence, without having regard to the heart and will. Man is a complete and
> unified whole, in spite of the variety of his functions. (Ferrer 1913, 29)

This statement reflects the anarchist educators' holistic concept of "integral
education": a union of intellectual and manual skills. They sought to educate the whole person as a means of eliminating personal distinctions based
on social class. The anarchists deeply opposed the culture of professionalism and believed that all people should be educated for productive work as
well as critical thinking. The Modern School sought to integrate working-
and middle-class children. In addition, Ferrer also opposed social distinctions based on gender (his sexist language is misleading); the Modern
School was coeducational, a shocking innovation in its time and place.

Ferrer said that true education comes from the student's spontaneous
involvement in the world. "Vital impressions" rather than "wearisome
reading" were the focus of his school. Grades, exams, rewards, and punish-
ments had no place in his scheme. Children could learn to rely on their own

interests, abilities, and experiences rather than perform according to adults' expectations.

> I would rather have the free spontaneity of a child who knows nothing than the verbal knowledge and intellectual deformation of one that has experienced the existing system of education. (Ferrer 1913, 73)

This is surely the pedagogy of anarchism, with its willful disregard for the established culture. It is not surprising that the ruling class in Spain found Ferrer's ideas threatening; similarly, mainstream American culture rejected them as well.

Liberal intellectuals throughout the world spoke out indignantly against Ferrer's execution, bringing attention to his ideas. In the United States, Ferrer's work found only a small audience: a lively group of radicals in prewar Greenwich Village (mentioned in the last chapter) which included the anarchist activists Emma Goldman and Alexander Berkman; artists and writers such as Alfred Steiglitz, George Bellows, Jack London, Upton Sinclair, Lincoln Steffens, and Eugene O'Neill; social reformers like Margaret Sanger and Clarence Darrow; and a provocative journal, *The Masses*, edited by Max Eastman. In 1910 members of this circle formed the Francisco Ferrer Association, and in 1911 opened a school based on Ferrer's model. The movement is thoroughly described in a fascinating study by Paul Avrich (1980).

Of course, Ferrer's criticism of his highly conservative society cannot be applied directly to the American situation, for in this country there was no similarly entrenched elite with such dominant power over the masses. Yet even in this more democratic society there is an implicit social hierarchy: small groups of people who benefit most from the established culture, who seek to maintain it at all costs, even at the cost of human development. The anarchist, like the holistic educator, objects that this cost is far too high.

Indeed, the American anarchists launched a passionate critique against mainstream education in this country. One of the teachers at the Ferrer School in New York charged that public schools

> exist for the specific purpose of making good citizens of our children. A good citizen is naturally one who submits to exploitation in the proud hope of being an exploiter himself some day; one who takes off his hat to the flag and stands reverently on his feet when the national song is being played, but who believes in jail for anyone who says anything is wrong in the land. (in Avrich 1980, 77)

The guardians of culture dismiss anarchists, like all romantics, as foolish, sentimental rebels who simply cannot accept legitimate authority or the needs of an organized society. But I would argue that this casual dismissal, like the Cold War conservatives' ridicule of progressive education, obscures the insightful criticisms which the radicals may be making. Granted, it is generally a society's most sensitive, troubled souls who gravitate to the romantic ranks, but the guardians of culture almost never address what it is about their worldview that so troubles these rebels. By dismissing social criticism as "un-American," they ensure that it will not be taken seriously.

In fact, the anarchists made some very penetrating criticisms about American culture.

The Modern School movement was basically a working class movement; it repudiated the middle class, conservative, Progressive, "social efficiency" solution to the problems of corporate industrialism. The New York radicals were actively involved in the labor agitation that so troubled the middle class during these years. For example, during the bitter strike at the textile mills of Lawrence, Massachusetts, in 1912, children of the strikers were welcomed by families at the Ferrer School. Anarchism was a deeply felt response to the human costs of modern industrial society, a total questioning of the underlying values of American culture. The anarchists were the most socially and politically radical of the holistic educators; they were anything but accommodating. They sought nothing less than a complete transformation of the American worldview,

> a new world of passion, diversity and freedom ... from the drab commercialism of conventional society.... They imagined themselves at the dawn of an epoch-making revolution, cultural as well as social and political. (Avrich 1980, 115, 129)

But of course, their idealism was crushed by the patriotic crusade that occurred during and after the First World War; anarchist and radical labor leaders were rounded up in the Red Scare, and either imprisoned or deported. As Avrich points out, there were other factors in the decline of anarchism, such as a serious split with other radicals after the Russian revolution, but I would argue that even had the movement endured, there was no hope for its success in American culture. The Ferrer School, which had moved to the countryside in Stelton, New Jersey, in 1915, continued to operate until 1953, but under a variety of directors, it lost its radical emphasis and was affiliated with the progressive education movement in the 1920s. About twenty other "modern" schools were scattered in various locations, but most lasted only a few years, and all had collapsed by the end of the 1950s. Still, Avrich observes that many of their ideas were carried forward by the free school movement of the 1960s.

The anarchist school movement was a brief but colorful chapter in the story of holistic education. These educators were passionately committed to the unfolding humanity of the child:

> Personal relationships were the most important thing. People were allowed to develop their own potentialities. (in Avrich 1980, 229)

Like all other holistic educators, they held a deep faith in the latent integrity of human nature, which one of them expressed quite lyrically:

> If the natural instincts of the child, uncorrupted by the conventional discipline, were given free play, we would have a race of men and women that could build a new, beautiful life on this earth. (in Avrich 1980, 248)

Clearly, the Protestant-nationalist-capitalist worldview has no place for anarchist idealism. The "Modern School" movement has been largely forgotten, and its only familiar legacy has been the historical books of Will and Ariel Durant, who were teacher and student at the Ferrer School in New

York. The "new world," the "new, beautiful life" envisioned by the anarchists awaits some future transformation of American culture.

The Montessori Movement

During the period of social and intellectual ferment before the First World War, American educators also encountered the work of Maria Montessori (1870–1952). Although an initial burst of interest between 1909 and 1915 declined rapidly, the Montessori method reemerged half a century later, and by the 1970s was the most widespread, best organized independent alternative movement in American education. Montessori was one of the premier theorists of the holistic philosophy, and yet, unlike other holistic approaches, her method has been preserved intact for eighty years and has been welcomed in middle class communities. Today there are approximately four thousand Montessori schools in the United States. To understand its success, we need to carefully evaluate the history of the Montessori movement in this country.

Montessori was the first woman ever to enter an Italian medical school, and after winning high honors, graduated in 1896. A practicing physician, she was also a student of psychiatry and physical anthropology. This intellectual background — unique among leading educational thinkers — emphasized an empirically disciplined approach to pedagogy and a therapeutic interest in the individual child. Consequently, her educational ideas were not so much derived from philosophical or ideological convictions as they were from a clinical perspective. In treating institutionalized children — the mentally retarded, learning disabled, emotionally disturbed, and delinquents who were, in those years, simply lumped together — she became convinced that social and intellectual deprivation in early childhood, rather than organic defect, was the leading cause of these children's difficulties. She went on speaking tours around Italy, and established a national reputation as "the apostle of a new movement on behalf of unfortunate children" (in Kramer 1976, 82).

In 1900, as a result of her efforts, an institute was founded for training teachers to work with these children, and Montessori was appointed its first director. The methods she used were based on the work of two of her predecessors in the medical profession — Jean Itard and his student Edouard Seguin — who had treated deaf-mute and "mentally defective" children early in the nineteenth century. (Itard was the teacher of the "wild boy of Aveyron.") Seguin's work was especially inspiring to Montessori; he realized that he could best reach so-called "idiot" children through concrete, sensory activities geared to their individual needs. He rejected "the violent sameness of most of education" and stated, "Respect for individuality is the first test of a teacher" (in Kramer 1976, 61).

Montessori experimented with the sensory materials devised by Seguin, refined them, and developed more of her own. The deficient child-dren taught by these methods exceeded all expectations; they learned to read and write, and often equalled the achievements of normal children. Observers were awed by this apparent miracle, but Montessori, like Seguin, realized that this was less a miracle than a powerful revelation about accepted educational practices. What if a sensorially based pedagogy were used in the education of normal children? Montessori turned her medical practice into an educational crusade; after engaging in an intensive study of educational philosophy (finding Pestalozzi and Froebel especially relevant) and experimental psychology, and conducting anthropological observations of schools, she was ready to try out her ideas with normally functioning children.

In 1907 she was given the opportunity: A housing project in a Roman slum asked her to help set up a day care program. It was called the Children's House — and it was the first Montessori school. Observing how the children used the materials, Montessori established the principles and procedures that henceforth would be used in every Montessori classroom. As before, she obtained dramatic results: young children (three to seven years old) who had been listless or destructive in their impoverished surroundings began to work with intense concentration, took a joyful interest in the world around them, and "exploded" into writing and reading by the age of four and five. Educators and social reformers from across Italy, and soon from around the world, came to see the "transformed" children, and soon Children's Houses were founded in more than a dozen countries. Eventually the methods would be extended to meet the needs of older children as well.

Montessori was a worldwide celebrity, sought out by a constant stream of visitors and even hailed by some as a prophet. At this point, she began to withdraw from the academic and scientific circles within which she had worked, and, surrounded by a devoted group of followers, became more of an authoritative and even charismatic figure. Claiming that she alone could teach the methods she had devised, Montessori began writing (starting with *The Method of Scientific Pedagogy Applied to the Education of Young Children in the Childrens' Houses* in 1909 [published in English in 1912 as *The Montessori Method*]) and offering international training courses to prospective teachers. With the establishment of the Association Montessori Internationale (AMI) in 1929, the worldwide Montessori movement was given authoritative direction. This deliberate isolation from the mainstream educational establishment has helped preserve the classroom practice of the Montessori method in essentially the same form as she devised it, but it has also had adverse effects, which we will consider below. First, we will explore the development of Montessori's ideas and their place in the holistic tradition.

Montessori's central concern was the natural development of the child, the healthy formation of the physical, mental, and spiritual qualities which are latent in the human being and which unfold, she believed, according to a purposeful, even divine, life force (for which she used the word *hormē*).

Despite her scientific training, Montessori retained this mystical faith in the spiritual force that guides human development. Behind the outward manifestations of the child's behavior and interests,

> there must be an individual spiritual embryo that is developing according to a definite plan.... The most urgent task facing educators is to come to know this unknown child and to free it from all entanglements. (Montessori 1972, 109-110)

Given the proper nurturing environment, *hormē* impels the child to unfold his or her potential personality, to expand his powers, assert his independence, and create an adult identity. Children *spontaneously* seek growth and learning because that is the (spiritual) nature of their humanness. What adults regard as misbehavior is caused by their own failure to provide the proper environment or by their own misguided efforts to direct human unfolding according to their prejudices. In traditional education

> a man has substituted himself for God, desiring to form the minds of children in his own image and likeness; and this cannot be done without subjecting a free creature to torture.... He who interrupts the children in their occupations in order to make them learn some predetermined thing; he who makes them cease the study of arithmetic to pass on to that of geography and the like, thinking it is important to direct their culture, confuses the means with the end and destroys the man for a vanity.... Our care of the child should be governed, not by the desire "to make him learn things," but by the endeavor always to keep burning within him that light which is called the intelligence. (Montessori 1965, 54, 180, 240)

Montessori reminds the educator that "we are no more the creators of spiritual than of physical forms"; just as the growth of the body unfolds naturally if given proper nourishment and suffers when unnaturally cramped or coerced, the growth of the personality must be given freedom to unfold. The teacher, said Montessori, must *follow the child*, for the direction of its life is contained within its own soul.

The job of the educator, then, is not to instruct, but to provide a learning atmosphere appropriate to the needs of the unfolding child, and then to allow the child to explore this "prepared environment."

> Education is not something which the teacher does, but ... a natural process which develops spontaneously in the human being. It is not acquired by listening to words, but in virtue of experience in which the child acts on his environment. (Montessori 1973, 6)

Every pedagogical practice must be grounded in empirical knowledge about the needs and tendencies of the growing child. "In order to educate," she wrote, "it is essential to know those who are to be educated" (in Kramer 1976, 98). What Montessori realized, years before developmental psychologists such as Piaget (who, by the way, was active in the Montessori movement early in his career), was that cognitive growth occurs in distinct stages. The first six years are especially crucial; during this period of "the absorbent mind," the young child literally "incarnates" the world around him. "The things he sees are not just remembered; they form part of his soul" (Montessori 1973, 63). The prime example of this power of absorption is the young child's effortless learning of his native language(s).

It is at this stage that sensory materials are most useful; the young child does not have the power of abstract reasoning and learns through concrete impression and manipulation. Writing, reading, and arithmetic can be taught during this period through sensorial experiences: sandpaper letters to trace, the "moveable alphabet" to manipulate, and an elaborate system of colored beads (the forerunners of the now widely used Cuisenaire rods) in learning about numbers. At first, Montessori was reluctant to emphasize these intellectual skills in the Children's House, but was convinced by the children's own excitement that around the age of four and five, the absorbent mind is particularly receptive to writing, reading, and number work if they are presented concretely. In fact, throughout the early years of life, there are a series of "sensitive periods" when the mind is finely attuned to specific sensory experiences (language, color, musical pitch, movement, etc.) as well as social habits. The Montessori materials are designed to appeal to these sensitivities, and the teacher's role is to observe each child closely enough to know exactly when to introduce each material.

The elementary (ages six to twelve) and then the adolescent years (twelve to eighteen) are characterized by their own developmental needs. Trying to learn basic skills after the absorbent mind period is like learning a foreign language, and

> imposes upon children an arid mental effort which breeds a certain disgust towards study and all intellectual instruction. (Montessori 1978, 95)

In the Montessori approach, since basic skills have been mastered at the concrete stage, the elementary child is free to turn his or her imagination loose. All areas of human experience (history, mythology, technology) and scientific discovery (the whole universe itself) are included in Montessori's vision of "cosmic education." The teacher introduces self-correcting materials which lead the children to greater awareness of their environment. And although the elementary child is beginning to think abstractly, the materials continue to emphasize purposeful movement, i.e., manipulation. "The hands are the instruments of man's intelligence," said Montessori. She argued that the person best engages the environment through meaningful work, especially when it involves intense concentration. Learning is an integration of mind, body, and soul, not a passive reception of abstract words (Montessori 1978, 26).

During adolescence the consuming interest in intellectual discovery gives way to more personal concerns about social, moral, and sexual identity. Montessori recognized this, and proposed for this age the *erdkinder*, a self-sufficient rural retreat where young people could experience for themselves the building of a community. Academic skills which traditional educators struggle to impress into unwilling teenagers have already been mastered by the Montessori student, who is free to address the more urgent problems of his or her own life.

It may seem as though Montessori advocated the complete freedom of the student to follow his or her impulses. But her thought was far more subtle than this; the prepared environment is a very deliberately structured place.

> In order to expand, the child, left at liberty to exercise his activities, ought to find in his surroundings something *organized* in direct relation to his internal organization which is developing itself by natural laws. (Montessori 1965, 70)

The prepared environment has rules and procedures which aim to encourage the child's "normalization" (optimum natural growth), even when the individual child is straying from this ideal path. Whether he is actually disruptive or *simply using the materials inappropriately*, the authority of the teacher is

> the support which is needed by the child, who having lost control of himself owing to temporary lack of balance, needs a strong support to which he can cling, just as one who has stumbled needs to hang on to something to maintain his balance. (Montessori 1966, 191)

Recall that it is the "unknown child" or "spiritual embryo" whom the teacher is bade to follow, not the child's outward behavior. This distinction created an implicit tension in Montessori's thought, which has left her work open to contradictory interpretations. On the one hand, she harshly criticized traditional educational methods which impose the adults' will on the child's embryonic personality. But then she has left it up to the adult — or more specifically, to her own view of human development — to evaluate whether the child is properly furthering his or her own growth. Montessori deeply believed that liberty and discipline were inextricably linked, that no person could truly be free if one were violating the natural laws — the inherent order or discipline — of one's own development. Adult intervention is withheld only to the extent that the child can act responsibly and independently in the prepared environment. It is interesting to note that this is a classic religious view; one achieves freedom only through a certain discipline. Montessori was a devout Catholic, not a romantic libertarian.

But this is a delicate pedagogical formula indeed, and it explains why the Montessori approach has been criticized as both too free and too rigid. From the point of view of the traditional educator, the open Montessori classroom is a noisy, chaotic place where children of various ages work together or alone unsupervised, and where there are no exams or grades. But the committed child-centered teacher finds it too structured, controlled, and focused on academic work. Even the ideal Montessori environment is subject to these interpretations, and in the hands of an inexperienced or mediocre teacher, a Montessori classroom can give an even more vivid impression of either chaos or rigidity.

Now we have clues to help explain the dramatic rise, fall, and rebirth of the Montessori movement in the United States. First the rise: From 1909 to 1915 Montessori's ideas made a sensational appearance. They were enthusiastically discussed in the popular press. *The Montessori Method* was a leading bestseller, and only two years after the first American Montessori school was founded in 1911, there were almost a hundred. A Montessori Educational Association was supported by influential patrons, including Mr. and Mrs. Alexander Graham Bell, the daughter of President Wilson, the U.S. Commissioner of Education, and various "bankers, attorneys, and foundation executives" (Kramer 1976, 180). Montessori herself came to the United States in December 1913, and made a triumphal tour. Her lectures, held in such places as Carnegie Hall, attracted huge audiences; the press covered her extensively; and leading academics as well as socialites feted her at a stream of banquets. She returned for the San Francisco Exposition in 1915, where a model Montessori classroom, enclosed by glass walls, was a tremendous success.

Montessori had struck a chord in the middle class Progressive movement. Like them, she proposed that social reform could be brought about by the application of science to human problems. Furthermore, education *in itself* would be sufficient to solve the problems of the modern world. As she later wrote,

> If education be conducted on scientific lines, we can effectively reduce the differences that divide men ... and this would lead to a greater harmony of life upon the earth. In other words, civilization can produce changes in man himself, just as it has produced changes in the surroundings offered him by nature. Magic powers are thus conferred upon the human race.... The new education is a revolution, but without violence. It is *the* non-violent revolution. After that, it triumphs, violent revolution will have become forever impossible. (Montessori 1973, 181, 214)

This was just the kind of reassurance middle class Americans needed, with violent strikes and demonstrations in the streets and anarchism and socialism knocking at the door! Science or (for many, the same thing) "magic powers" would obviate the need for fundamental social change. Montessori's *accommodating* approach brilliantly answered American culture's need to find educational solutions to social problems.

While some of the enthusiasts (such as Bell) understood and welcomed Montessori's radical challenge to traditional pedagogy, it is clear that middle class interest in the method was predominantly attracted by Montessori's emphasis on order and, more importantly, by her promise of accelerated learning. Kramer's excellent study confirms this observation. A newspaper reported that the crowds attending Montessori's 1913 lectures

> were eager to hear Dr. Montessori explain how she was able to make children advance rapidly in learning, make them polite, self-reliant and charming. (in Kramer 1976, 194)

Two thousand families had applied to have their children in the San Francisco demonstration class,

> eager to enroll their children in a class to be held under the supervision of the world-famous educator whose method promised to turn their offspring into what one enthusiastic journalist described as "the perfect mental and physical child" — and all in four months. (Kramer 1976, 216)

As we saw in Chapter Three, mainstream educators during these years were caught up in the "cult of efficiency," and one NEA report approved of the Montessori approach because it could "lessen effort while at the same time increasing output" (in Kramer 1976, 218). It seems as though American education was ripe for Montessori's ideas — or more accurately, for its own narrow interpretation of them.

However, after 1915, America's interest in Montessori suffered a rapid decline and an almost fifty-year lull. There were several factors involved: First, Montessori's own insistence on controlling the use of her method and materials, combined with her increasingly prophetic attitude, isolated the movement from academic circles and teacher-training institutions, and caused dissension among her own followers, a point Kramer emphasizes repeatedly. Not until the founding of the American Montessori Society in 1960 was there an alternative source of teacher training and school accreditation that was more sensitive to developments in the academic and educational community.

Secondly, Montessori's approach was out of step with other current trends in educational theory. The social efficiency movement had little use for Montessori's individualized teaching method, and even her approach was not sufficiently "scientific" (i.e., quantifiable) to satisfy the intelligence testers and curriculum planners. On the other hand, progressive educators rejected Montessori education as too mechanical, narrowly focused on cognitive skills, and isolated from social life. Kilpatrick's *The Montessori System Examined* (1914) probably turned many educators away from it. Margaret Naumburg (whom I discussed in the last chapter) and Helen Parkhurst, originator of the Dalton Plan, were both Montessorians (Parkhurst, the teacher in the San Francisco model classroom, was a favorite of Montessori) — before finding more room for their original and creative ideas in the progressive education movement.

Finally, there is a cultural explanation. In the United States, World War I and its aftermath aroused disillusionment with all cheerful theories of social progress and led to an anti-European isolationism that lasted until the Second World War. Even had the other two factors not been present, the Montessori movement would have found a great deal of resistance in the postwar years.

However, by the end of the 1950s, Montessori would become popular again and considered worthy of another look by Americans because

> the Russians had launched Sputnik, Johnny couldn't read as well as Ivan, and the progressive education movement was blamed for stressing social and psychological adjustment at the expense of the systematic development of cognitive skills — the three R's. (Kramer 1976, 230)

Once again, it was the efficient and accelerated learning achieved by Montessori's approach that caught the interest of middle class Americans. Yet Montessori had not been interested in promoting nationalistic competition, just as she had not been concerned with the "output" of the child. To use her method as a shortcut to academic success, or as a tool for efficiency or national prestige, is to adopt the letter of her approach without its holistic spirit. It is interesting to note that Benito Mussolini also found what he wanted in Montessori's ideas. Mussolini surely did not want "a nation of independent thinkers," but in order to build a modern industrial state, he had to make sure that "everyone could read and write efficiently, just as he would have to see that the trains were to run on time." Similarly, many of Montessori's supporters never actually understood what Montessori really meant by "order" or "discipline" — the sight of all those good, neat little children, so busily occupied and so well behaved. (Kramer 1976, 282, 283)

The point is not that middle class Americans are fascists, but that Montessori's ideas are subject to various interpretations, some of which are not holistic. The revival of the movement in the United States since the 1950s has certainly included a large share of social and educational idealism, but its success in suburban middle class communities, I believe, is due more to its academic results than to its holistic philosophical foundations.

Nevertheless, Montessori's ideas continue to stimulate the holistic tradition. Empirical research has reaffirmed her observation that the growing child does unfold in definite stages, each with its particular needs. Even outside the Montessori movement itself, the practices of early childhood education have been greatly modified by her insights. And while mainstream educators are reluctant to apply these ideas to elementary and secondary schooling, many holistic and various religious educators have been significantly influenced by them. In my interviews with holistic educators around the country, I found a large number — even among those who were not Montessori trained or working in Montessori schools — who named the work of Maria Montessori as their major inspiration. Like Naumburg and Parkhurst, Piaget and Erik Erikson, many people have been encouraged by Montessori's work to further explore the inner unfolding of the human being.

The Waldorf Schools

Another pioneering educator, whose ideas are far less familiar than Montessori's but in many respects more deeply challenging, was the Austrian thinker Rudolf Steiner (1861-1925). Steiner's collected works fill more than 350 volumes. He wrote and lectured on an astounding variety of subjects, including theology, history, psychology, political theory, agriculture, medicine, and education. His insights came from two sources: he was a scientist and philosopher, thoroughly versed in the scholarly literature of his time, and he was a mystic. Any understanding of his ideas must take both sources into account.

As Colin Wilson points out, many sensitive people in late nineteenth century Europe, in the face of the triumph of scientism and industrialism, experienced an emotional hunger, a "deep and powerful craving" stirred by "the natural religious impulses of man" (Wilson 1985, 57). Steiner was one of several thinkers to give voice to this hunger. He belonged to the minority but intellectually legitimate tradition of philosophers who have challenged scientism, such as Bergson, Whitehead, Husserl, Merleau-Ponty, William James, and Aldous Huxley. Steiner's thought was highly influenced by Goethe, whose writings on science he edited. Goethe opposed materialism — the view that physical matter is the only reality, and fixed natural law the only "purpose" — and saw nature as "God's living garment ... constantly in a process of creation." He affirmed "the positive role of subjectivity, individuality, and volition in the process of attaining scientific knowledge" (Wilson 1985, 37; McDermott 1984, 37). The idealism of Fichte and the concept of "intentionality" (purposefulness of consciousness) taught by Franz Brentano also helped Steiner develop his thought. So, while Steiner called into question the basic underpinnings of the Western worldview, he was not simply anti-intellectual. He was a disciplined and well-informed thinker.

Yet he was also a mystic. From an early age, he had experiences of clairvoyance and intuitions of spiritual realms beyond everyday awareness. It is difficult to assess the validity of such experiences solely from the perspective of sober scholarship. Skeptics have tried to explain how such an apparently gifted thinker could have launched into his long discussions of occult matters; they thought he had to be a fraud, if not a psychotic. Few considered the possibility that Steiner might in fact have been perceiving aspects of reality outside the "consensus consciousness" of the Western, scientific-materialistic worldview. Wilson concludes that although much of Steiner's elaborate cosmology seems to have sprung from an amplified imagination, there is no doubt that he was a "genuine seer" of supersensory, inner reality, comparable to other Western mystics such as Eckhart, Boehme, Swedenborg, and Blake.

After spending the first part of his career in scholarly research, around 1900 Steiner became involved with the Theosophy movement, which at the time was the major avenue (outside established churches) open to spiritual seekers in the West. He was recognized as a "genuine Initiate" and became a popular lecturer and active proselytizer; in 1904 he published his *Theosophy* (which some students consider the single best introduction to his ideas). By 1913, however, he broke away to found his own movement, which he called Anthroposophy. He continued to attract disciples (as well as critics) and built a headquarters at Dornach, Switzerland. In 1919, he was asked by one of his followers, the owner of the Waldorf-Astoria cigarette factory in Stuttgart, Germany, to inaugurate an adult education program for employees and then a school for their children. The Waldorf School was the prototype for a worldwide movement which today includes over 400 schools in over twenty countries, including about a hundred in the United States — with the number growing. This is probably the most radically holistic approach ever attempted; before we consider it, we need to understand more of Steiner's ideas.

Steiner's major teaching is that Western scientific materialism is too narrow to encompass the full reality of the universe. There is a spiritual, supersensible (we might add archetypal, transpersonal, transcendent) reality which only seems "occult" and inaccessible because we have not developed our latent ability to perceive it.

> There slumber in every human being faculties by means of which he can acquire for himself a knowledge of higher worlds. Mystics, Gnostics, Theosophists — all speak of a world of soul and spirit which for them is just as real as

the world we see with our physical eyes and touch with our physical hands....
This esoteric knowledge is no more of a secret for the average human being
than writing is a secret for those who have never learned it. (Steiner 1947, 1, 3)

Steiner recognized that his teachings would be hard to accept and said that
they should not be taken on faith, but subjected to the test of empirical
validation. He saw no conflict between spiritual experience and scientific
method — as long as science was not narrowly defined. Steiner believed
that science must expand to include supersensible phenomena; in other
words, it must become a "spiritual science" which takes *all* human experience seriously. In his writings Steiner repeatedly emphasized that further
progress in civilization demands a radical shift from a materialistic to a
spiritual worldview.

This requires, first of all, a wholly different method of gaining knowledge. Materialistic science can only know what is spiritually *transparent*,
such as the workings of a machine. Steiner asserted that there is nothing
human in such knowledge, that it is "dead," and Western culture's preoccupation with it can only drain the life out of the human spirit (Steiner 1969, 9;
1967, 55). According to one Waldorf educator,

> Life is calling to be understood but the call cannot be answered with the
> thinking that became dominant in the nineteenth and twentieth centuries.
> (Barnes 1980, 336)

Or as Steiner put it,

> man is thought of exclusively in terms of what the senses can teach us about
> the phenomena of nature.... But all the knowledge that has been acquired in
> recent times about the world of nature does not really lead us to man himself.
> (in McDermott 1984, 315)

Anthroposophy teaches that the inner life of the human being — the soul —
contains the deepest truths about human existence. Each person must
develop his or her own spiritual sensitivity, for it is through the individual
soul that spiritual awareness is gained. Worldly knowledge needs to be
acquired in harmony with the spiritual development of the person.

Like Montessori, Steiner saw human development as an unfolding
from within, following a succession of distinct stages. Although they are in
agreement on some facets of development, Steiner's conception is less
focused on sensorial and cognitive growth and more thoroughly oriented to
the manifestation of the inner spiritual being. From birth to around age
seven, said Steiner, the child's energy is devoted to constructing its physical
body, primarily through sensation, imitation, and activity — a non-
cognitive "impersonal consciousness" (Harwood 1958, 16). The moral and
psychological environment provided for the young child is vitally important, for the physical body will incarnate its qualities into the child's basic
temperament. This parallels Montessori's idea of the absorbent mind; but
Steiner opposed the teaching of cognitive skills as a diversion of energy
needed for physical growth, which is the first task of the young child. The
transition from infant to adult teeth is an important signal that the life force
has completed this task and is ready for its next stage.

From age seven to fourteen (puberty), it is the "etheric" body which emerges. This is the power of self-formation which vitalizes the inert matter of the physical body; Steiner described it as an inner sculptor. This is the first level of supersensible being, common to all life forms. It is not visible or measurable, but to Steiner it was no less real than the physical body. At this stage in human growth, the person is largely freed from one's primary concern with physical growth and begins to engage the world through imagination and feelings. The child is especially inspired by mythological stories and vivid pictures.

The next seven-year cycle is the emergence of the "astral" body or soul. The adolescent becomes conscious of his or her own inner world. Spirit is expressed through a deepening of thought and a quest for meaning. The person becomes attuned to the harmony of music and mathematics. At this stage the person develops more abstract thinking and, consequently, a greater ability to transcend the immediate and personal. Finally, with the emergence of ego at around age twenty-one, the individual can actually recognize oneself as a manifestation of spirit. Spirit as such is the ultimate divine being, the underlying laws of reality — perhaps what Plato was trying to express with his concept of the realm of "Ideas."

To summarize, Steiner saw human nature as comprised of body (physical matter and vital forces), soul (personal inner life) and spirit (ultimate being). He insisted that each of these levels of being exists independently, although interconnected, in every person. To ignore them, as does materialism, is an incomplete, reductionistic view.

> You can never explain the life of feeling and passion by natural laws and so-called psychological methods... I can very well understand that there may be many people who will consider what I have set forth as purely fantastic if not half-crazy. But a so-called "reasonable" way of thinking can unfortunately never portray man as he really is. We have to develop a new and wider reasonableness in these things. (in McDermott 1984, 349)

Waldorf education is the method based on this conception of human development. Its ruling principle is the spiritual unfolding of the individual. Steiner asserted that "a concrete knowledge of man" — i.e., the anthroposophical view just outlined —

> is the only possible basis for a true art of education — an art of education whereby men may find their place in life, and subject to the laws of their own destiny develop all their powers to the full. Education should never work against a person's destiny, but should achieve the full development of his own predispositions ... the fullest clarity of thought, the most loving deepening of his feeling, and the greatest possible energy and ability of will. (in McDermott 1984, 341-342)

It follows, then, that the individual must not be hindered by the materialist values of social institutions. The cultural/spiritual realm of life, which includes the arts, literature, law, and education, "should unfold freely and independently alongside the other realms" of politics and economics (in McDermott 1984, 297).

> For an education that has gradually been taken over by the State has deprived man of active striving; it has made him into a devoted member of the State structure.... He strives to fit this pattern because it is instilled in him.... Now it is

very uncomfortable to hear that salvation lies in free spiritual striving which must be independent of the State. (Steiner 1969, 108-109)

It is clear that Steiner's approach is at odds with mainstream American educational thought. His view that education is a spiritual endeavor, a process of personal growth, that can only be distorted if controlled by political institutions, is wholly opposed to the accepted definition of education in modern industrial societies. Waldorf education, like other holistic approaches, begins by insisting that the needs of the learning, developing person be given priority over social goals.

> One should not ask, "What does a person need to know and to be able to do for the existing social order?" but rather "What gifts does a person possess and how may these be developed in him?" (in Richards 1980, 31)

In fact, Steiner's conception of human development is probably the most inclusive, most "holistic" understanding of any of the movements in this tradition. Steiner believed that every facet of human experience is a manifestation of spirit, and thus *"the whole human body, and not the brain alone, is a vehicle of consciousness"* (Harwood 1958, 20). The body should be educated along with the intellect — or actually before it, in the first years of life, as we have seen. Steiner developed the exercises of "eurythmy" for this purpose, and even the more intellectual work done in the Waldorf school is accompanied by — or accomplished through — physical activity. Reaffirming a theme familiar to us by now, the Waldorf approach holds that life itself educates: "Let the children observe; teach them to read nature before books" (Richards 1980, 57).

Similarly, the Waldorf educator is oriented to the imaginative, emotional, and moral experience of children. The student is not seen as an empty intellect waiting to be filled with information, but as a feeling, aspiring individual with a uniquely personal style of learning. Steiner instructed Waldorf teachers to concentrate on refining their own spiritual sensitivity because they would be touching the spiritual depths of children. Thus, in the Waldorf method a teacher starts with a class in first grade and *stays with them* each year during the elementary school period. The teacher's goal is to reach an intimate familiarity with the personality of each child, in order to assist the unfolding spirit. Steiner held that education is not a science, not a professional technique, but an *art* requiring sensitivity and intuition.

> To give a picture of what Waldorf Education is, we must say that it speaks quite differently from the way in which people speak elsewhere in the sphere of education: Waldorf School Education is not a pedagogical system but an Art — the Art of awakening what is actually there within the human being. Fundamentally, the Waldorf School does not want to educate, but to awaken.... First of all, the teachers must be awakened, and then the teachers must awaken the children and the young people. (Steiner 1967, 23)

He declared that "pedantry" and "sharply defined ideas about life" were stultifying, that the teacher needs to welcome the "life-forming forces" of unfolding growth.

What Steiner meant by art, according to M.C. Richards, is a creative process: an openness to, and expression of, the unfolding life within oneself.

> It involves a certain way of seeing the child, a feeling for life, an intuition of the connections between the inner processes of forming and their outer expression.... A sense of awe rises in the presence of the child, as in the presence of a poem one hears forming in one's inner ear. (Richards 1980, 69)

For Steiner, art was not a pleasant diversion, a curricular frill, but the essence of life itself. In his autobiography he quoted a friend as saying

> People do not have as much as an inkling of the real significance of the creative power within the human soul. They do not realize that the creativeness of man is an expression of the same cosmic power that creates in nature. (in Wilson 1985, 72)

The Waldorf method calls for creative activities in virtually every facet of the program. Even subjects that are traditionally treated as academic are presented through one or another of the creative arts. However, Steiner did not seek to replace science with art, but to infuse intellectual skill with artistic and spiritual sensitivity. No limited way of knowing can adequately fathom "the ultimate unity of human experience" (Harwood 1958, 11).

As with Montessori, the Waldorf classroom is not the wide open environment which the child-centered educator would provide. There is a definite structure to the studies, a structure mainly chosen by the teacher. The children are not at liberty to come and go, or to move around the classroom at will. Steiner insisted — again, like Montessori — that human development (as he understood it) requires a particularly organized environment. The young child, moved by a strong will, needs a consistent social order, some regularity of rituals to imitate. The elementary age child needs a strong adult figure to emulate: a source of moral authority, an enforcer of rules. The teenager needs adults who hold to their ideals and challenge the young person to think out his or her own. To give the child excessive autonomy out of a preconceived ideal of "freedom" actually impairs the person's ability to achieve freedom as an adult; the child, Steiner argued, needs order and security to build a foundation of self-esteem and respect for other people. While the child-centered holistic educator sees this approach as unnecessarily rigid and restrictive, Waldorf educators, like Montessorians, apparently succeed, most of the time, in developing the autonomy of their students while keeping the joy of learning alive. There are many paths to the same goal.

In short, the Waldorf approach is radically holistic because it is so thoroughly rooted in a spiritual framework. The guidelines for educational practice are not derived from social values, nor even from some relatively objective, psychological-scientific study of children; the educator is asked to trust a source that at first appears wholly interior, subjective, hidden. Thus the Waldorf approach shuns the very rationale — objective science — that is currently the only approach capable of persuading American educators to focus more on the child's developmental needs. As I have argued, one reason the Montessori movement attained its early influence was that the public respected it as a new science of education; it will take a major cultural shift for Americans to understand the anthroposophical worldview as a scientific approach.

Unfortunately, as with any system based on esoteric understandings, Steiner's teachings contain a certain potential for cult-like imitation, and the Waldorf movement, even more than the Montessori movement, has in many ways become insulated from mainstream education and scholarship. This has, to be sure, helped ensure its integrity, but it has also prevented Steiner's ideas from having a wider hearing. This is most unfortunate because, for Steiner, Waldorf education was not meant to be a self-contained movement but the prototype for a wide reform of education. Ideally, the Waldorf educator does not see his or her purpose as the mere application of a preestablished method or curriculum. Steiner called any standardized school curriculum an

> instrument of murder for the real development of human forces.... We must no longer think that subjects exist in order to be taught *as subjects*. (Steiner 1969, 46)

Instead, the highest priority of the Waldorf approach is to encourage the individuality of both children and adults. Each school is run as a community of teachers, parents, and students, and should embody their particular values and ideals. Richards emphasizes that in Waldorf schools she visited across the U.S. "the relationship between adult and child is a real human connection" and that there is little use of hierarchical, authoritarian decision making or professional aloofness. Waldorf educators, she says, integrate personal and professional development, for they follow Steiner's belief that who they are is what they teach. Richards contrasts the Waldorf teacher, as an artist working out of love for children and their spiritual unfolding, with public school teachers, who are paid employees of large impersonal institutions. Of course, many individual public school teachers are sincerely devoted to their work; the point is that the structure of the system tends to frustrate rather than encourage such devotion (Richards 1980, 32, 53, 118).

In many ways, Rudolf Steiner's worldview is a powerful critique of mainstream American culture.

> That is one of the things I keep repeating, not only here but to myself: there is something expressed in Steiner/Waldorf educational impulses which does not come from mainstream culture. (Richards 1980, 84)

According to Richards, this something is an "innocence" — a faithfulness to one's inner creative powers, a reaching out to the distinctly human within other people. It is essentially the ability to transcend the limitations of consensus consciousness. In American culture,

> We can say that because we believe popularly in competition, our public schools are competitive.... The processes by which we learn in public schools perpetuate and aggravate acquisitiveness, anxiety, and mistrust. We are goaded into endlessly *adding*, as if growth were always measured by size.... Quantity, consumption, and competition — these are the natural consequences of a philosophy of materialism. (Richards 1980, 144, 180)

By "materialism," Steiner did not mean scientific reductionism merely, but the fundamental worldview which underlies Western civilization, of which he saw American culture as the most extreme manifestation (Steiner

1967, 33). The deepest problem with Western civilization is that it honors economic, technological, and intellectual dimensions of experience while discrediting the mythological, transcendent, and spiritual. In other words, the fundamental issue is *not* between capitalism and some kind of socialism, or between patriotism and anarchism. *It is between a preoccupation with the material world which can be measured and controlled — and a concern for the inner human world which must be respectfully contemplated and gently nurtured.* It is between a social discipline, imposed by those with economic and political power, which aims at economic advancement and national glory — and a spiritual unfolding from within each individual, which aspires toward personal wholeness and planetary peace. Whatever particular criticisms can be made of Steiner's esoteric teachings and the Waldorf School method, in this radical analysis of American culture his thought was explicitly and powerfully holistic.

The Education Crisis: 1967-1972

CHAPTER 8

In the 1960s, American society was subjected to the most searching criticism in its history. The eruption of several major social movements gave the 1960s a lasting reputation as an historic decade of protest and rebellion. For the first time, large numbers of people began to question the very foundations — the underlying worldview — of American society. The unsolved social and existential problems of materialism and industrialism seemed to call for radical answers.

This social ferment was the setting for an educational uprising which by 1970 came to be regarded as a "crisis." Public education came under intense attack from all points of view. Never, since the formation of the statewide school systems in the 1830s, had there been such a sweeping examination, such a willingness to rethink all aspects of educational theory and practice. Young activists were joined by scholarly observers in their questioning of educational traditions. Teacher strikes, extremely rare up until then, reached an alarming peak between 1968 and 1972, and student dissent broke out around the country. Alternative and experimental programs were organized in school districts around the country, and "free" schools — a repudiation of public education entirely — suddenly blossomed. According to one observer, there were about 30 free schools in 1967; between 1968 and 1972 approximately five hundred more were started (Graubard 1974). Foundations, government agencies, informal networks, and universities established programs to study — as well as advance — the new approaches.

The crisis had its origins between 1967 and 1970, when a number of radical educators applied the 1960s critique of society to the public schools. They were inspired by a group of social critics that included Paul Goodman, Jules Henry, and Edgar Friedenberg, and further influenced by A.S. Neill's account of his experimental Summerhill school in England. The leading radical critics — John Holt, Jonathan Kozol, Herbert Kohl, James Herndon, George Dennison, Ivan Illich, and Neil Postman and Charles Weingartner — examined the social, cultural, and political foundations of public schooling, and some found these foundations so rotten that they called for the dismantling of public schools altogether.

The radical writers expressed their ideas forcefully, with biting social criticism, deep moral outrage, and highly personal and moving accounts of children's experience in schools. Their work was often more passionate and polemical than tightly reasoned, and at times they can be justly criticized for overstating their case (for example, in presenting an exaggerated child-centered position). But however unscholarly their writings, they expressed heartfelt anguish over the state of education and American society; like the Transcendentalists, their criticism expressed a personal yearning for wholeness in a culture that frustrated them. Their observations revealed, as few writers had done before, the inhumane conditions of life in schools — schools supposedly humanized by progressive education and scientific pedagogy — and their criticism drove to the core of the social purposes of public schooling.

The radical critique centered on several major themes. Most basically, this literature insisted that schools are primarily concerned with *controlling masses of students*, and only secondarily with their learning and growth. School systems are massive bureaucracies, with petty rules, prescribed roles, and rigid procedures which serve the smooth operation of the system, but not the spontaneous, joyful growth of either children or adults.

> Testing, grading, seating arrangements according to the teacher's conven-
> ience, predigested textbooks, public address systems, guarded corridors and
> closed rooms, attendance records, punishments, truant officers — all this
> belongs to an environment of coercion and control. Such an environment has
> not consulted the needs of normal growth, or the special needs of those whose
> growth has already been impaired. (Dennison 1969, 102)

The radical critics asserted that the perpetuation of such an environment was *not*, as mainstream reformers would contend, merely an accidental byproduct of bureaucracy. The use of bureaucratic structure was itself a deliberate choice, reflecting cultural priorities.

> A student in a traditional school learns before long in a hundred different
> ways that the school is not on his side; that it is working, not for him, but for
> the community and the state; that it is not interested in him except as he
> serves its purposes; and that among all the reasons for which the adults in the
> school do things, his happiness, health, and growth are by far the least
> important. (Holt 1972, 88)

In such a system, decision making is autocratic and hierarchical rather than democratic. Curricula, textbooks, rules are determined by distant, anonymous figures (by "Noman," said Herndon) and imposed on teachers and students regardless of their interests, needs, or styles of learning and personal interaction.

> So we treat those decisions precisely as if dead men made them, as if none of
> them are up to us live people to make, and therefore we determine that we are
> not responsible for any of them. (Herndon 1971, 102)

The radical literature called for a major overhaul of school administration: the replacement of hierarchical bureaucracy with democratic processes involving parents, teachers, and students.

> The idea of "full-time administrators" is palpably a bad one — especially in
> schools — and we say to hell with it.... If schools functioned according to the
> democratic ideals they pay verbal allegiance to, the students would long since

have played a major role in developing policies and procedures guiding its [sic] operation. (Postman & Weingartner 1969, 153)

A few alternative schools adopted the Summerhillian method of determining school policy at open meetings where everyone, including every child, had a vote.

The critics also pointed out that the definition of subject matter — that is, the answer to the philosophical question "what knowledge is of most value?" — is likewise arbitrary, rigid, and beyond the teachers' or students' determination. Schooling has more to do with memorizing and reciting "right answers" than with critical thinking, intelligent problem-solving, experiment, or discovery. Holt's *How Children Fail* (1964), one of the earliest works in the literature, documented how students' efforts are spent devising strategies for appeasing teachers rather than gaining any critical understanding. One boy, explaining why he was willing to accept a nonsensical answer on a math problem,

> shrugged his shoulders and said, "Well, that's the way the system worked out." Precisely. He has long since quit expecting school to make sense. They tell you these facts and rules, and your job is to put them down on paper the way they tell you. Never mind whether they mean anything or not. (Holt 1964, 144)

Achievement is wholly defined in terms of these "right answers." Evaluation is impersonal, authoritarian, and quantitative, based on a "closed" definition of learning goals rather than recognizing the individual's unique potential for growth. Students who do not adjust to the school routine are "failures," no matter how creative, intuitive, and adaptable they are in real-life situations. Many children, observed the radical critics, enter school alert and inquisitive; yet within a few years, because their ideas, interests, and needs are ignored, they become apathetic and "stupid." Holt observed that classroom life creates a constant fear of being wrong.

> There are very few children who do not feel, during most of the time they are in school, an amount of fear, anxiety, and tension that most adults would find intolerable. (Holt 1964, 63-64, 142)

He described one scene where a teacher dismissed a child's attempt to argue a point by saying, "Now, Jimmy, I'm sure we don't want to hear any *wrong* answers." In the same vein, Kozol complained that from seasoned teachers

> I cannot say that I learned anything at all except how to suppress and pulverize any sparks of humanity or independence or originality in children. (Kozol 1967, 14)

Another point the radicals made was that school subjects are too abstract and predigested, too far removed from the real problems and moral issues that students must face in the world. Herbert Kohl wrote that schools

> teach "objective" knowledge and its corollary, obedience to authority. They teach avoidance of conflict and obeisance to tradition in the guise of history. They teach equality and democracy while castrating students and controlling teachers. Most of all they teach people to be silent about what they think and feel, and worst of all, they teach people to pretend that they are saying what they think and feel. (Kohl 1969, 116)

Kozol called schooling "the moral ether of our lives" because it smothers authentic personal responsiveness and fosters an alienated, competitive striving to succeed. This allows the middle class professional, for example, to drive contentedly through the urban ghetto on the way to his comfortable suburb, and encourages military officials to talk about "metadeaths and metacorpses, with scarcely a thought to the blood and suffering these words imply" (Kozol 1975; Holt 1964, 169; Holt 1972, 266-267). In other words, modern industrial society has lost any true sense of community, any concern for true connections between people. Schooling is not the primary cause, but it is a powerful agent of alienation in modern life.

It is not only the content of the curriculum, but the implicit social structure of the school — the "hidden curriculum" — that cause a separation between personal experience and required role behavior. Students may be taught about democracy in civics classes, but from their school experience they learn that they must be obedient to authority in order to earn praise and necessary credentials, that the source of "right answers" is always vested in authority figures. Because school is compulsory as well as hierarchically ruled, it is, like prison, a "total institution" with almost unchecked power over the lives of its inmates. This point was made dramatically in a little book (aptly titled *The Crisis in American Education*) put out in 1970 by the Sudbury Valley School in Massachusetts.

> A student has no right of free speech, no right of dissent, no right of peaceful assembly, no right to confront his accuser, no right of privacy.... During the entire formative period of his growth, a youth is committed ... to serve time in educational institutions which, like prisons, simply do not recognize the existence of individual rights. (Sudbury Valley School 1970, 31)

Like many of the progressive educators, the radicals asked how Americans expected to teach democratic citizenship by subjecting children to such undemocratic practices.

Moreover, they said, this authoritarian environment breeds what I have called the "culture of professionalism" in American education — the sanctification of "expert" knowledge and behavior. Teachers, themselves subservient to the authoritarian system, have learned to band together to maintain their professional dignity and to resist criticism or change. In the process, they sacrifice a person-to-person relationship with the students. Kozol documented this from his own experience within the public schools. He was actively discouraged (by his peers no less than by administrators) from having nonprofessional relationships with students; one teacher even told him that "you cannot teach them if you are going to be in the position of a friend" (in Kozol 1967, 115). George Dennison was the most insistent critic on this point.

> Where the public school conceives of itself merely as a place of instruction, and puts severe restraints on the relationships between persons, we conceived of ourselves as an environment for growth, and accepted the relationships between the children and ourselves as being the very heart of the school.... The teachers must be themselves, and not play roles. They must teach the children, and not teach "subjects." The child, after all, is avid to acquire what he takes to be the necessities of life, and the teacher must not answer him with mere professionalism and gimmickry. (Dennison 1969, 8, 79)

Like Rudolf Steiner, Dennison claimed that the teacher is an artist, and thus should cultivate self-awareness and personal growth rather than mere pedagogical technique. In a true human encounter between teacher and student, issues such as discipline and control are minor, even irrelevant. Dennison, Holt, and other critics asserted that adults have a "natural authority," simply because they are for young people the gateway to the vast unknown world; they must wield this authority with care and sensitivity rather than brute force. But authentic encounter is discouraged in a traditional school environment.

> What a vast perversion of the natural relations of children and adults has been worked by our bureaucratized system of public education!... No teacher is just a teacher, no student just a student. The life meaning which joins them is the *sine qua non* for the process of education, yet precisely this is destroyed in the public schools because everything is standardized and the persons are made to vanish into their roles. (Dennison 1969, 118-119)

The radicals' answer to this moral alienation, expounded most forcefully by Paul Goodman and Ivan Illich, was to attack the culture of professionalism itself. Their ultimate goal was to get students *out* of the schools and into the community to learn about social reality firsthand, in direct relationships with adults. (Indeed, one of the characteristic features of free and alternative schools has been their common use of daily excursions, field study, apprenticeships, and the use of storefronts for schools.) But this strategy cannot work on a large scale until Americans overcome their faith in professionalism. This is the main argument Illich made in *Deschooling Society*.

> Health, learning, dignity, independence, and creative endeavor are defined as little more than the performance of the institutions which claim to serve these ends.... (Illich 1970, 1)

This causes a "progressive underdevelopment of self- and community-reliance" and the net effect is to place the young, the poor, and the powerless under the permanent control of the social elites who run the institutions. The radicals questioned the common sense belief that young people *belong* in school because the adult world is too complicated or dangerous for them. They insisted that young people have the inherent desire and ability to learn about the world through active participation, but are frustrated by the elitist, bureaucratic mentality of American society.

The radicals argued that the inhumane, bureaucratic structure of the schools was not an aberration, but a distinct consequence of the values of American culture. They claimed that authoritarian control and moral alienation in schools are directly related to the inequality and racism of society at large. It was clear to them that public schooling was fulfilling, not liberal reformers' hopes of providing equal opportunity, but the conservative "social efficiency" plan to funnel youths smoothly into their "probable destinies." Schooling, they said, reinforces the severely imbalanced distribution of wealth in American society. Wealthy communities have better schools; impoverished communities have dilapidated school buildings and uninspiring educational offerings. Furthermore, schools for minority youth are permeated with racism, from textbooks to staff attitudes. Public schools have always devalued the ethnic subcultural experience of minority groups, and continued to do so in the 1960s.

All these glaring problems in American education, argued the radicals, result directly from the impersonal, bureaucratic mentality of a mass industrial society, which mandates that individuals must be taught to conform to organizational behavior and standardized consumerism. It is no accident that the standardized credentials required for advancement are awarded on the basis of school performance. The school serves the larger social purpose of culling the "winners" (those who perform school tasks obediently and efficiently) from the "losers." It is through schooling that the young learn to participate in a ritualized competition for coveted positions of status, to accept failure passively, and to become morally indifferent to the fate of others. The use of grades and IQ and achievement tests to "track" students shows that "the school's purpose is not teaching. The school's purpose is to separate sheep from goats" (Herndon 1971, 96).

Radical educators argued passionately that a bureaucratic, hierarchical society is wrong — not abstractly and ideologically, but profoundly and humanly wrong. To control and sort young people for the sake of institutional efficiency is to crush the human spirit.

> Being bottled up for seven hours a day in a place where you decide nothing, having your success or failure depend, a hundred times a day, on the plan, invention, and whim of someone else, being put in a position where most of your real desires are not only ignored but actively penalized, undertaking nothing for its own sake but only for that illusory carrot of the future — maybe you can do it, and maybe you can't, but either way, it's probably done you some harm. (Herndon 1969, 197)

The problem, as Holt pointed out, is that schools cannot be places of learning and discovery, or of growth and healing, while they are serving the functions of sorting, jailing, and indoctrinating in patriotism and values. Holt reached the conclusion that is my thesis in this study:

> What is there about this particular system that makes humane reforms have such a short and uneasy life?... I think the answer is plain enough, and that we would see it if we did not keep turning our heads away from it. Universal compulsory schools are not and *never were meant to be* humane institutions, and most of their fundamental purposes, tasks, missions, are not humane. (Holt 1972, 261, 253)

It is because these critics were so deeply concerned with human development and personal growth that I consider them to be part of the holistic tradition. Like Rousseau, Pestalozzi, and their pedagogical descendants, the radical educators of the 1960s were humanists; they believed that human nature is basically good, that evil is not caused by insufficient discipline but, on the contrary, by repression and deprivation. A.S. Neill stated this position forcefully in *Summerhill* (1960). Paul Goodman, a Gestalt therapist and anarchist, also taught this basic trust in human psychology and emotions. His student Dennison wrote that

> I have been urging one simple truth through all these pages: that the educational function does not rest upon our ability to control, or our will to instruct, but upon our human nature and the nature of experience.

According to Dennison, this means trusting

> such principles as our inherent sociability, our inherent rationality, our inherent freedom of thought, our inherent curiosity, and our inherent (while vigor lasts) appetite for more. What this means concretely is that we must rescue the individuals from their present obscurity in the bureaucratic heap.... (Dennison 1969, 252, 253)

The radical educators came under heavy criticism for their romantic, "sentimental" defense of human nature against the presumably stifling forces of society. Critics pointed out that an individual's impulses are not always desirable, and in any event are never purely separate from social influences that begin at birth. But according to my reading, the major radical critics did *not* say that adults should let children do anything they like because their impulses are always correct; they did *not*, as critics charged, say that adults should "abdicate" all responsibility and let children grow up by themselves. What they said, and what the guardians of culture could not afford to hear, is that educators should be more concerned about the human possibilities that are repressed by conventional schooling. Holt, for example, wrote that

> people, and above all children, may not only have much greater learning powers than we suspect, but also greater self-curing powers. Our task is to learn more about these powers, and how we may create conditions in which they may have a chance to work. This is one of the things that children may be able to teach us, if we are not always busy teaching them. (Holt 1972, 77-78)

Traditional schooling obscures the unique abilities of the person; the supposedly objective means of classifying students — grades, IQ and achievement tests, tracking — are self-fulfilling: Students predefined as less capable are treated accordingly — and then act appropriately. In the radical writings are many examples of "dumb" students who blossomed when they were treated as individuals rather than with generic labels. It would appear that if children actually do have greater potential for learning, growth and self-discovery than the cultural view is willing to admit, then the radical critique is not simply "romantic," it is powerfully correct! To argue that society or its schools should not repress human possibilities is a stinging criticism of the Protestant-conservative belief that the best human powers are limited to a select few, and a serious challenge to the hierarchical society that necessarily follows that belief.

This is really why the guardians were alarmed by the radicals, and why they have always rejected the holistic approach. One conservative critic charged that

> They deplore the evils of capitalism and wish to promote egalitarian values that could eventually lead to the dismantling of many institutions in our society. (Troost 1973, 5)

It could not be more clear: the conservative Protestant-capitalist worldview is not as interested in promoting democracy or personal development as in preserving the social order. Even the *evils* of capitalism are preferable to any alternative worldview! For good measure, this writer accused the radical educators of encouraging

> thrill-seeking behavior related to drugs, sex, violence, and crime.... By indulging the individual learner, by exalting his choices, by dismissing the hard-won standards of civilization, the open-classroom devotee contributes to the dissolution of our civilization. (Troost 1973, 3, 188)

Here is the utter distrust of human nature and spontaneity characteristic of Protestant-capitalist culture. "Civilization" (that is, the current social order presided over by economic and political elites) must be protected from the undisciplined impulses of human nature. Just as the radical progressives' criticism was swept away with the charges of "Red" and "Communist," the radical criticism of the 1960s was dismissed with the epithets of "drugs, sex, violence, and crime." The charges were irrelevant and misleading, but they were guaranteed to arouse middle class fears.

As a matter of fact, the radicals themselves were highly distressed by the "dissolution of our civilization," which they witnessed firsthand in the schools. But they believed that, like so-called "stupidity," the problems of "thrill-seeking behavior," delinquency, and rebellion were symptoms of the *repression* of human growth. Herbert Kohl argued that "the problems of motivation and discipline are intricately involved with the authoritarian role of the teacher" (Kohl 1969, 77). Such problems, traditionally blamed on the student, frequently disappeared when the learning environment was made more democratic, when relationships between people were personal and genuine rather than hierarchically structured. This is a common discovery among educators in alternative schools (see Gold & Mann, 1984), and was reported to me often when I interviewed holistic educators. The implications for social policy are enormous: the "dissolution" of civilization may not be stemmed, but worsened, by the further regimentation and standardization of individuals' lives.

The radical literature then, was not a call for tinkering with the curriculum or seating arrangements, but a profound critique of the traditional conception of schooling itself. While only Holt, Illich, Everett Reimer, and a few others proposed the total abolition of public education, the movement as a whole made a strong plea for fundamental, as opposed to merely cosmetic, reform. The free school movement was an expression of this radical dissent — although even here the split between "accommodating" and radical educators was evident. Many free schoolers were simply "dropping out" of the system to obtain their own freedom, but by 1972, the more socially radical among them reminded their peers of their broader purpose. Allen Graubard wrote

> In order to create a truly humane and liberating education, we must be in the process of creating a truly humane and liberating social order.... The real problems of educational reform are social, political, economic, and ideological. (Graubard 1974, xi, 35)

And in a passionate critique, Kozol (1972) accused affluent free schoolers of fleeing from the real social problems of inequality and poverty. The radicals were understandably disturbed by the political indifference of many free schoolers. But Graubard and Kozol were not criticizing their colleagues for disagreeing with the radical analysis, only for not fully living out its implications. (This tension between personal freedom and social change continues to exist in the free school movement today.)

The mainstream of American society, however, did not agree with the radical analysis. Even at its peak, according to one writer, the free school movement reached about 10,000 students, or only ¼ of 1% of the school population. He says that the radical/free school movement was "doomed to failure" because it was a political and not just a pedagogical critique; his interpretation affirms my own:

> The fundamental purpose of education has always been to transmit the culture: The purpose behind many alternatives was to transform the culture. (Rosenfeld 1978, 486-489)

The radical critique and free school movement were, like other holistic approaches, countercultural — and hence rejected by American society and education.

However, the upheaval of the 1960s had frightened the guardians of culture, and they turned once again to their favorite remedy: educational reform. The problems in American schools, so passionately decried by the radical critics, were finally perceived as a *crisis* when the mainstream establishment decided, around 1970, that the social ferment demanded some kind of reform in response. The perennial conservative response — a call for greater efficiency, better academic results, and more discipline — was already being made in the 1960s by such figures as James B. Conant and Mortimer Adler; they sought to strengthen the system with more challenging curricula or more rigorous teacher training. But around 1970, there emerged another group, whom we may call mainstream liberals; they responded to social and educational dissent with less radical — yet still quite potent — ideas for reform such as open classrooms and "public schools of choice." Among the figures in this group were Charles Silberman, Joseph Featherstone, Mario Fantini, Lilian Weber, Vincent Rogers, Vito Perrone, Roland S. Barth, and Ewald Nyquist.

The open classroom movement was a rare case of mainstream educators advocating a largely holistic approach. At the outset, it was inspired by a strong conviction that traditional educational practices were *inhumane* and must therefore be changed. Silberman, for example, claimed

> It is not possible to spend any prolonged period visiting public school classrooms without being appalled by the mutilation visible everywhere — mutilation of spontaneity, of joy in learning, of pleasure in creating, of sense of self.... The pervasive atmosphere of distrust, together with rules covering the most minute aspects of existence, teach students every day that they are not people of worth, and certainly not individuals capable of regulating their own behavior. (Silberman 1970, 10, 134)

On this point the liberals were not far from the radical analysis; they admitted that curriculum reforms already undertaken in the previous decade were superficial.

> We know that it is not enough to rewrite the math program, or the English, or the science, or all of them together. It is not enough to put TV sets in the

> classroom, to install movable walls, or to institute team teaching.... A preoccupation with technology, programs, and "things" may, in fact, tend to forestall serious confrontation of the basic problems which, we believe, are essentially human. (D.E. Armington, in Nyquist & Hawes 1972, 65; cf. J. Featherstone, ibid., 94)

This is a remarkable admission by a mainstream educator, a rejection of scientistic professional expertise. The liberal reform movement, surprisingly enough, shared to a large extent the holistic concern for human development. This is the historic significance of the education crisis.

The open classroom approach may be considered holistic because its starting point was a faith in the natural unfolding of human development. According to Nyquist, "Respect for and trust in the child are perhaps the most basic principles underlying the open classroom" (Nyquist & Hawes 1972, 10). Barth listed twenty-nine "assumptions about learning and knowledge" shared by these educators, the first of which was *"Children are innately curious and will explore without adult intervention."* These writers recognized that their faith held true only in a learning environment which nurtured the child's emotional well-being and self-esteem. Traditional schooling does not provide such an environment. According to Barth:

> The entire affective, emotional domain of learning remains underdeveloped in American classrooms.... We continue to be self-conscious, inhibited, and repressed about exposing our feelings either through words or bodily movement. (Barth 1972, 18, 53)

He attributed this situation to the atmosphere of distrust that pervades the classroom, where teachers devote their energy to maintaining control and students remain in a continuous state of anxiety.

> Thus the conventional relationship between teacher and child is essentially one of adversaries in a constant struggle. (Barth 1972, 89)

The liberals, like the radical educators, called upon teachers to act as whole persons, to open themselves to spontaneity and to express feelings honestly in the classroom. They asked teachers to give up their "pathological professionalism"; Featherstone, Silberman, and others were highly critical of the education "establishment," with its self-serving teacher-training and credentialing procedures. In short, it is evident that the open classroom approach was not simply another mainstream attempt to borrow a few humanistic techniques to make learning more efficient. There was instead a genuine interest in promoting holistic human development.

The mainstream liberals did not, however, draw upon American holistic models, such as the 1960s radical literature, free schools, or the discredited approach of progressive education. Instead, they discovered a fresh approach in Britain. Only a few Americans had known about the open classroom (or "integrated day") experiments taking place in many of the primary schools there — until 1967, when the British Plowden Commission reported favorably on them, and Featherstone told Americans about them in a series of articles in *The New Republic*. By 1971, when a volley of books and articles touted this approach, it had become the model that foundations, researchers, and school officials sought to emulate.

These educators were among the first to apply the insights of the developmental psychologist Jean Piaget. The foundation of Piaget's voluminous work was that human intelligence unfolds in stages, and (especially during the early stages) that people learn best through *activity*, by engaging the world through meaningful interaction which is physical and emotional as well as cognitive. In essence, Piaget had given empirical sanction to a core idea of the holistic tradition since Pestalozzi: "Education" must not be defined as a dry transmission of information, but as the creation of an environment which stimulates exploration and discovery. As Featherstone put it, "Formal schools train children to take achievement tests, whereas informal ones teach more important things" (Featherstone 1971, 40). When the open classroom advocates, in Britain and America, applied Piaget's research to classroom practice, the result was a beehive of children freely choosing among different activity areas, similar in some ways to the Montessori "prepared environment." This was no coincidence; as we have seen, Piaget himself was influenced by Montessori.

Yet it is clear that the liberal, open classroom approach was an "accommodating" holistic movement. Like the 1960s radicals, the liberals were sincerely concerned with the optimal growth of the individual, but unlike them, the liberals assumed hopefully that individual growth through educational reform could take place without significant social change. The liberals gave most of their attention to exploring techniques for creating more humane classrooms; they did not, like the radicals, seek a major overhaul of American culture. They did not believe that the problems of the schools reflected deep-seated social problems, but simply resulted from "mindlessness" (as Silberman argued) or well-intentioned error. Although they did occasionally recognize that social issues larger than schooling were at stake, these writers did not share the radicals' feeling that much of American society was "all wrong," as Herndon once put it. In fact, they often sought to reassure their middle class constituency by specifically distancing themselves from the radicals (Silberman 1970, 141; Nyquist & Hawes 1972, 3-4; Barth 1972, 12-13).

Rosenfeld suggests that the liberal reformers defused the education crisis by substituting their own reforms for the radical proposals:

> Reform was effectively depoliticized, and schools remained essentially the same as they have been for the past century.... Reform, as always, centered on techniques to improve efficiency; the reforms were not aimed at the foundations of the educational system. (Rosenfeld 1978, 487)

I agree that the liberals' "depoliticized" reforms relieved Americans of the need to take the radicals too seriously. Once again, the panacea of educational reform deflected attention from the more serious criticisms being made against American culture. Still, as I have pointed out, the open classroom movement was not essentially conservative; it did not aim for social conformity and efficiency in the sense that the common school and mainstream Progressive movements did. Genuine conservatives, in fact, lumped the mainstream liberals with the radicals, seeing both as subversive, because the open classroom movement did contain many truly holistic elements. If the liberals extinguished the reform efforts of the radical educators, it was because of their faith that a presumably democratic, humanistic American culture would welcome their ideals. This is the danger of the "accommodating" approach to holistic education; American culture does *not* welcome holistic ideas, and accommodation usually leads to fatal compromise.

This is exactly what happened by the mid-1970s. As even some of its proponents realized, the open classroom approach had been adopted as the latest educational panacea and carelessly grafted onto the existing school structure (Nyquist & Hawes 1972, 89). It suffered the same fate as Pestalozzi's and Parker's ideas: It was diluted by compromise with mainstream educational expectations until it was reduced to a caricature, and then roundly condemned as ineffective (Raywid 1981). As John Holt observed, an approach that is concerned with the unfolding personality of every child is fundamentally at odds with the public schools' mission of sorting and social efficiency. Thus, when studies indicated that open classrooms made no significant difference in terms of *traditional* educational goals, the approach was discredited, like all previous holistic attempts to enter the mainstream. As Ira Shor has argued, conservative forces reasserted their control over education and society in the 1970s, effectively frustrating the social protest of the 1960s. Social efficiency and international economic competition required higher achievement scores, not holistic human development (Shor 1986).

By the mid-1970s, American education had weathered its most serious crisis without making any major concessions to its critics. The "back-to-basics" movement, emphasizing test scores, "time-on-task" and other heavy-handed control over the lives of children, continued to gain momentum through the 1980s. In the past fifteen years, educational "reform" has not meant making schools more humane or democratic, or making learning more meaningful, joyful, or spontaneous; it means raising test scores, improving "cultural literacy" (what "every American must know"), and reestablishing discipline. Just as the mainstream Progressive movement reasserted American culture against radical discontent with urban industrialism, educational "reform" in the 1980s responded repressively to the culturally threatening criticism of the 1960s.

The education establishment did introduce one innovation: "public schools of choice," alternative or magnet schools designed to satisfy critics of the mainstream. There were about one hundred such programs in 1970, and there are many hundreds today. While the alternative school movement could represent an historic opening for holistic approaches (several Montessori programs, for example, have been introduced into public schooling, although not without danger of compromise), for the most part "the concept of alternative schools has changed from a radical idea to a conservative response to local school problems" (Barr 1981). Indeed, a large number of alternative programs serve dropouts or potential dropouts; their main purpose is to make school palatable enough to keep dissatisfied students in the system, not to address the fundamental problems that cause such alienation in the first place. They serve to draw trouble-makers and vandals out of the regular schools, so that the business of education can efficiently continue. Also, voluntary magnet schools are a convenient way to achieve racial integration in urban systems.

Consequently, while alternative programs can be (and often are) somewhat more personalized, democratic, and responsive to community and student needs, they usually endorse traditional educational goals: academic and vocational skills and the transmission of cultural values. They do not, for the most part, constitute a holistic movement. If they did, I believe they would not be as attractive to political and educational leaders. Public "schools of choice" are a hopeful step toward a desperately needed decentralization of education, but they are far from being the fundamental educational reform which the Bush administration considers them to be. They are yet another substitute for serious rethinking of educational goals.

The radical educational critique, like the turmoil of the 1960s, has receded into history. For part of a decade, many Americans had so lost confidence in their institutions that they were willing to consider the unfamiliar path of radical social reform. As had happened before in times of crisis, the guardians of culture reaffirmed the sustaining mythology of American culture, and the person-centered vision of the holistic educators was repudiated once again. But as the twenty-first century nears, there are signs that it will return with unprecedented strength.

Education for the Twenty-First Century

CHAPTER 9

In this book, I have sought to re-assess the significance of a diverse group of educators whose work has not received serious attention in mainstream educational practice. I have identified this group as "holistic" educators, even though few of them (until recently) have used the term themselves. Indeed, holistic education draws on a variety of intellectual and pedagogical influences. But I would argue that several core themes characterize the educational approaches I have described. Despite variations in teaching methods or styles or particular philosophical differences, several themes define an educational approach as "holistic."

An Emphasis on the Wholeness of Human Experience

Holistic educators recognize that all aspects of human life are fundamentally interconnected. They contend that education must be concerned with the physical, emotional, social, esthetic/creative, and spiritual qualities of every person, as well as traditionally emphasized intellectual and vocational skills. They argue that our present culture's emphasis on rational intellect, economic achievement, competition, and the uncomplaining performance of social roles is lopsided. To be "well-educated" in the modern industrial world means to be well disciplined; it is to be alienated from one's own spontaneous, creative, self-actualizing impulses. Holistic education calls for a new recognition of the organic, subconscious, subjective, intuitive, artistic, mythological, and spiritual dimensions of our lives.

A traditionalist would argue that, even if these human qualities need to be addressed, *schools* are not the proper place to do so. (Recall Rickover's statement that educating the whole child is "something very close to propagandizing your children.") The conservative claims that such education is the responsibility of the home and church. But there are at least two responses to this complaint. First, the holistic approach points out that human experience is integrated; we cannot isolate facets of children's lives without doing violence to their healthy development. Children do not simply learn through their minds, but through their feelings and concerns, their imaginations and their bodies. To focus only on one aspect of experience is, quite simply, a symptom of the reductionism of our culture; its implicit message is that our latent spiritual qualities are not as highly valued as rational, calculating intellect.

Second, we must consider the declining state of our culture: Many families are crumbling under tremendous stress, and children are subjected to a proliferation of crudely hedonistic and violent messages through mass marketing and entertainment. Given this milieu, *schools may be the only place in the present culture where the developmental needs of young people can be given the highest priority* and the attention and care they require. (The rapidly growing homeschool movement and the small but growing "co-housing" and intentional community movement are positive and promising exceptions.) Holistic educators recognize the need for cooperation with parents, and in the schools I visited around the country, they had a much more open, cooperative relationship with parents than do teachers in most public schools. Yet because children spend much of their time in school — and a staggering amount of their time at home under the influence of television — it is imperative that we make their school experience as fully nurturing as possible. To argue that schools should only be concerned with the "3 Rs" is to ignore the vast changes that are taking place in the world! Today's children *need* a holistic education if they are to develop into emotionally healthy, morally secure, and democratically inclined citizens.

A Spiritual Worldview

A basic premise of holistic education is the belief that our lives have a meaning and purpose greater than the mechanistic laws described by science, and greater than the "consensus consciousness" of any one culture. This transcendent purpose is a creative, self-guiding energy which we ought not attempt to suppress. No ideology, no social order devised by wealth- or power-seeking factions should be allowed to corrupt the delicate, miraculous unfolding of this creative energy. The needs of commerce, the roles imposed by vocation or social class, the prejudices that divide groups of people from each other — all tragically obscure the essential humanity that is inherent in every person.

Thus, a spiritual worldview is a *global* paradigm: It emphasizes the human connections between persons across political boundaries, and hence stands in opposition to this culture's obsession with national economic success. It is an *ecological* paradigm, emphasizing our connections to all of life and opposing the destructive anthropocentrism and materialism of modern Western culture. Ultimately, a spiritual worldview is a *reverence for life*, an attitude of wonder and awe in the face of the transcendent Source of our being.

As I have pointed out before, two quite different languages have been used to describe this spiritual attitude. One is primarily religious or theistic, and describes the transcendent in terms such as "God," "divine," and "soul." (The word *spiritual* itself is derived from this tradition.) The other is a more empirical, down-to-earth language, taken from twentieth century psychology, which uses terms such as "archetype" and "individuation" and "self-actualization." There are significant and interesting differences between these two conceptions. For example, religious approaches tend to seek the transcendent through various *disciplines*, and holistic education methods developed in these traditions (such as Waldorf, Montessori, and schools affiliated with religious sects) are often quite highly structured and disciplined. On the other hand, empirical psychological approaches are more interested in the *spontaneity* of creative expression, and educators who draw upon this point of view (Neef, Ferrer, Neill, Goodman, Holt, etc.) are the "child-centered" libertarians in the holistic tradition.

But I would argue that such differences are not as significant as the fundamental respect which both groups hold for the transcendent creative Source. Both approaches are guided by a central conviction that human nature, as an expression of this Source, is fundamentally good rather than evil and should be nurtured rather than repressed. In this light, *the "child-centered" educators are not centered on childishness as such, but on the vital energies that children express with more spontaneity than do most adults*. These educators, then, are more accurately described as *spirit-centered* or *life-centered*. I would argue that this is a significantly revised understanding of the child-centered tradition in education; it is the major theme of this book.

One tradition which has achieved a remarkable balance between the religious and empirical perspectives is the Religious Society of Friends. The Quakers clearly draw from deep theological, Christian roots, and yet their emphasis on the "Inner Light" — a direct experience of the creative Source — leads them to honor the fresh, spontaneous expression of this energy. This emphasis has profound implications for education. According to Thomas S. Brown,

> our Quaker experience of education is different from education understood as the transmission of the group's inherited wisdom and the proven techniques of survival and the refining of intellectual manipulations.... Every moment bears in it the dynamic of new truth, a life-changing insight, a hitherto unexplored perspective often coming through unexpected and unlikely channels. (in Dorrance 1982, 9-10)

Parker J. Palmer, a Quaker-inspired writer, has commented:

> We must commit ourselves to being authentic adults — that is, persons whose lives are built around caring for new life ... [because] the children are an incarnation of God's continuing revelation. (Palmer 1978, 18)

Quaker educational theory has not been influenced by the holistic tradition described in this book, yet its profound similarity is confirming evidence that when young people are honored as essentially spiritual beings, the ruling purpose of education is *to care for new life* rather than "to make possible the survival of our country" or to convince young people "that their skills are a product" which serve their employers' interests. This brings us to the next fundamental theme of holistic education.

A Community that Nurtures Individuals

Because spiritual unfolding is an inner, personal process of discovery, holistic approaches are highly concerned with the integrity of the individual person. Holistic education emphasizes the development of each individual's unique and characteristic potentials, not the preservation of cultural belief systems and social institutions. In direct opposition to the nationalistic "social efficiency" orientation of American education, holistic educators insist that human development must be served before the economic and political goals of those in power. The more radical holistic educators demand that social institutions be changed if they fail to serve human needs first.

But this emphasis on the individual is not a "sentimental" individualism; it is not a celebration of the "noble savage." As anthropology has quite clearly established, "human nature" cannot exist free from enculturation; human development *requires* culture to activate and direct its natural potentials. *But it is within our power to create a culture that encourages the fullest development of human potentials, rather than one which arbitrarily cuts off an entire range of them*. We can create a social order that respects the inherent uniqueness and originality of the person, rather than one which attempts to impose a uniformity of belief and behavior.

This raises issues of authority, as well as issues of community. Holistic educators have been accused of "abdicating" adult authority, yet in reality, most of them have recognized that children naturally look to caring adults as their guides. The *real* issue is whether educators will wield this authority through force or through a genuine respect for the developmental needs of the child. As Palmer writes:

> Adults will always have the power to coerce children. But caring rests on the power of hope and trust, not on the power of containment. If we try to keep our children within safe boundaries, we prevent them from undertaking any great experiment with truth. (Palmer 1978, 9-10)

Holistic educators *do* emphasize the need for community, cooperation, and common values. But they observe that cooperation arises naturally in a healthy, supportive environment. Human beings *seek* fellowship and cooperation when their developmental needs are satisfied; they do not need to be socialized by moralistic authority. The holistic approach asserts that genuine personal encounter, resting on a firm foundation of mutual respect and concern, is the basis for a true human community. Like Emerson, holistic educators offer "the power of love" as the basis for social order. Is this idealistic? Of course it is — in this hierarchical, materialistic, competitive culture. But as a vision for a possible post-industrial culture, it stirs the soul.

Learning Through Experience

In our culture, "education" is implicitly equated with the transmission of information, particularly through written sources. But the holistic educators have, for two centuries, asserted that education is *an active engagement between a person and a vastly complex world*. Holistic education emphasizes experience, not "Great Books" or a few "basic skills." Experience is as profound and unlimited and exciting as the universe itself! Why limit students to a curriculum of academic subjects when the entire cosmos is at hand? Education, as John Dewey so eloquently argued, must not be seen as "preparation" for life — it *is* life! Education is growth, discovery, and a widening of horizons. This is just the opposite of traditional educational goals — discipline, order, high test scores — that aim to prepare young people for the limited world which the adult generation has created. The educator can guide students as they take on this vast realm of experience, but this is precisely where educating is an art rather than a technique. Ultimately no teacher can step in between a learner and his or her experience of the world. The role of a teacher is to facilitate an active engagement between a person and the universe.

Education is a meaningful encounter, sustained by interest, curiosity, and personal purpose. In this sense, education is not the mere acquisition of information, but a joyful, exhilarating and enriching exploration of the world and one's intricate relationships to it. For decades, holistic educators had defined education in this way, only to be dismissed as incurably sentimental romantics. But in the twentieth century, this insight of the holistic educators was first supported by the sophisticated thought of Dewey, and later by the empirically substantiated work of Jean Piaget, Howard Gardner, and dozens of other researchers who have explored the nature of intelligence, learning, and the functioning of the human brain. It is now obvious that human beings, children as well as adults, learn in a variety of ways, involving physical activity, imagination, emotional concern, and implicit connections to their physical and social (and spiritual) environments. Education defined exclusively as book learning is a patently obsolete concept.

As I argued before, this research in itself is not holistic education. Often the findings in neuroscience and learning style research are incorporated into traditionally structured classrooms in order to more effectively instill traditional curricula for traditional cultural purposes. But this empirical research, when combined with the other essential themes I am describing here, offers a new educational approach that I believe will answer the educational needs of the coming post-industrial age.

Education for the Twenty-First Century

For the past century and a half, holistic educators have been deemed "romantic" and therefore irrelevant to the educational goals of a scientific, industrial, nationalistic age. But if the holistic critique of Western culture is indeed accurate — and I believe it is — then this age is coming to a close. The educational needs of the now-emerging post-industrial age will be radically different from those this culture has chosen to serve for almost two hundred years. These new educational goals cannot be served by our present educational practices; they require approaches that honor a global, ecological, and spiritual worldview. Holistic education is an approach whose time has come.

Industrial-age education seeks to provide information to young people, and measures students' vocational and social value in terms of how much information they can manage. Conventional education seeks to impose a particular worldview on each new generation — a worldview limited by certain themes such as conservative Protestant Christianity, scientific reductionism, restrained democratic ideals, capitalism, and nationalism. Traditional education sees young people as undisciplined, uninformed, unmotivated little creatures in need of authoritative adult direction.

But in the post industrial age, these foundations of mainstream education are becoming obsolete. We are drowning in information, which grows and changes so rapidly that an education which only passes information along soon becomes outdated. But we are desperately lacking meaning; we are lacking purpose; we are lacking a social vision that can inspire us to determine which information is appropriate to the needs of human life (Roszak 1986; Fox 1988; Oliver & Gershman 1989; Purpel 1989). The themes of American culture are increasingly unable to provide a sustaining cosmology; in a world increasingly knitted more tightly together by communications, trade, and *a shared ecological fate*, the limited vistas of the American worldview become more dangerously restrictive. It is increasingly apparent that the competitive, materialistic urge to control nature and human nature leads only to the trivialization of our human potentials, to the desecration of the Earth, and ultimately to the destruction of life.

The holistic paradigm, then, is essentially radical, and those holistic educators who have adopted an "accommodating" attitude have, in my view, failed to recognize the profound implications of their beliefs. Holistic education is not just a different way of teaching children; it is implicitly a statement that the values and beliefs of our culture are fundamentally impoverished and unsatisfactory. Education alone will not change our culture. The first lesson to be gained from the social history of education is that changes in schools do *not* produce changes in society, but are doomed to failure unless society itself is transformed. Holistic education will not be adopted on any meaningful scale until the industrial age is eclipsed by a more ecological, global worldview.

Holistic education, while radical, is not simply another ideology. It does not seek to indoctrinate a young generation in its values, but to educate them for a new world that will welcome and honor their highest possibilities. To be radical may not achieve our goals more quickly, but it will at least keep them intact. The Quakers have been described as a "holding company" for humankind's highest ideals while the rest of humanity struggles to free itself of old ideologies, and I think the holistic tradition can be described in the same way. The danger in accommodation is that these ideals are compromised by a culture that cannot appreciate them. We have seen this occur again and again in the holistic tradition, from Pestalozzi's object method to progressive education to Montessori's work to the "open classroom."

We are approaching a crucial point in history: Humankind *must* soon choose between total destruction of the ecosystem or a new worldview that strives for peace, cooperation, and justice based upon a reverence for life. There is no more room for compromise; we cannot muddle through much longer, as we have so far, with our faith in technology and professional expertise. At this time, humankind is in transition. We are in a confusing and frightening abyss between worldviews. There will probably be a great deal of resistance, and possibly violence, before the holistic paradigm will be fully accepted. As each day brings more news of wars and revolts, corruption and drugs, terrorism and hostages, repression and torture, we may become discouraged and come to feel that humanity is beyond redemption. The world is in agony now and it is often difficult to believe that it can be saved at all. But all it takes is a shift of consciousness. A new worldview would create a new reality. Transformation is possible.

Bibliography

Aikin, Wilford M. (1942). *The Story of the Eight-Year Study*. New York: Harper.

Albanese, Catherine L. (1977). *Corresponding Motion: Transcendental Religion and the New America*. Philadelphia: Temple University.

Alcott, A. Bronson (1938). *The Journals of Bronson Alcott* (Odell Shepard, Ed.). Boston: Little, Brown.

Alcott, A. Bronson (1960). *Essays on Education by Amos Bronson Alcott* (Walter Harding, Ed.). Gainesville, FL: Scholars' Facsimiles & Reprints.

Alcott, A. Bronson (1972). *Conversations with Children on the Gospels* (1836). New York: Arno/New York Times.

Allender, Jerome S. (1982). Affective Education. In H.E. Mitzel (Ed.), *Encyclopedia of Educational Research* (5th ed.). New York: Free Press.

Archdeacon, Thomas J. (1983). *Becoming American: An Ethnic History*. New York: Free Press.

Arieli, Yehoshua (1964). *Individualism and Nationalism in American Ideology*. Cambridge: Harvard.

Arons, Stephen (1983). *Compelling Belief: The Culture of American Schooling*. New York: McGraw-Hill.

Avrich, Paul (1980). *The Modern School Movement: Anarchism and Education in the United States*. Princeton, NJ: Princeton University.

Barlow, Thomas A. (1977). *Pestalozzi and American Education*. Boulder, CO: Este Es Press/University of Colorado.

Barnes, Henry (1980, Spring). An Introduction to Waldorf Education. *Teachers College Record* 81(3).

Barr, Robert D. (1981, April). Alternatives for the Eighties: A Second Decade of Development. *Phi Delta Kappan* 62(8).

Barth, Roland S. (1972). *Open Education and the American School*. New York: Agathon.

Bercovitch, Sacvan (1975). *The Puritan Origins of the American Self*. New Haven: Yale.

Bernstein, Richard J. (1966). *John Dewey*. New York: Washington Square Press.

Bestor, Arthur (1953). *Educational Wastelands*. Urbana: University of Illinois Press.

Bestor, Arthur (1955). *The Restoration of Learning*. New York: Knopf.

Bledstein, Burton W. (1976). *The Culture of Professionalism: The Middle Class and the Development of Higher Education in America*. New York: Norton.

Bode, Boyd (1927). *Modern Educational Theories*. New York: Macmillan; reprinted by Vintage Books.

Bourne, Randolph (1965). *The World of Randolph Bourne* (Lillian Schlissel, Ed.). New York: Dutton.

Brown, George Isaac (1971). *Human Teaching for Human Learning: An Introduction to Confluent Education*. New York: Viking.

Butts, R. Freeman (1978). *Public Education in the United States: From Revolution to Reform*. New York: Holt, Rinehart & Winston.

Callahan, Raymond E. (1962). *Education and the Cult of Efficiency*. Chicago: University of Chicago.

Capra, Fritjof, & Spretnak, Charlene (1986). *Green Politics: The Global Promise*. Santa Fe, NM: Bear.

Carbone, Peter F., Jr. (1977). *The Social and Educational Thought of Harold Rugg*. Durham, NC: Duke University.

Channing, William Ellery (1900). *Works*. Boston: American Unitarian Association.

Channing, William Henry (1880). *Life of William Ellery Channing*. Boston: American Unitarian Association.

Church, Robert L., & Sedlak, Michael (1976). *Education in the United States*. New York: Free Press.

Clark, Edward T., Jr. (1988, Spring). The Search for a New Educational Paradigm: The Implications of New Assumptions About Thinking and Learning. *Holistic Education Review* 1(1), 18-30.

Conn, Sandra (1986, September 15). Education's Failure Stirs Small Business Ire. *Crain's Chicago Business*.

Cott, Nancy F. (1977). *The Bonds of Womanhood: "Women's Sphere" in New England 1780-1835*. New Haven: Yale.

Counts, George S. (1930). *The American Road to Culture*. New York: Day.

Counts, George S. (1932). *Dare the School Build a New Social Order?* New York: Day.

Cremin, Lawrence (1961). *The Transformation of the School*. New York: Knopf.

Cronin, Joseph M. (1973). *The Control of Urban Schools*. New York: Free Press.

Curti, Merle (1968). *The Social Ideas of American Educators* (1935). Totowa, NJ: Littlefield, Adams.

Dahlstrand, Frederick C. (1982). *Amos Bronson Alcott: An Intellectual Biography*. East Brunswick, NJ: Associated University Presses.

Dennison, George (1969). *The Lives of Children: The Story of the First Street School*. New York: Random House.

Dewey, John (1938). *Experience and Education*. New York: Macmillan.

Dewey, John (1939). *Intelligence in the Modern World: John Dewey's Philosophy* (Joseph Ratner, Ed.). New York: Random House.

Dewey, John (1940). *Education Today* (Joseph Ratner, Ed.). New York: Putnam.

Dewey, John (1957). *Human Nature and Conduct* (1922). New York: Modern Library.

Dewey, John (1966a). *Democracy and Education* (1916). New York: Free Press.

Dewey, John (1966b). *Lectures in the Philosophy of Education* (1899; Reginald D. Archambault, Ed.). New York: Random House.

Dorrance, Christopher A. (Ed.). (1982). *Reflections from a Friends Education*. Philadelphia: Friends Council on Education.

Downs, Robert B. (1975). *Heinrich Pestalozzi: Father of Modern Pedagogy*. Boston: Twayne/G.K. Hall.

Downs, Robert B. (1978). *Friedrich Froebel*. Boston: Twayne/G.K. Hall.

Duberman, Martin (Ed.). (1965). *The Anti-Slavery Vanguard: New Essays on the Abolitionists*. Princeton, NJ: Princeton University.

Edwards, Newton, & Richey, Herman (1963). *The School in the American Social Order* (2nd ed.). Boston: Houghton Mifflin.

Eisler, Riane (1987). *The Chalice and the Blade*. New York: Harper & Row.

Elkins, Stanley M. (1968). *Slavery* (2nd ed.). Chicago: University of Chicago.

Emerson, Ralph Waldo (1965). *Selected Writings* (William H. Gilman, Ed.). New York: New American Library.

Faler, Paul G. (1981). *Mechanics and Manufacturers in the Early Industrial Revolution: Lynn, Massachusetts 1780–1860*. Albany: SUNY Press.

Featherstone, Joseph (1967). *Schools Where Children Learn*. New York: Liveright.

Ferrer, Francisco (1913). *The Origin and Ideals of the Modern School* (Joseph McCabe, Trans.). New York: Putnam.

Fox, Matthew (1983). *Original Blessing*. Santa Fe, NM: Bear.

Fox, Matthew (1988). *The Coming of the Cosmic Christ*. San Francisco: Harper & Row.

Froebel, Friedrich (1893). *The Education of Man* (1826; W.N. Hailmann, Trans.). New York: Appleton.

Gardner, Howard (1984). *Frames of Mind: The Theory of Multiple Intelligences*. New York: Basic Books.

Geertz, Clifford (1973). *The Interpretation of Cultures*. New York: Basic Books.

Geiger, George R. (1958). *John Dewey in Perspective*. New York: Oxford.

Glenn, Charles Leslie, Jr. (1988). *The Myth of the Common School*. Amherst: University of Massachusetts Press.

Gold, Martin, & Mann, David W. (1984). *Expelled to a Friendlier Place: A Study of Effective Alternative Schools*. Ann Arbor: University of Michigan.

Goldman, Eric. F. (1966). *Rendezvous With Destiny: A History of Modern American Reform* (1952). New York: Knopf.

Gordon, Thomas (1989). *Teaching Children Self-Discipline: At Home and at School*. New York: Times Books.

Graham, Patricia Albjerg (1967). *Progressive Education: From Arcady to Academe*. New York: Teachers College Press.

Graubard, Allen (1974). *Free the Children*. New York: Vintage.

Greene, Maxine (1965). *The Public School and the Private Vision*. New York: Random House.

Griffin, Clifford S. (1960). *Their Brothers' Keepers: Moral Stewardship in the United States 1800-1865*. New Brunswick, NJ: Rutgers University.

Griffin, Clifford S. (1967). *The Ferment of Reform*. New York: Crowell.

Gutek, Gerald Lee (1970). *The Educational Theory of George S. Counts*. Columbus: Ohio State University.

Gutek, Gerald Lee (1978). *Joseph Neef: The Americanization of Pestalozzianism*. Tuscaloosa: University of Alabama Press.

Gutman, Herbert (1976). *Work, Culture and Society in Industrializing America*. New York: Knopf.

Handy, Robert T. (1984). *A Christian America: Protestant Hopes and Historical Realities* (2nd ed.). New York: Oxford.

Harding, Walter (1982). *The Days of Henry Thoreau* (1965). New York: Dover.

Hartz, Louis (1955). *The Liberal Tradition in America*. New York: Harcourt, Brace & World.

Harwood, A.C. (1958). *The Recovery of Man in Childhood: A Study in the Educational Work of Rudolf Steiner*. Spring Valley, NY: Anthroposophic Press.

Herndon, James (1969). *The Way it Spozed to Be*. New York: Bantam.

Herndon, James (1971). *How to Survive in Your Native Land*. New York: Simon & Schuster.

Higham, John (1970). *Strangers in the Land: Patterns of American Nativism* (1955). New York: Atheneum.

Hofstadter, Richard (1955a). *The Age of Reform*. New York: Vintage.

Hofstadter, Richard (1955b). *Social Darwinism in American Thought*. Boston: Beacon Press.

Holt, John (1964). *How Children Fail*. New York: Pitman.

Holt, John (1972). *Freedom and Beyond*. New York: Dell.

Hugins, Walter (Ed.) (1972). *The Reform Impulse, 1825-1850*. New York: Harper & Row.

Illich, Ivan (1970). *Deschooling Society*. New York: Harper & Row.

Jones, Maldwyn Allen (1960). *American Immigration*. Chicago: University of Chicago.

Jones, Rufus M. (1931). *Pathways to the Reality of God*. New York: Macmillan.

Kaestle, Carl F. (1983). *Pillars of the Republic: Common Schools and American Society 1780-1860*. New York: Hill & Wang.

Kallen, Horace M. (1949). *The Education of Free Men*. New York: Farrar, Straus.

Kandel, I. L. (1943). *The Cult of Uncertainty*. New York: Macmillan.

Karier, Clarence J. (1986). *The Individual, Society, and Education* (2nd ed.). Urbana: University of Illinois Press.

Karier, Clarence J., Violas, Paul C., & Spring, Joel (1973). *Roots of Crisis: American Education in the Twentieth Century*. Chicago: Rand McNally.

Katz, Michael (1968). *The Irony of Early School Reform*. Cambridge: Harvard.

Kestenbaum, Victor (1977). *The Phenomenological Sense of John Dewey: Habit and Meaning.* Atlantic Highlands, NJ: Humanities Press.

Kliebard, Herbert M. (1986). *The Struggle for the American Curriculum 1893-1958.* Boston: Routledge & Kegan Paul.

Kohl, Herbert (1969). *The Open Classroom: A Practical Guide to a New Way of Teaching.* New York: New York Review.

Kozol, Jonathan (1967). *Death at an Early Age.* Boston: Houghton Mifflin.

Kozol, Jonathan (1972). *Free Schools.* Boston: Houghton Mifflin.

Kozol, Jonathan (1975). *The Night is Dark and I am Far From Home.* Boston: Houghton Mifflin.

Kramer, Rita (1976). *Maria Montessori: A Biography.* New York: Putnam.

Kuhn, Thomas (1970). *The Structure of Scientific Revolutions* (2nd ed.). Chicago: University of Chicago Press.

Lasch, Christopher (1965). *The New Radicalism in America 1889- 1963: The Intellectual as a Social Type.* New York: Knopf.

Lazerson, Marvin (1971). *Origins of the Urban School: Public Education in Massachusetts 1870-1915.* Cambridge: Harvard.

Leonard, George B. (1968). *Education and Ecstasy.* New York: Delacorte.

Link, Arthur S., & McCormick, Richard L. (1983). *Progressivism.* Arlington Heights, IL: Harlan Davidson.

Lynd, Albert (1953). *Quackery in the Public Schools.* Boston: Little, Brown.

McDermott, Robert A. (Ed.). (1984). *The Essential Steiner: Basic Writings of Rudolf Steiner.* San Francisco: Harper & Row.

McCluskey, Neil G. (1958). *Public Schools and Moral Education: The Influence of Mann, Harris, and Dewey.* New York: Columbia University.

McCuskey, Dorothy (1969). *Bronson Alcott: Teacher* (1940). New York: Arno/ New York Times.

Mendelsohn, Jack (1971). *Channing: The Reluctant Radical.* Boston: Little, Brown.

Messerli, Jonathan (1972). *Horace Mann.* New York: Knopf.

Metzger, Milton, & Harding, Walter (1962). *A Thoreau Profile.* Concord, MA: Thoreau Foundation.

Meyers, Marvin (1957). *The Jacksonian Persuasion.* Palo Alto: Stanford University.

Miller, John P. (1988). *The Holistic Curriculum.* Toronto: Ontario Institute for Studies in Education.

Miller, Perry (1960). *The Transcendentalists.* Cambridge: Harvard.

Monroe, Will S. (1969). *History of the Pestalozzian Movement in the United States (1907).* New York: Arno/New York Times.

Montessori, Maria (1965). *Spontaneous Activity in Education* (1917; F. Simmonds, Trans.). New York: Schocken.

Montessori, Maria (1966). *The Discovery of the Child* (M.A. Johnstone, Trans.). Madras, India: Kalakshetra.

Montessori, Maria (1972). *The Secret of Childhood* (M.J. Costelloe, Trans.). New York: Ballantine.

Montessori, Maria (1973). *The Absorbent Mind* (1949; Claude Claremont, Trans.). Madras, India: Kalakshetra.

Montessori, Maria (1978). *The Formation of Man* (A.M. Joosten, Trans.). Madras, India: Kalakshetra.

Nasaw, David (1979). *Schooled to Order: A Social History of Public Schooling in the United States.* New York: Oxford.

Nash, Paul (1964, April). The Strange Death of Progressive Education. *Educational Theory* 14 (2), 65-75.

Nash, Roderick (1970). *The Nervous Generation: American Thought 1917-1930.* Chicago: Rand McNally.

Naumburg, Margaret (1928). *The Child and the World.* New York: Harcourt, Brace.

Neef, Joseph (1969). *Sketch of a Plan and Method of Education* (1808). New York: Arno/New York Times.

Nyquist, Ewald, & Hawes, Gene R. (1972). *Open Education: A Sourcebook for Parents and Teachers.* New York: Bantam.

Oliver, Donald W., & Gershman, Kathleen W. (1989). *Education, Modernity, and Fractured Meaning: Toward a Process Theory of Teaching and Learning.* Albany: SUNY Press.

Ostrander, Gilman M. (1970). *American Civilization in the First Machine Age 1890-1940.* New York: Harper & Row.

Palmer, Parker J. (1978). And a Little Child Shall Lead Them. Philadelphia: *Friends Journal.*

Parker, Francis W. (1969). *Talks on Pedagogics* (1894). New York: Arno/New York Times.

Peabody, Elizabeth P. (1969). *Record of a School* (1836). New York: Arno/New York Times.

Pearce, Joseph Chilton (1971). *The Crack in the Cosmic Egg: Challenging Constructs of Mind and Reality.* New York: Julian Press.

Pearce, Joseph Chilton (1980). *Magical Child: Rediscovering Nature's Plan for Our Children* (1977). New York: Bantam.

Pearce, Joseph Chilton (1986). *Magical Child Matures* (1985). New York: Bantam.

Postman, Neil, & Weingartner, Charles (1969). *Teaching as a Subversive Activity.* New York: Dell.

Pratt, Caroline (1948). *I Learn From Children: An Adventure in Progressive Education.* New York: Simon & Schuster.

Progressive Education magazine. 1924-1930.

Purpel, David E. (1989). *The Moral and Spiritual Crisis in Education: A Curriculum for Justice and Compassion in Education.* Granby, MA: Bergin & Garvey.

Rafferty, Max (1962). *Suffer, Little Children.* New York: Devin, Adair.

Ravitch, Diane (1983). *The Troubled Crusade: American Education 1945-1980.* New York: Basic Books.

Raywid, Mary Anne (1981, April). The First Decade of Public School Alternatives. *Phi Delta Kappan* 62(8), 551-554.

Richards, Mary C. (1980). *Toward Wholeness: Rudolf Steiner Education in America*. Middletown, CT: Wesleyan University.

Rickover, H. L. (1959). *Education and Freedom*. New York: Dutton.

Roberts, Thomas B. (Ed.). (1975). *Four Psychologies Applied to Education*. Cambridge, MA: Schenkman.

Rogers, Carl (1969). *Freedom to Learn*. Columbus, OH: Merrill.

Rose, Ann C. (1981). *Transcendentalism as a Social Movement 1830–1850*. New Haven: Yale.

Rosenfeld, Stuart (1978, March). Reflections on the Legacy of the Free Schools Movement. *Phi Delta Kappan* 59(7), 486-489.

Rosenstone, Robert A. (1975). *Romantic Revolutionary: A Biography of John Reed*. New York: Knopf.

Roszak, Theodore (1973). *Where the Wasteland Ends: Politics and Transcendence in Postindustrial Society*. Garden City, NY: Anchor/Doubleday.

Roszak, Theodore (1978). *Person/Planet: The Creative Disintegration of Industrial Society*. Garden City, NY: Anchor/Doubleday.

Roszak, Theodore (1986). *The Cult of Information: The Folklore of Computers and the True Art of Thinking*. New York: Pantheon.

Roth, Robert J. (1962). *John Dewey and Self-Realization*. Englewood Cliffs, NJ: Prentice-Hall.

Rothman, David (1971). *The Discovery of the Asylum: Social Order and Disorder in the New Republic*. Boston: Little, Brown.

Rousseau, Jean Jacques (1911). *Emile* (1762). London: Dent.

Rudolph, Frederick (Ed.). (1965). *Essays on Education in the Early Republic*. Cambridge: Harvard.

Rugg, Harold O. (Ed.). (1939). *Democracy and the Curriculum*. New York: Appleton-Century.

Salomon, Louis B. (1962, Spring). The Straight-Cut Ditch: Thoreau on Education. *American Quarterly* 14, 19-36.

Satin, Mark (1979). *New Age Politics: Healing Self and Society*. New York: Dell.

Shor, Ira (1986). *Culture Wars: School and Society in the Conservative Restoration 1969-1984*. London: Routledge and Kegan Paul.

Silber, Kate (1965). *Pestalozzi: The Man and His Work* (2nd ed.). London: Routledge & Kegan Paul.

Silberman, Charles (1970). *Crisis in the Classroom*. New York: Random House.

Sloan, Douglas (1983). *Insight-Imagination: The Emancipation of Thought and the Modern World*. Westport, CT: Greenwood Press.

Smith, Mortimer (1949). *And Madly Teach*. Chicago: Regnery.

Smith, Mortimer (1954). *The Diminished Mind*. Chicago: Regnery.

Spretnak, Charlene (1986). *The Spiritual Dimension of Green Politics*. Santa Fe, NM: Bear.

Spring, Joel (1972). *Education and the Rise of the Corporate State*. Boston: Beacon.

Spring, Joel (1976). *The Sorting Machine: National Educational Policy Since 1945*. New York: McKay.

Steiner, Rudolf (1947). *Knowledge of the Higher Worlds and Its Attainment.* (G. Metaxa, Trans.). Hudson, NY: Anthroposophic Press.

Steiner, Rudolf (1967). *The Younger Generation.* Spring Valley, NY: Anthroposophic Press.

Steiner, Rudolf (1969). *Education as a Social Problem.* Spring Valley, NY: Anthroposophic Press.

Sudbury Valley School (1970). *The Crisis in American Education: An Analysis and a Proposal.* Framingham, MA: Sudbury Valley School.

Susman, Warren I. (1984). *Culture as History: The Transformation of American Society in the Twentieth Century.* New York: Pantheon.

Swift, Lindsay (1904). *Brook Farm.* New York: Macmillan.

Tart, Charles (1986). *Waking Up: The Obstacles to Human Potential.* Boston: New Science Library/Shambhala.

Thoreau, Henry David (1950). *Walden and Other Writings* (Brooks Atkinson, Ed.). New York: Random House.

de Tocqueville, Alexis (1954). *Democracy in America* (1840). (Henry Reeve & Francis Bowen, Trans.; Phillips Bradley, Ed.). New York: Vintage.

Troost, Cornelius J. (1973). *Radical School Reform: Critique and Alternatives.* Boston: Little, Brown.

Tyack, David (1974). *The One Best System.* Cambridge: Harvard.

Tyler, Alice Felt (1962). *Freedom's Ferment: Phases of American Social History from the Colonial Period to the Outbreak of the Civil War* (1944). New York: Harper & Row.

Washburne, Carleton (1952). *What is Progressive Education?* New York: Day.

Welter, Rush (1962). *Popular Education and Democratic Thought in America.* New York: Columbia University.

Wilber, Ken (1980). *The Atman Project.* Wheaton, IL: Quest.

Williams, Lloyd (1963). The Illegible Contours of Progressive Education: An Effort at Clarification. *Educational Forum* 27(2), 219-225.

Willson, Lawrence (1962). Thoreau on Education. *History of Education Quarterly* 11, 19-29.

Wilson, Colin (1985). *Rudolf Steiner: The Man and His Vision.* Wellingborough, England: Aquarian Press.

Wingo, G. Max (1965). *The Philosophy of American Education.* Lexington, MA: Heath.

Wishy, Bernard (1968). *The Child and the Republic: The Dawn of Modern American Child Nurture.* Philadelphia: University of Pennsylvania.

Wood, Gordon (1969). *The Creation of the American Republic 1776–1787.* Chapel Hill: University of North Carolina.

Woodring, Paul (1953). *Let's Talk Sense About Our Schools.* New York: McGraw-Hill.

Zilversmit, Arthur (1976). The Failure of Progressive Education, 1920-1940. In Lawrence Stone (Ed.), *Schooling and Society* (pp. 252-263). Baltimore: Johns Hopkins.

Additional Writings on the Holistic Paradigm

Barfield, Owen (1965). *Saving the Appearances*. New York: Harcourt, Brace & World.

Bateson, Gregory (1972). *Steps to an Ecology of Mind*. New York: Ballantine.

Berman, Morris (1981). *The Reenchantment of the World*. Ithaca, NY: Cornell University.

Bohm, David (1980). *Wholeness and the Implicate Order*. London: Routledge & Kegan Paul.

Capra, Fritjof (1976). *The Tao of Physics: An Exploration of the Parallels Between Modern Physics and Eastern Mysticism*. Boulder, CO: Shambhala.

Capra, Fritjof (1982). *The Turning Point: Science, Society, and the Rising Culture*. New York: Simon & Schuster.

de Chardin, Teilhard (1961). *The Phenomenon of Man* (1955). (Bernard Wall, Trans.). New York: Harper & Row.

Ferguson, Marilyn (1980). *The Aquarian Conspiracy: Personal and Social Transformation in the 1980s*. Los Angeles: Tarcher.

Harman, Willis (1988). *Global Mind Change: The Promise of the Last Years of the Twentieth Century*. Indianapolis: Knowledge Systems.

Houston, Jean (1982). *The Possible Human*. Los Angeles: Tarcher.

Huxley, Aldous (1945). *The Perennial Philosophy*. New York: Harper.

Johnston, Charles M. (1986). *The Creative Imperative: A Four-Dimensional Theory of Human Growth and Planetary Evolution*. Berkeley, CA: Celestial Arts.

Lemkow, Anna F. (1990). *The Wholeness Principle: Dynamics of Unity Within Science, Religion and Society*. Wheaton, IL: Quest.

Mumford, Lewis (1956). *The Transformations of Man*. New York: Harper.

Rifkin, Jeremy (1980). *Entropy: A New World View*. New York: Viking.

Rifkin, Jeremy (1987). *Time Wars*. New York: Holt.

Schumacher, E.F. (1974). *Small is Beautiful: Economics as if People Mattered*. Abacus.

Schumacher, E.F. (1977). *A Guide for the Perplexed*. New York: Harper & Row.

Sheldrake, Rupert (1981). *A New Science of Life*. Frederick Muller.

Swimme, Brian (1984). *The Universe is a Green Dragon*. Santa Fe, NM: Bear.

Theobald, Robert (1987). *The Rapids of Change: Social Entrepreneurship in Turbulent Times*. Indianapolis: Knowledge Systems.

Toffler, Alvin (1980). *The Third Wave*. New York: Morrow.

Wilber, Ken (1983). *Up From Eden: A Transpersonal View of Human Evolution*. Boulder, CO: Shambhala.

Wilson, Colin (1967). *Introduction to the New Existentialism*. Boston: Houghton Mifflin.

Index